WuMO

SOMETHING IS WRONG

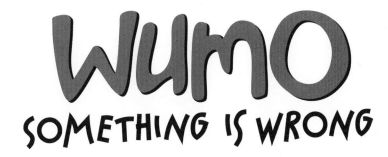

WuMo
SOMETHING IS WRONG

Wulff & Morgenthaler

Andrews McMeel
Publishing®

Kansas City • Sydney • London

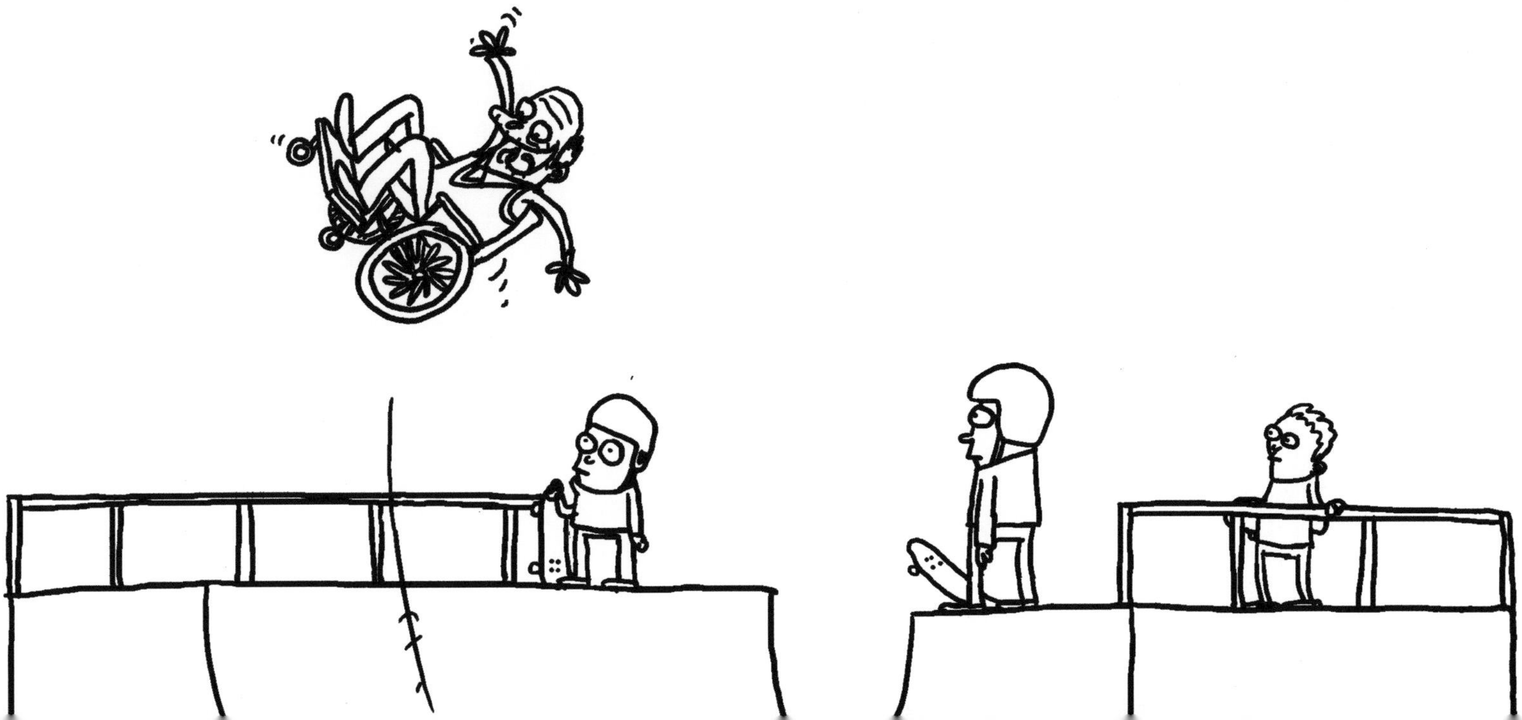

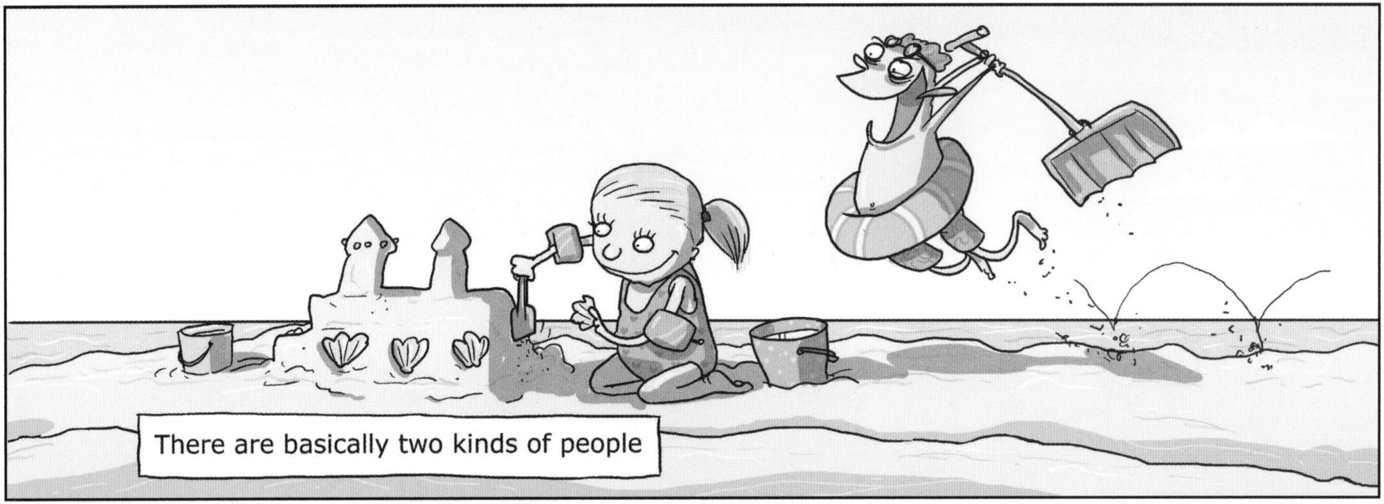
There are basically two kinds of people

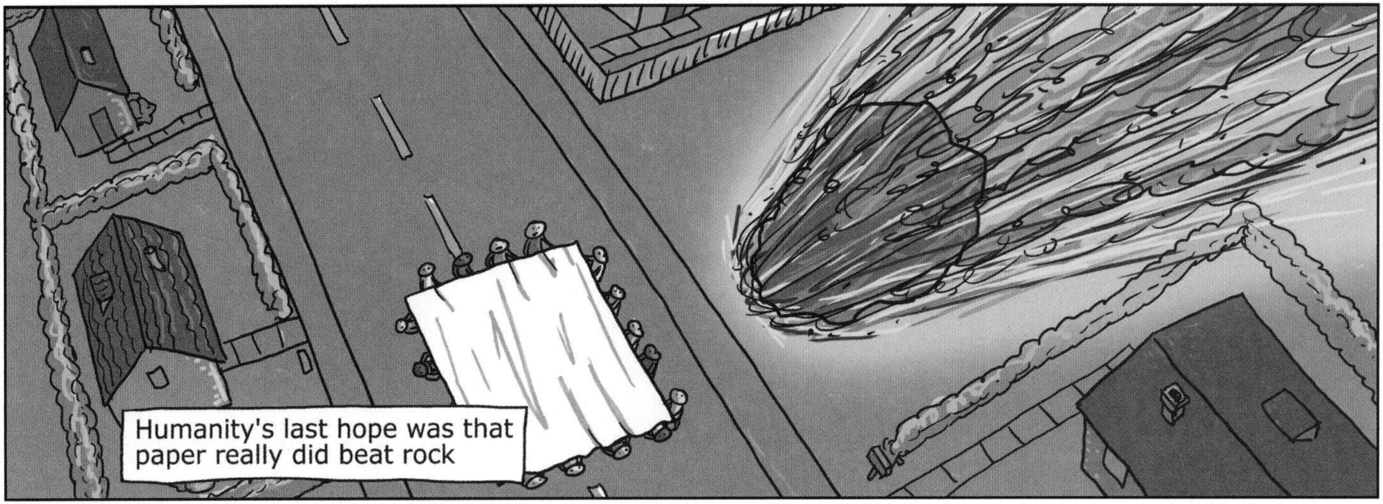
Humanity's last hope was that paper really did beat rock

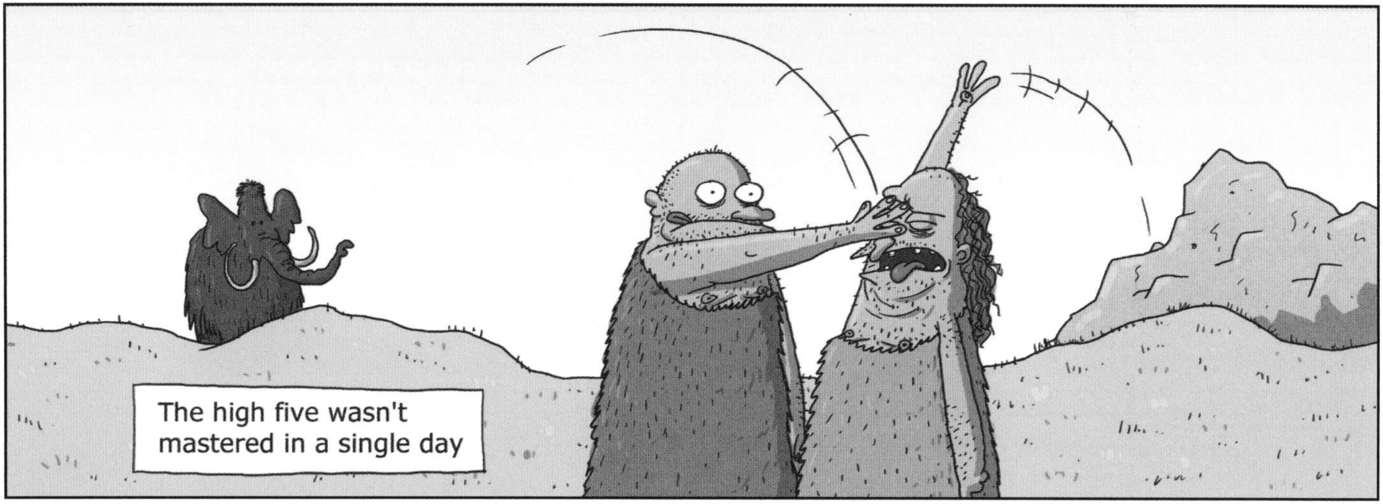
The high five wasn't mastered in a single day

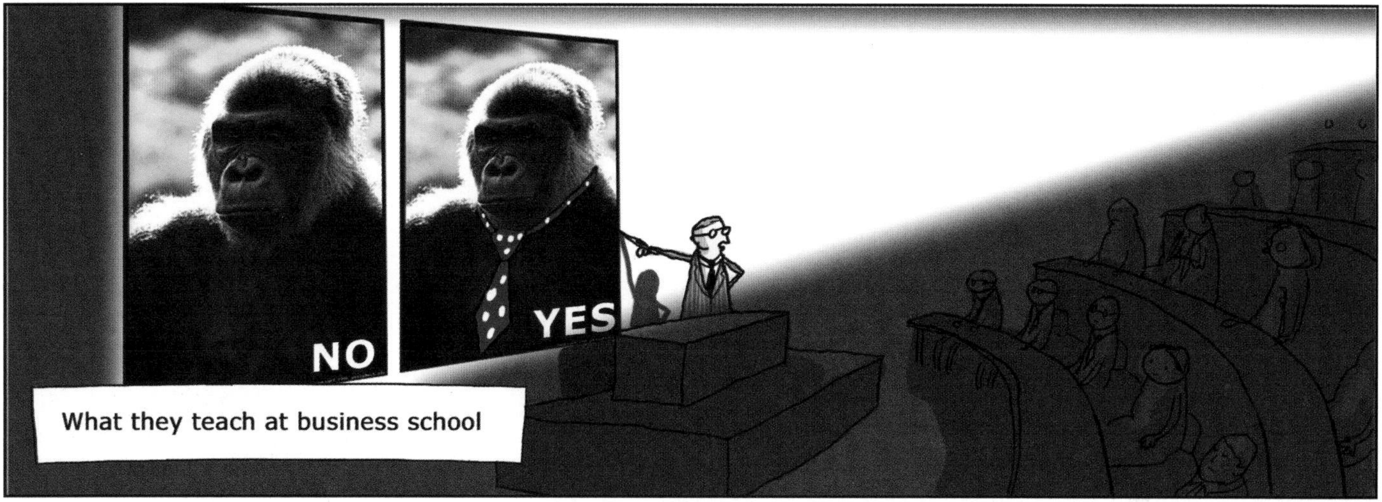
NO
YES
What they teach at business school

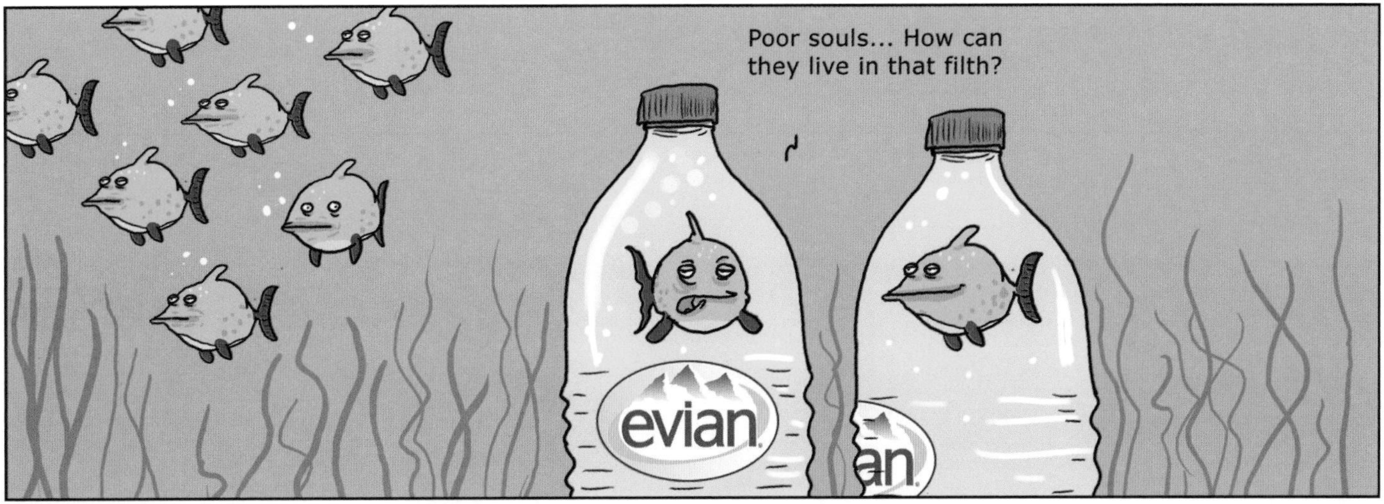
Poor souls... How can they live in that filth?
evian
an

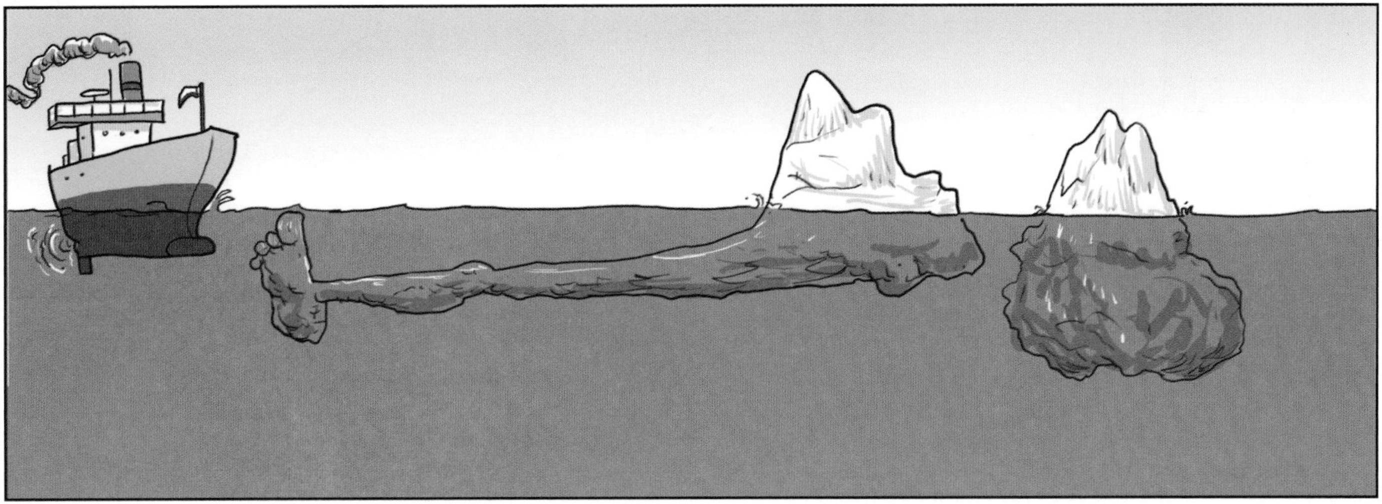

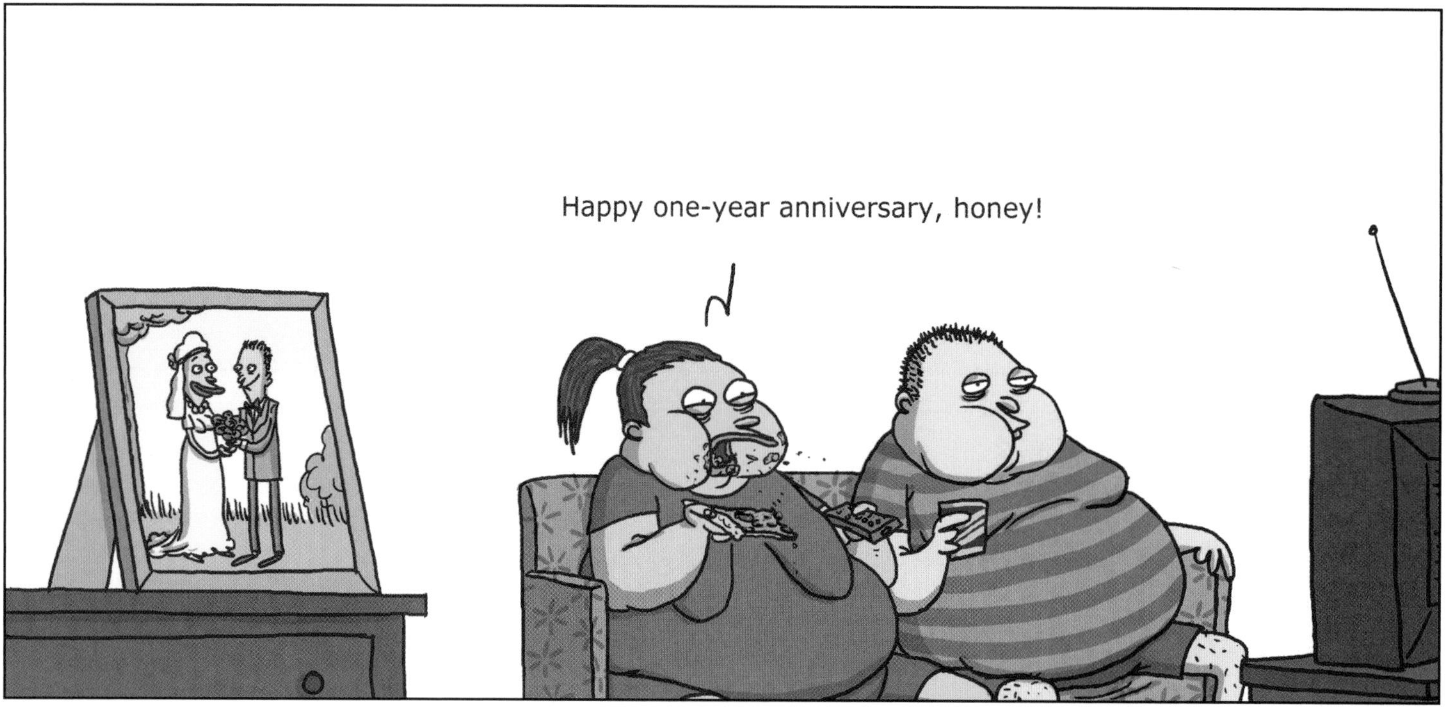
Happy one-year anniversary, honey!

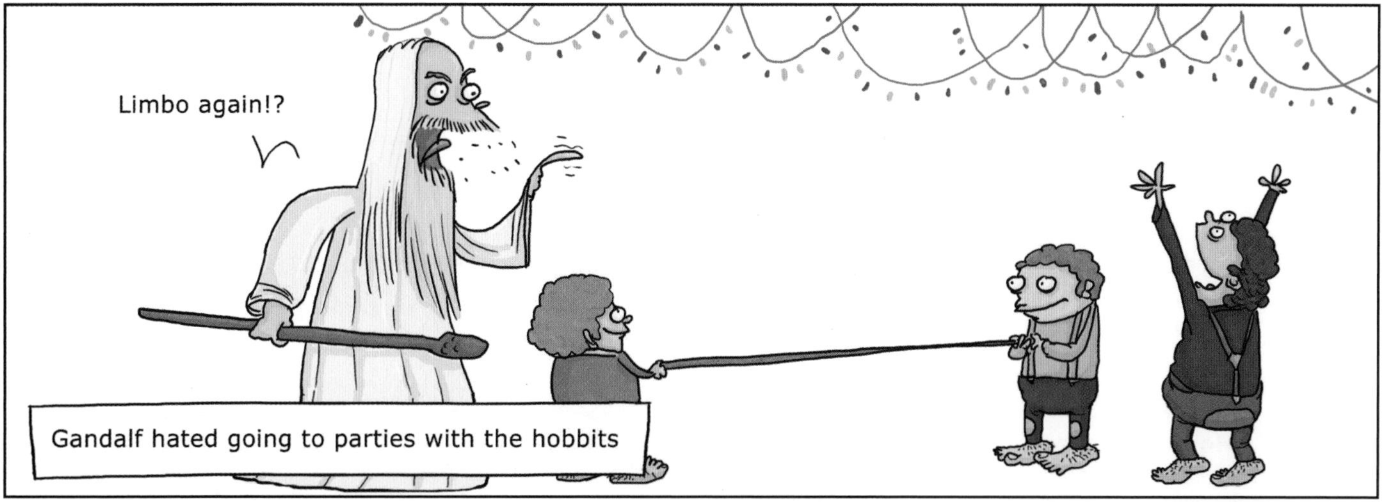
Limbo again!?
Gandalf hated going to parties with the hobbits

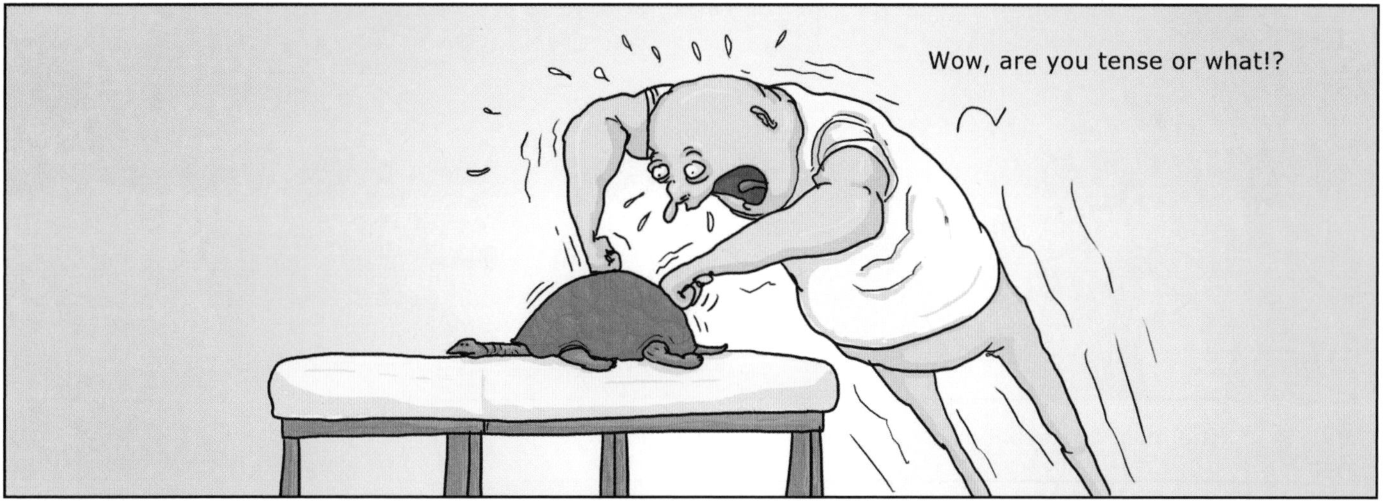
Wow, are you tense or what!?

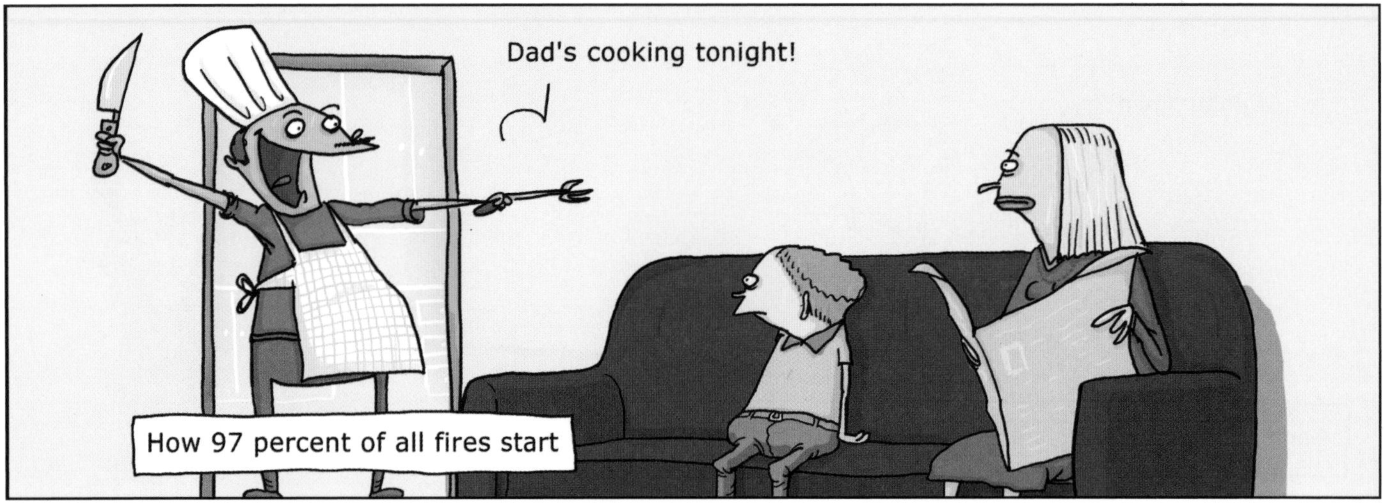
Dad's cooking tonight!
How 97 percent of all fires start

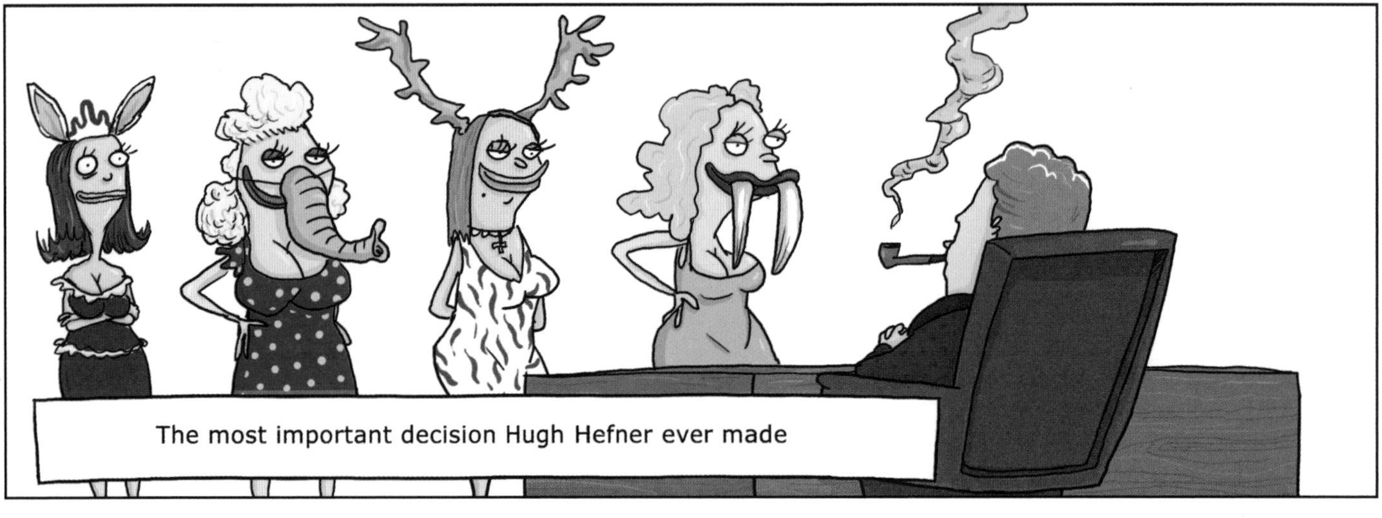
The most important decision Hugh Hefner ever made

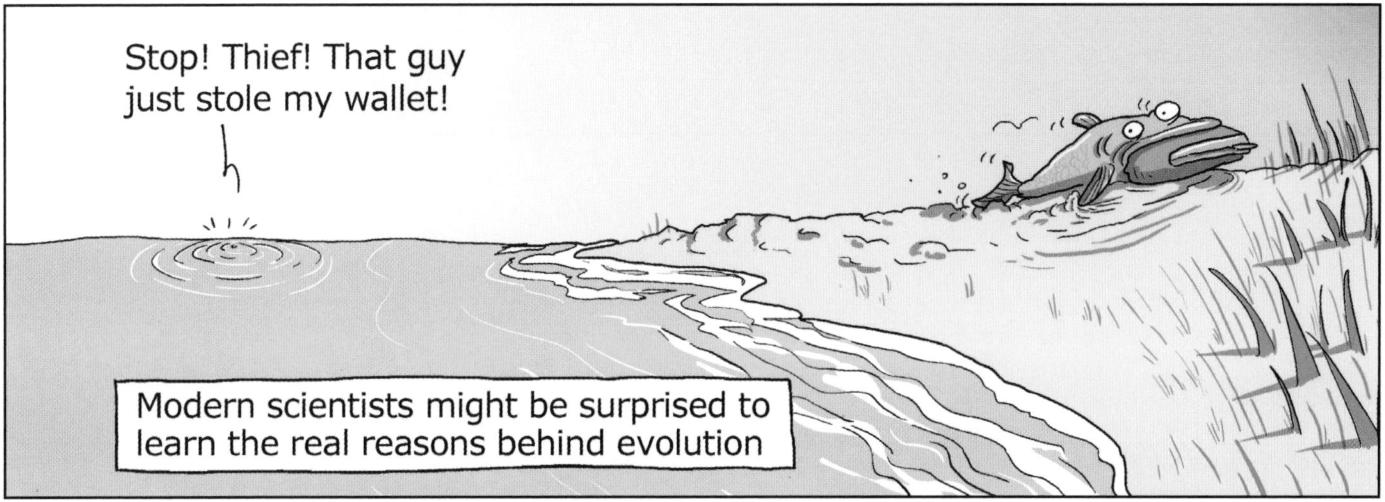
Stop! Thief! That guy just stole my wallet!
Modern scientists might be surprised to learn the real reasons behind evolution

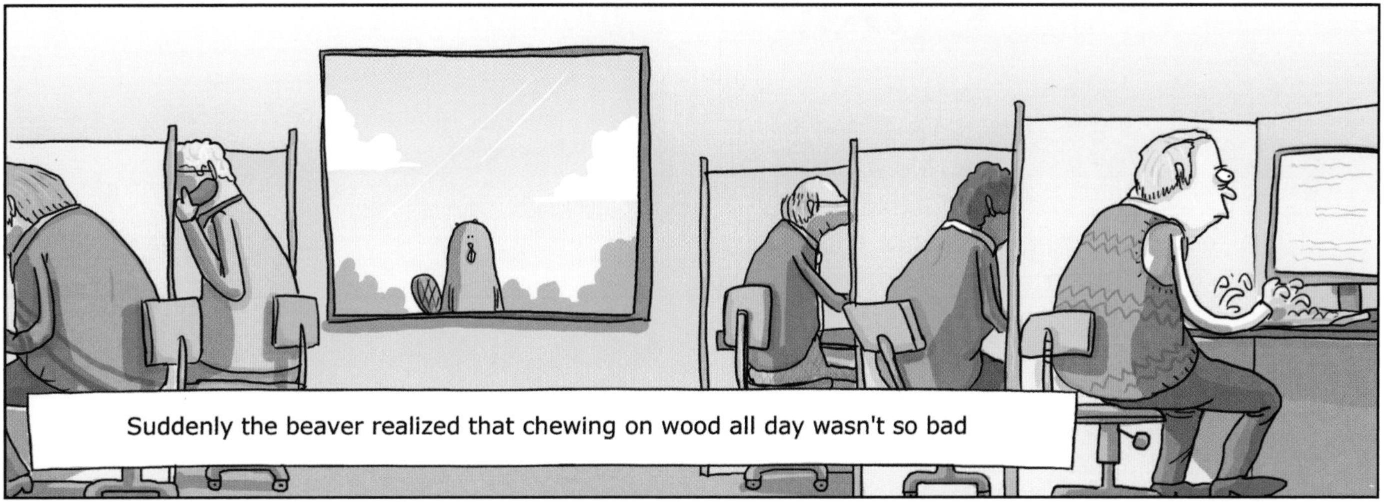
Suddenly the beaver realized that chewing on wood all day wasn't so bad

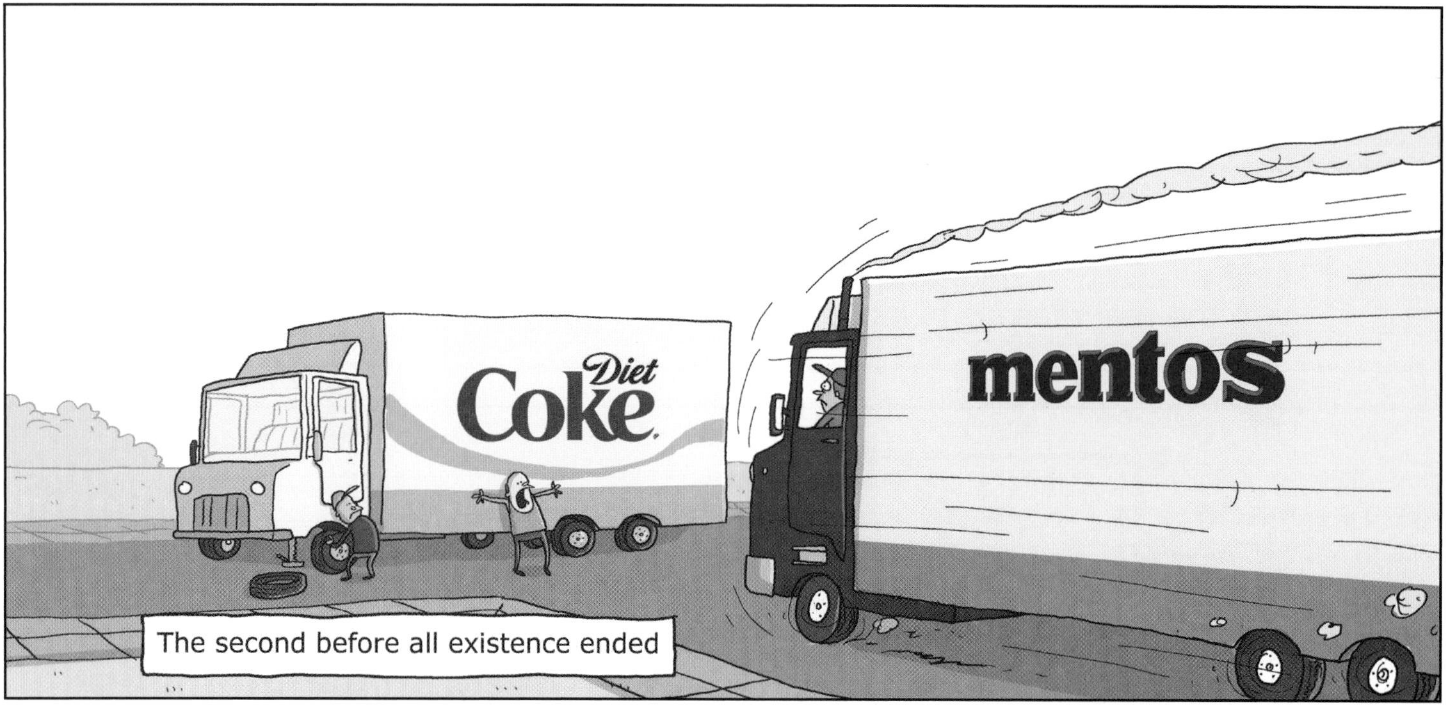
Diet Coke
mentos
The second before all existence ended

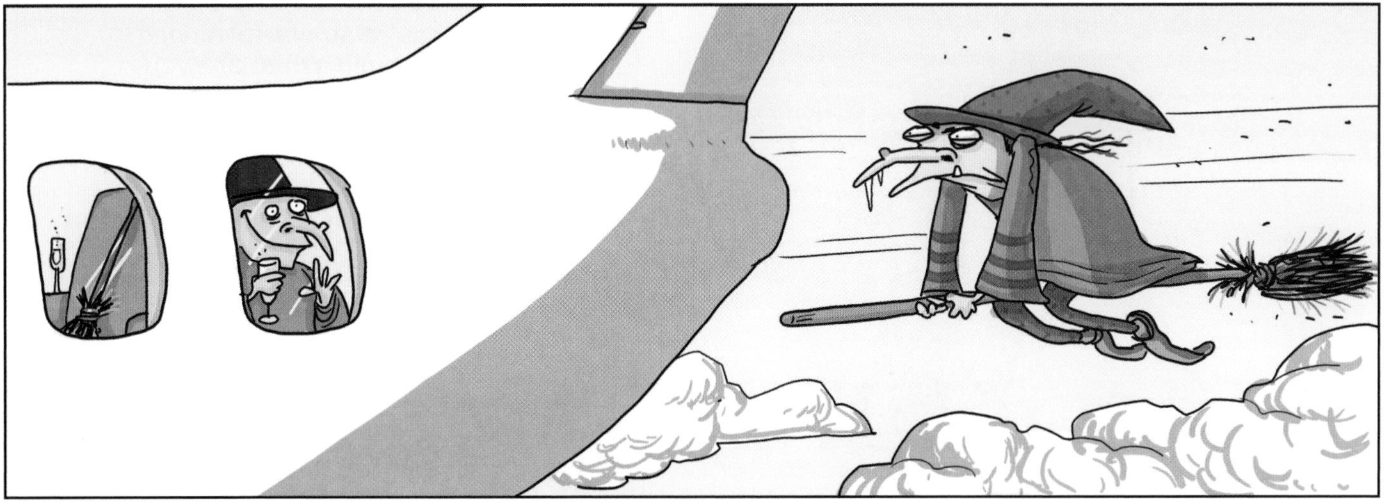

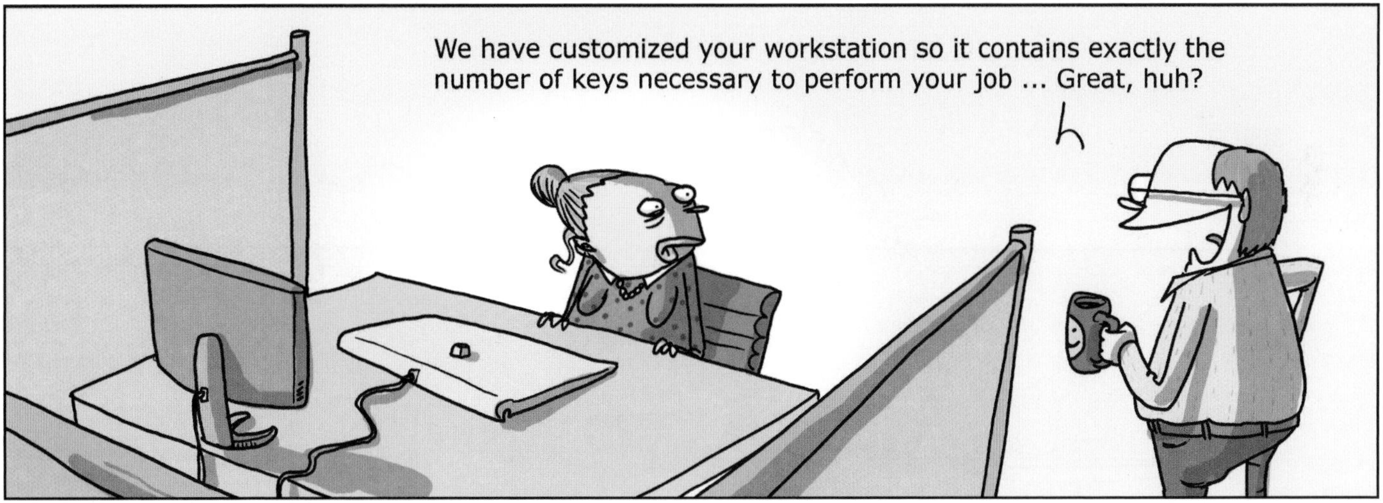
We have customized your workstation so it contains exactly the number of keys necessary to perform your job ... Great, huh?

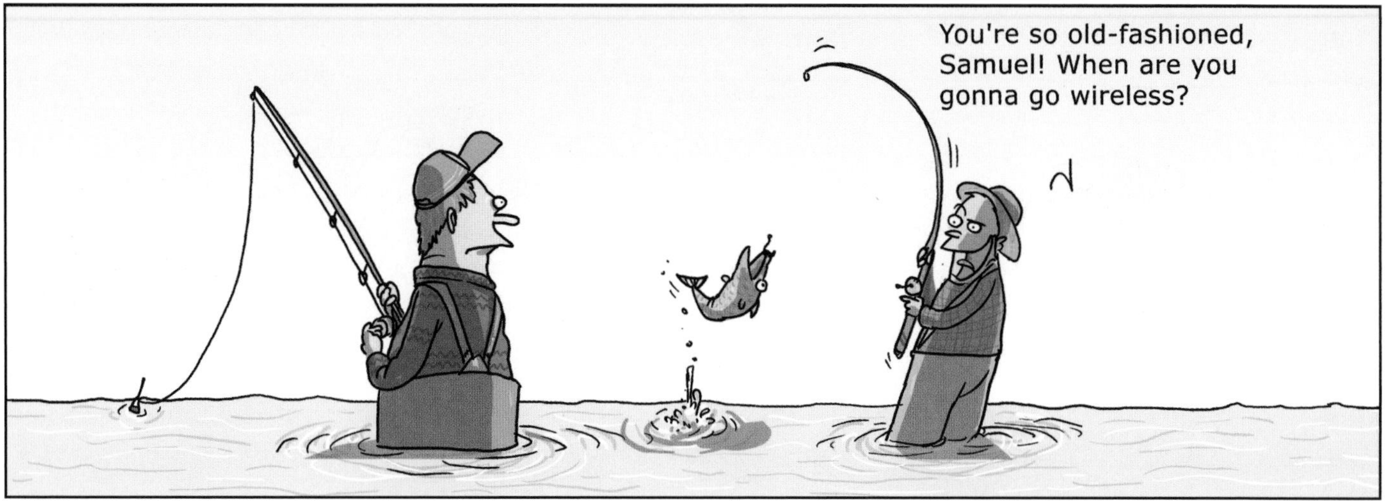
You're so old-fashioned, Samuel! When are you gonna go wireless?

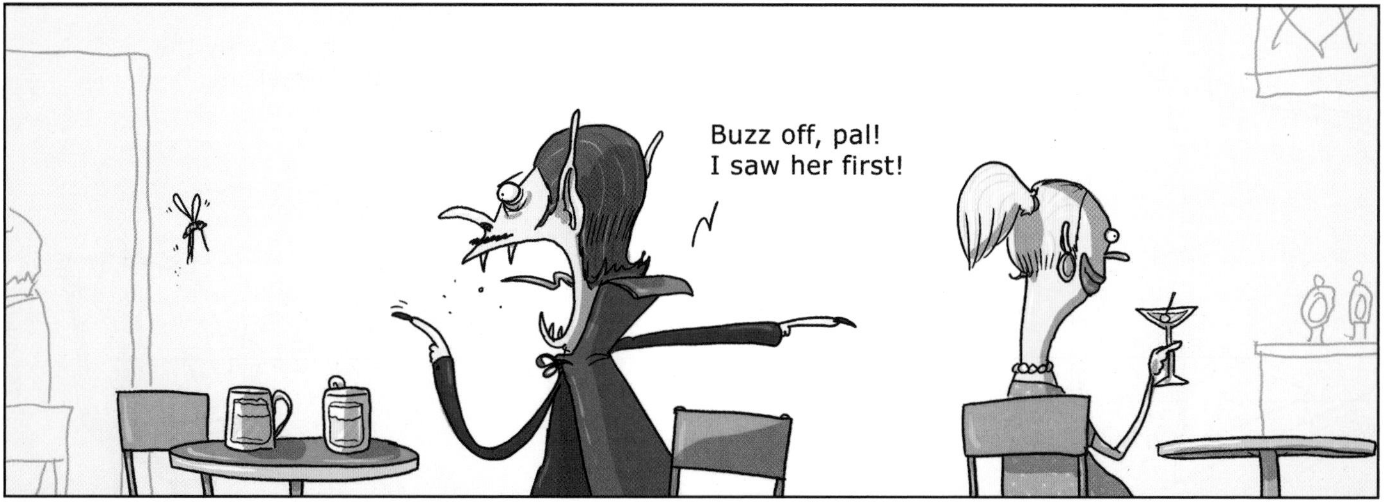
Buzz off, pal!
I saw her first!

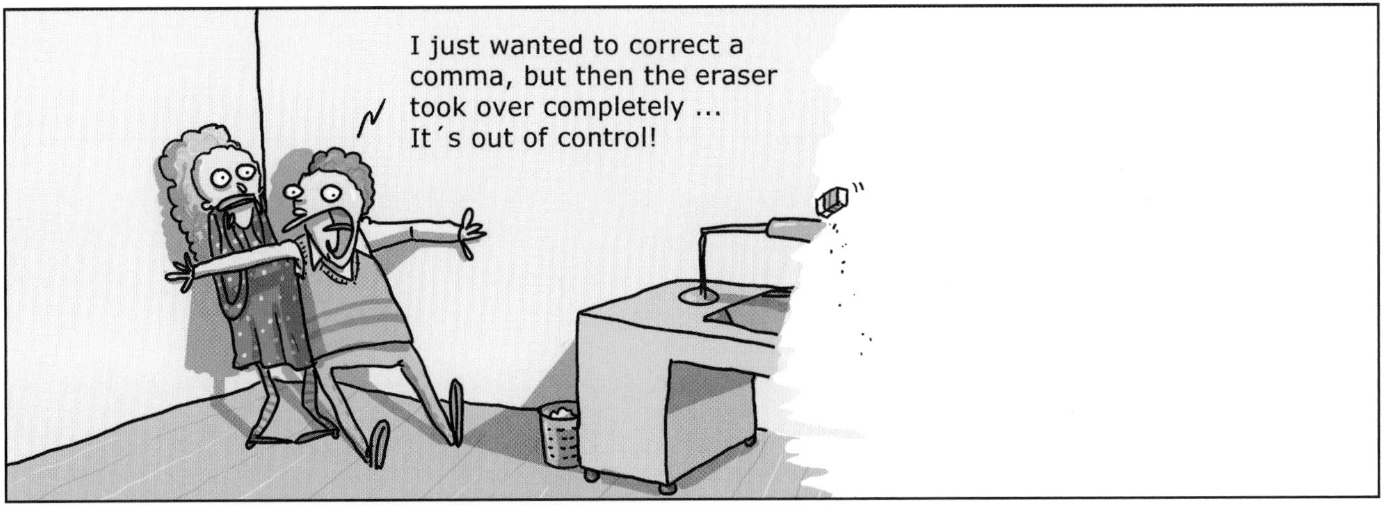
I just wanted to correct a comma, but then the eraser took over completely ... It´s out of control!

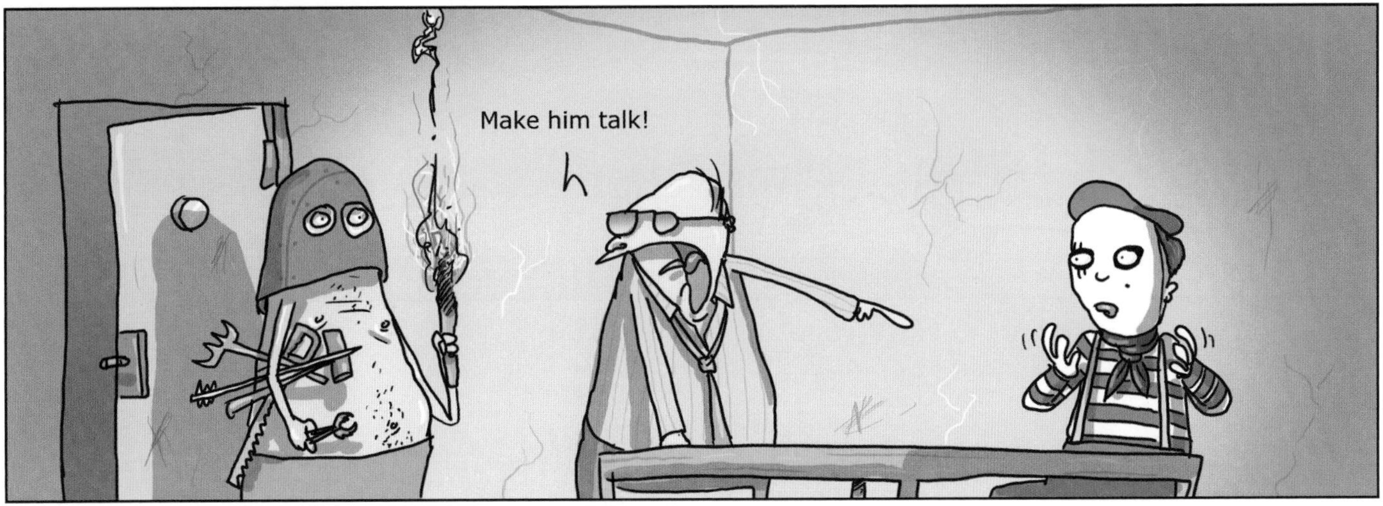
Make him talk!

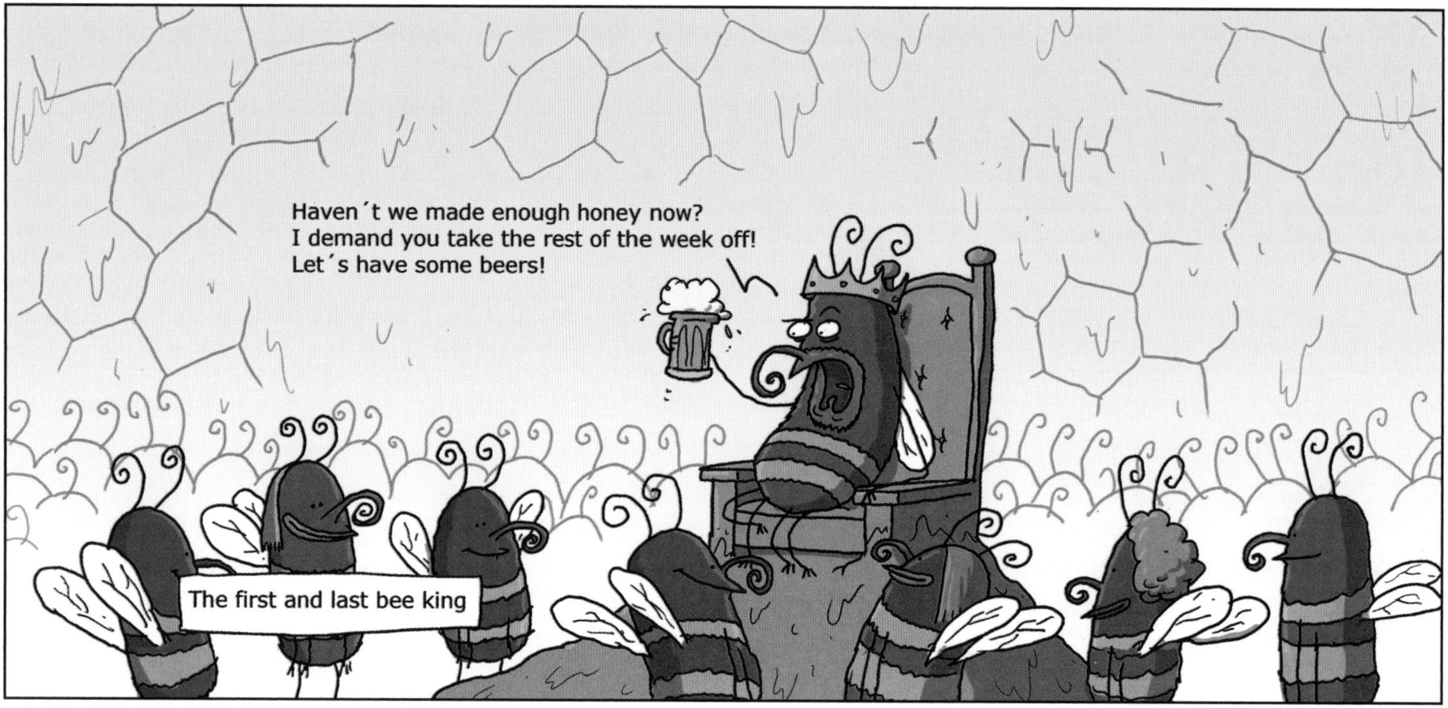
Haven´t we made enough honey now?
I demand you take the rest of the week off!
Let´s have some beers!
The first and last bee king

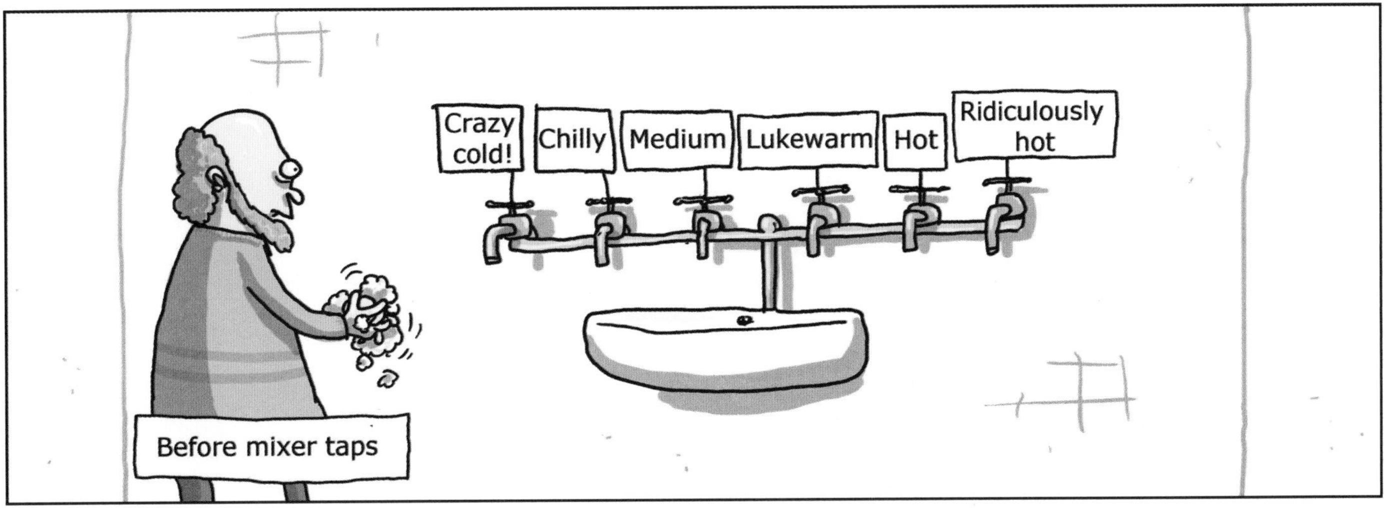
Crazy cold!
Chilly
Medium
Lukewarm
Hot
Ridiculously hot
Before mixer taps

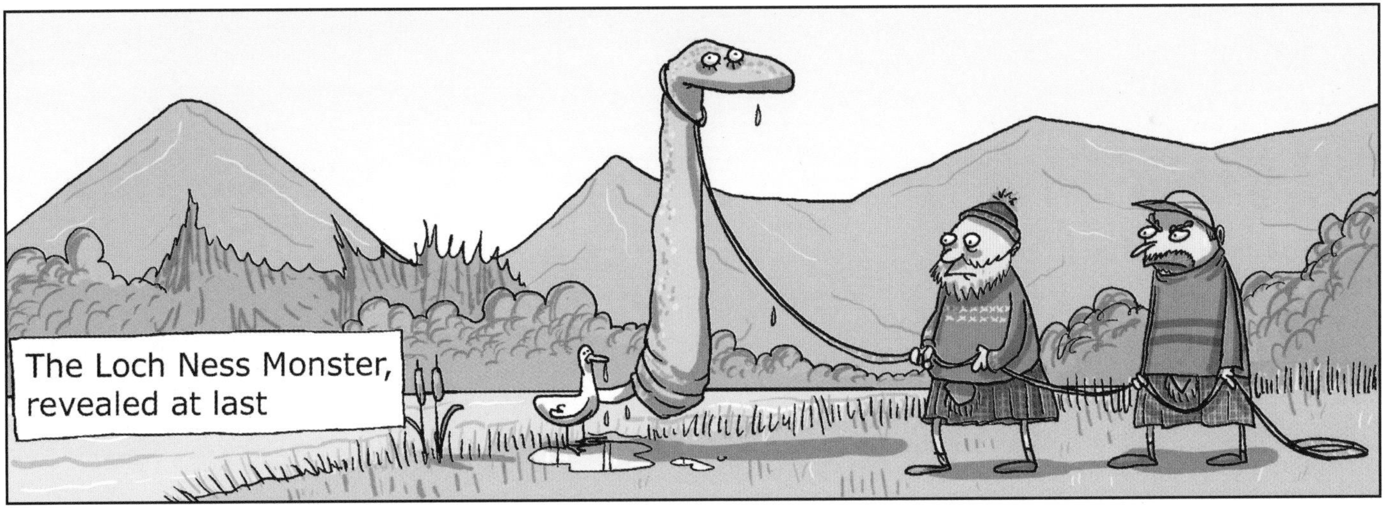
The Loch Ness Monster, revealed at last

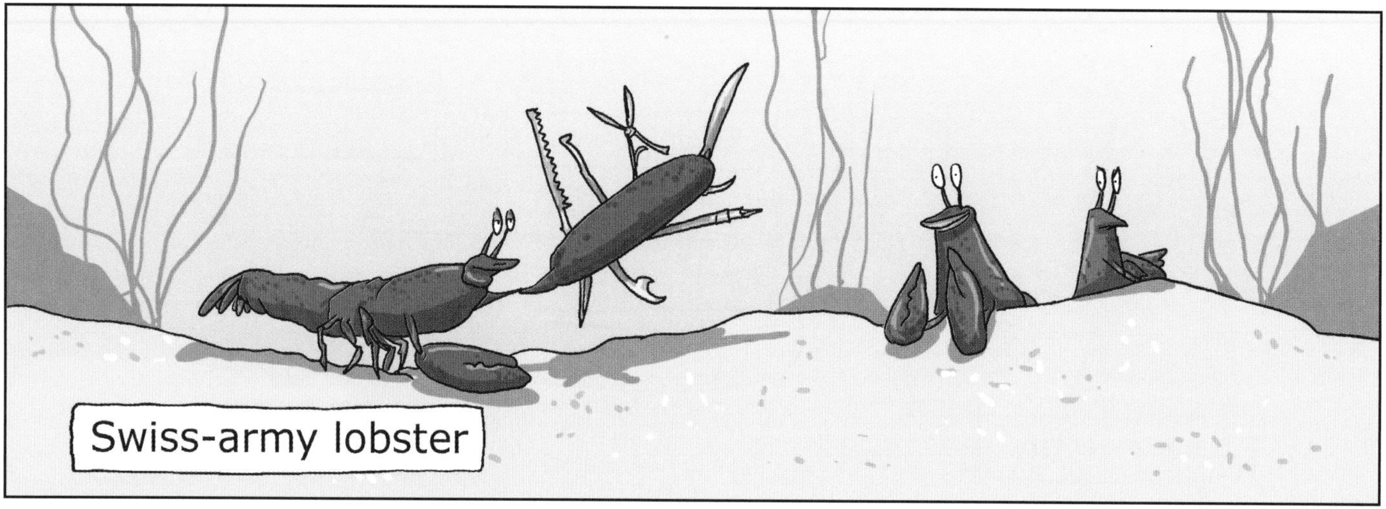
Swiss-army lobster

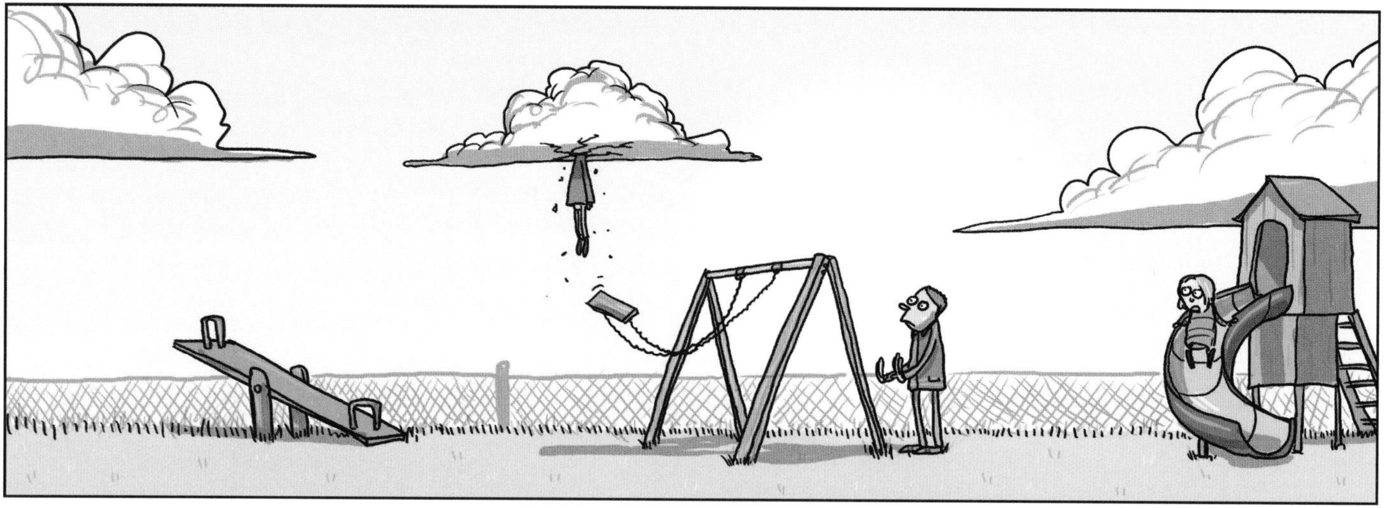

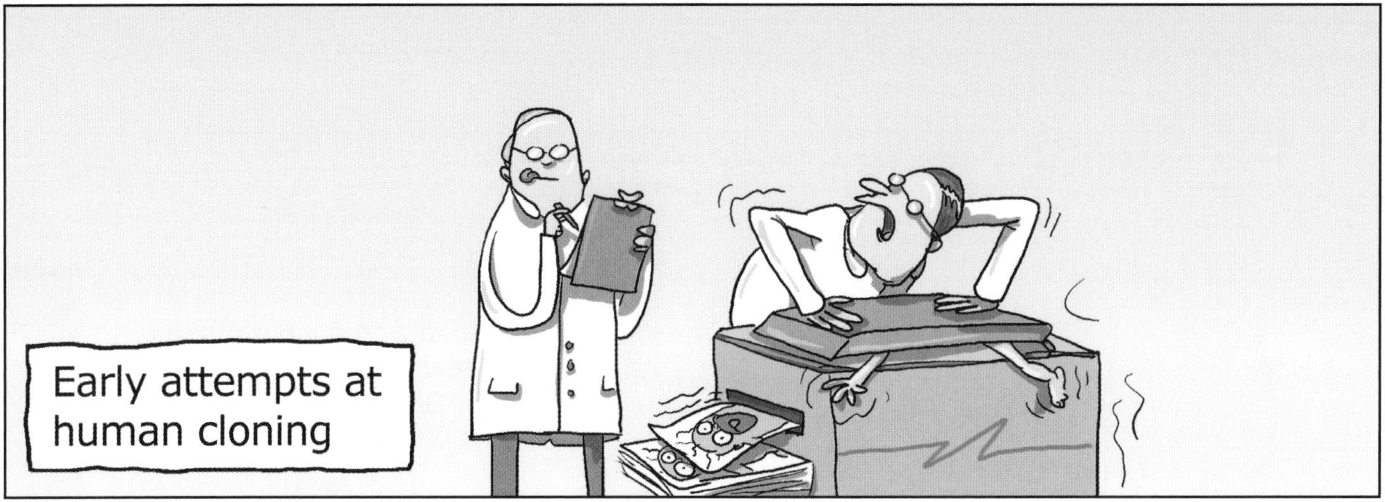
Early attempts at
human cloning

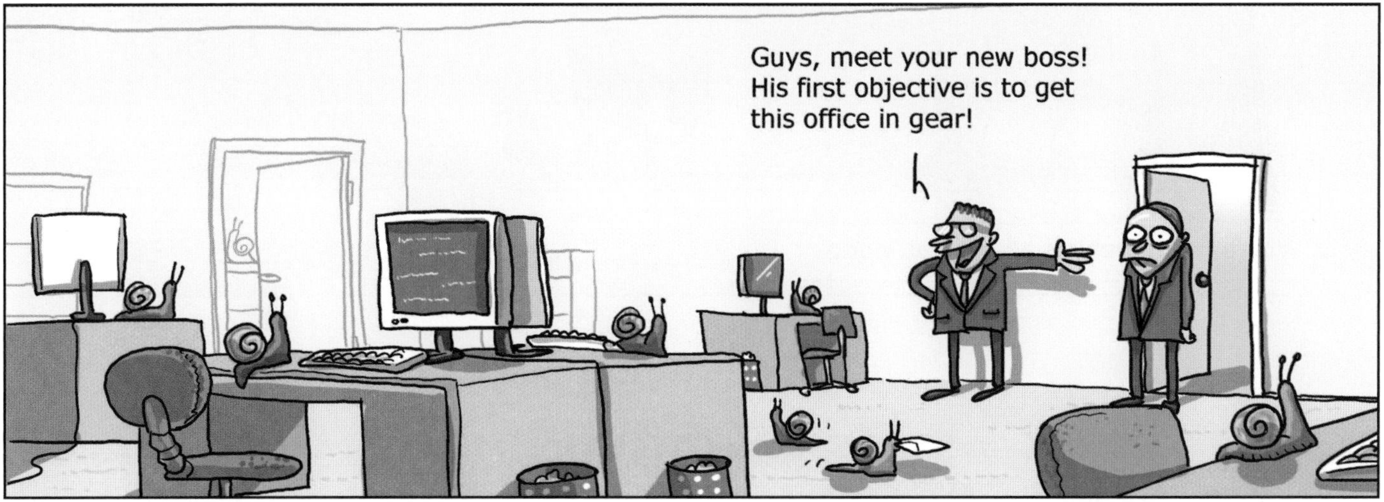
Guys, meet your new boss!
His first objective is to get
this office in gear!

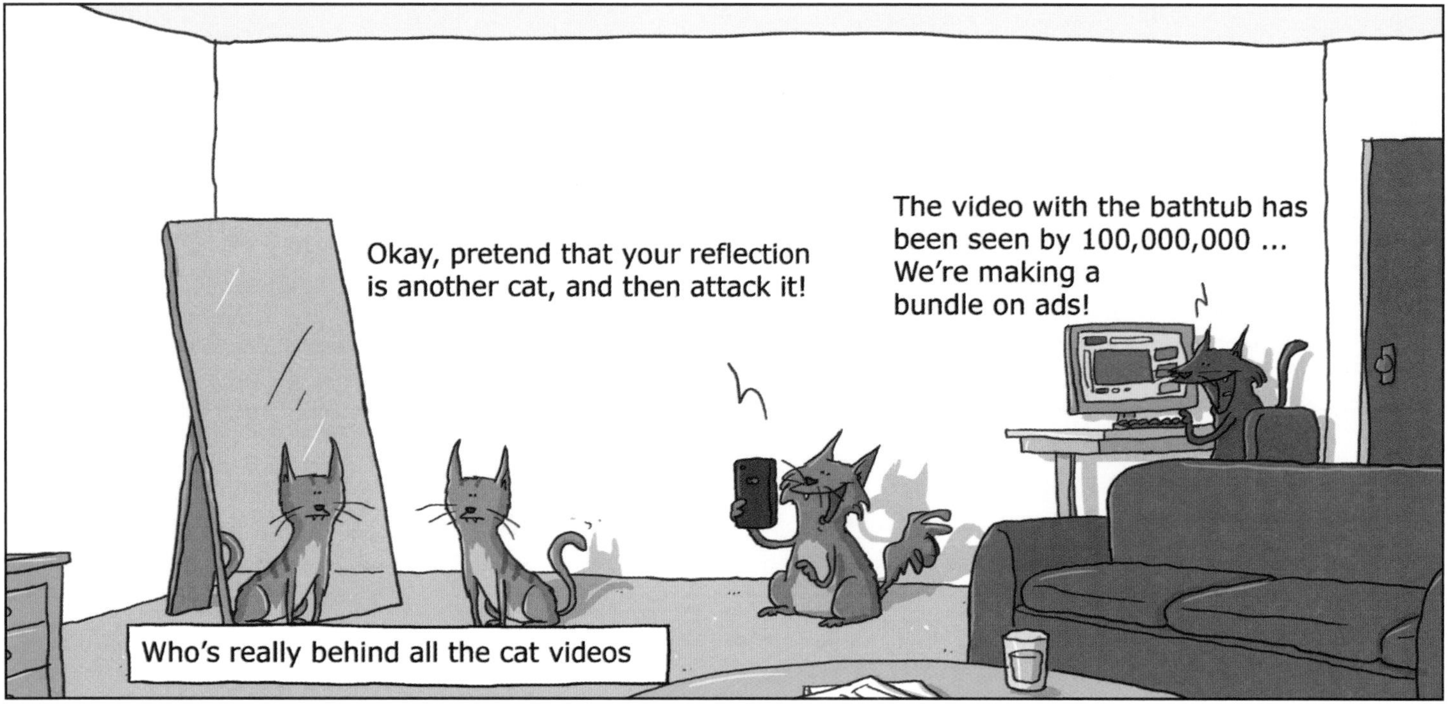
Okay, pretend that your reflection is another cat, and then attack it!
The video with the bathtub has been seen by 100,000,000 ... We're making a bundle on ads!
Who's really behind all the cat videos

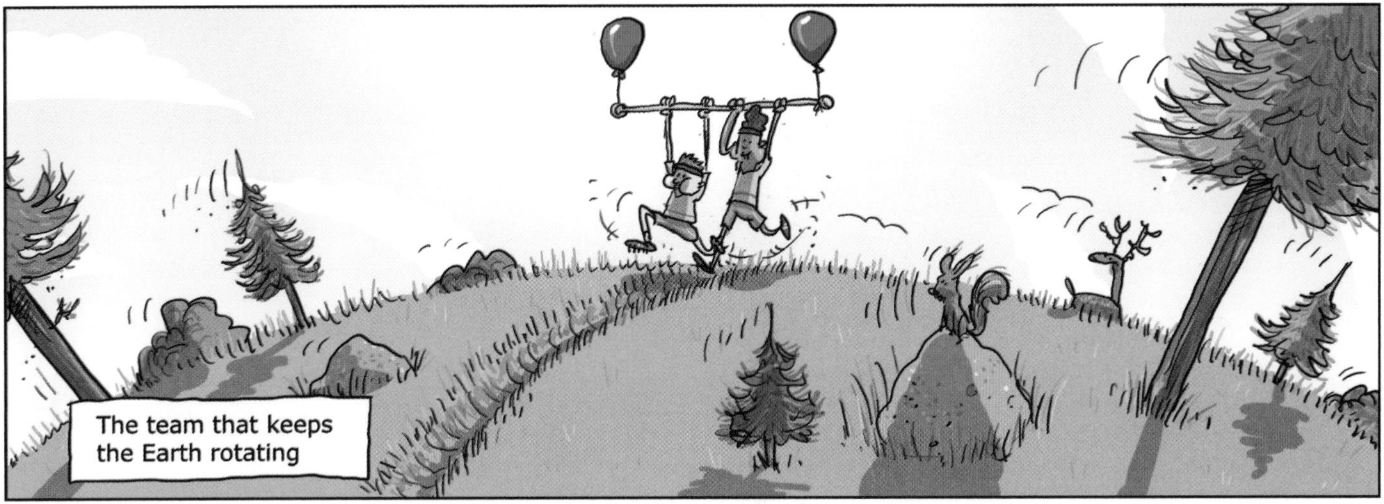
The team that keeps
the Earth rotating

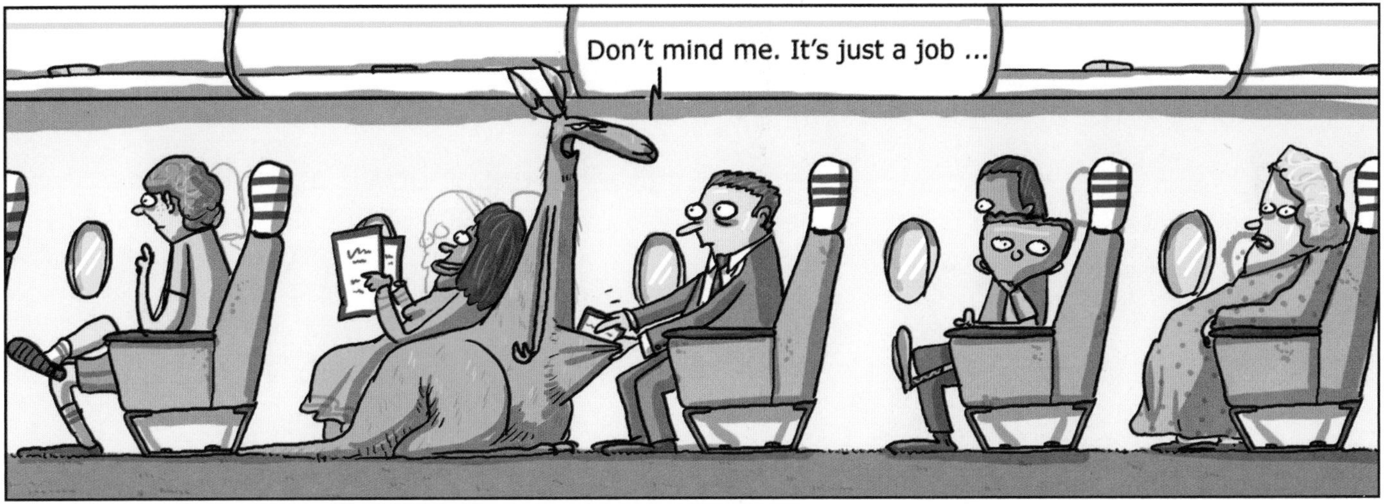
Don't mind me. It's just a job ...

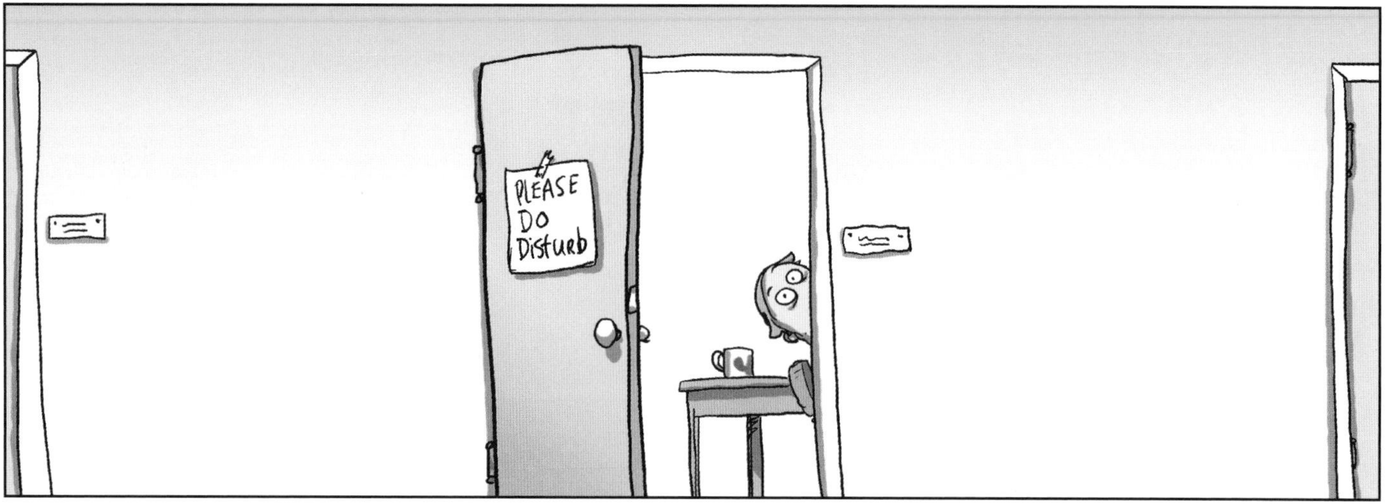
PLEASE
DO
DISTURB

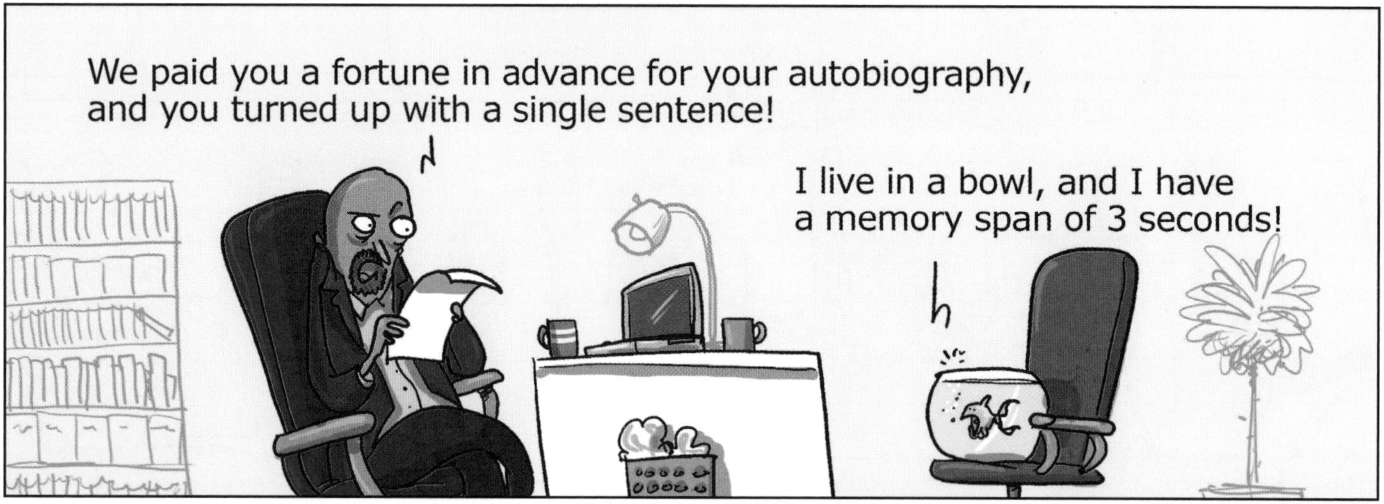
We paid you a fortune in advance for your autobiography, and you turned up with a single sentence!
I live in a bowl, and I have a memory span of 3 seconds!

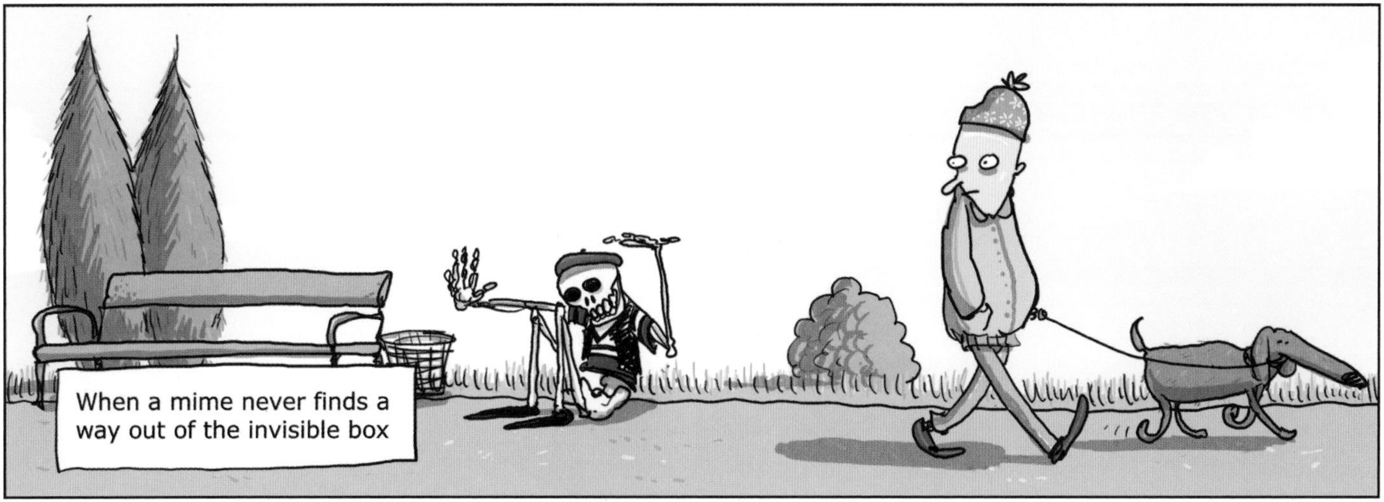
When a mime never finds a way out of the invisible box

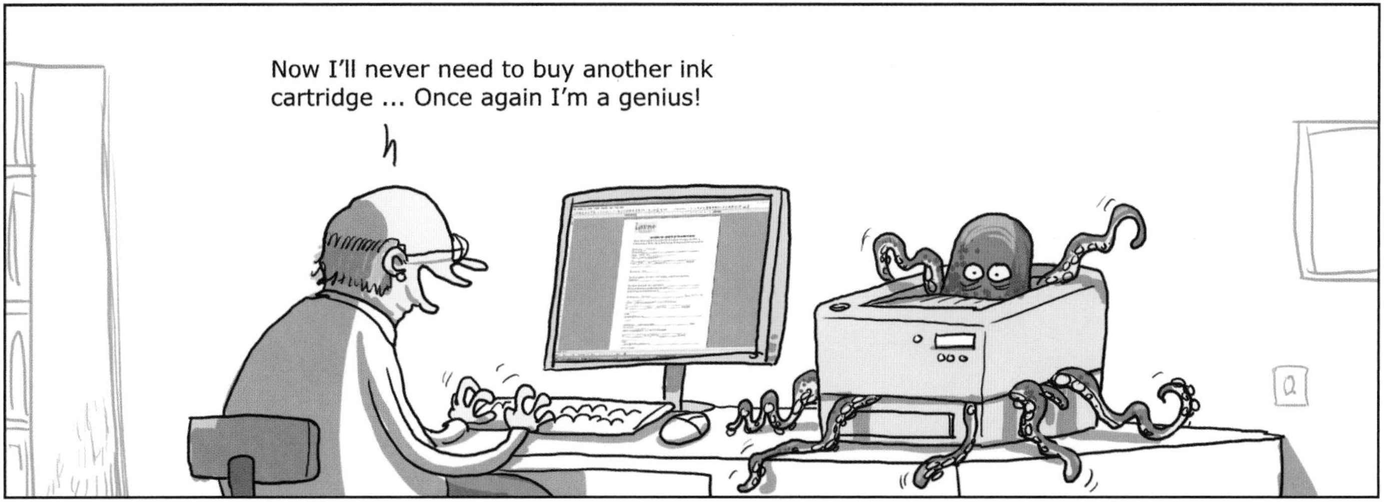
Now I'll never need to buy another ink cartridge ... Once again I'm a genius!

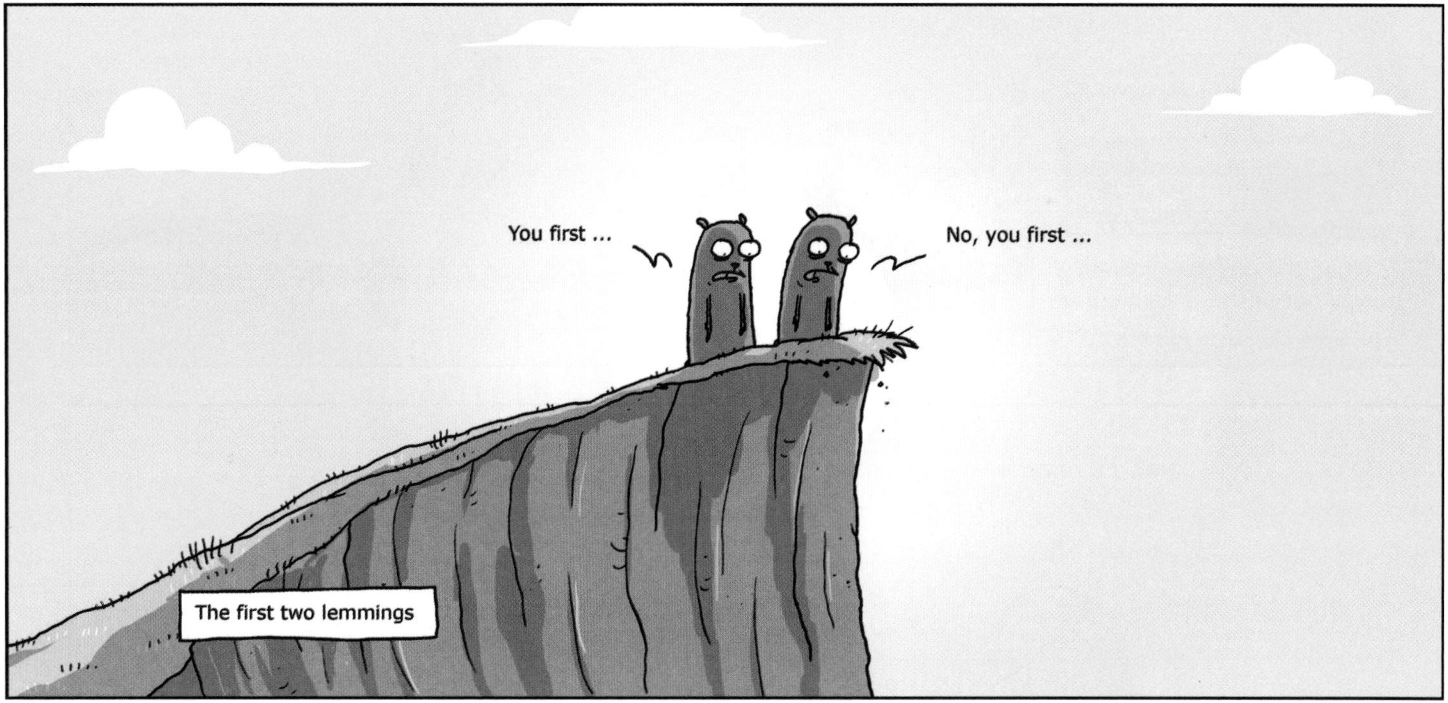
You first ...
No, you first ...
The first two lemmings

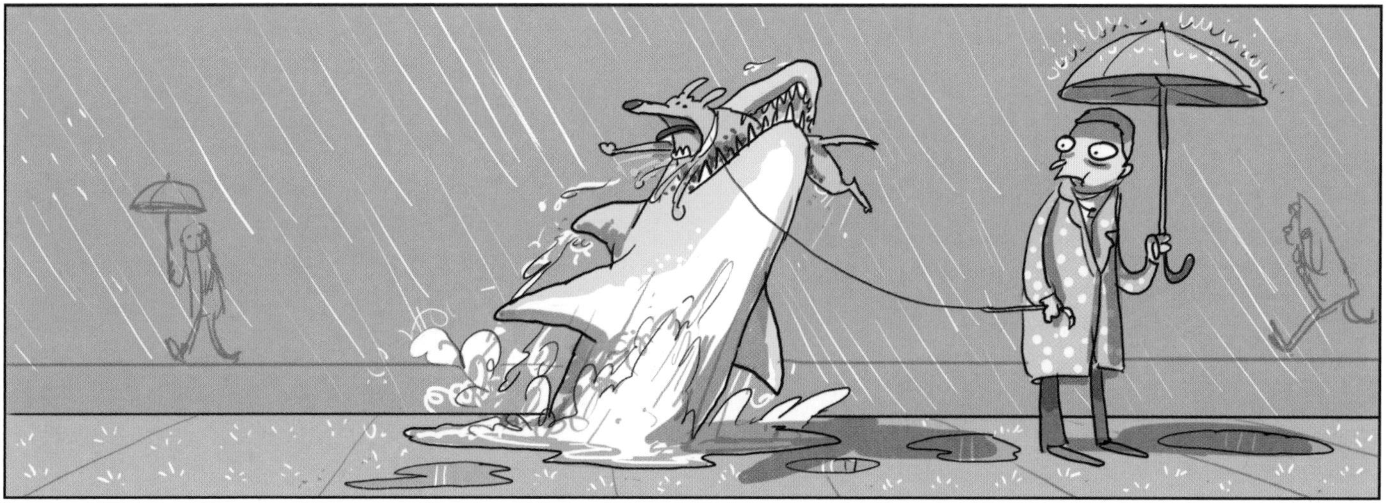

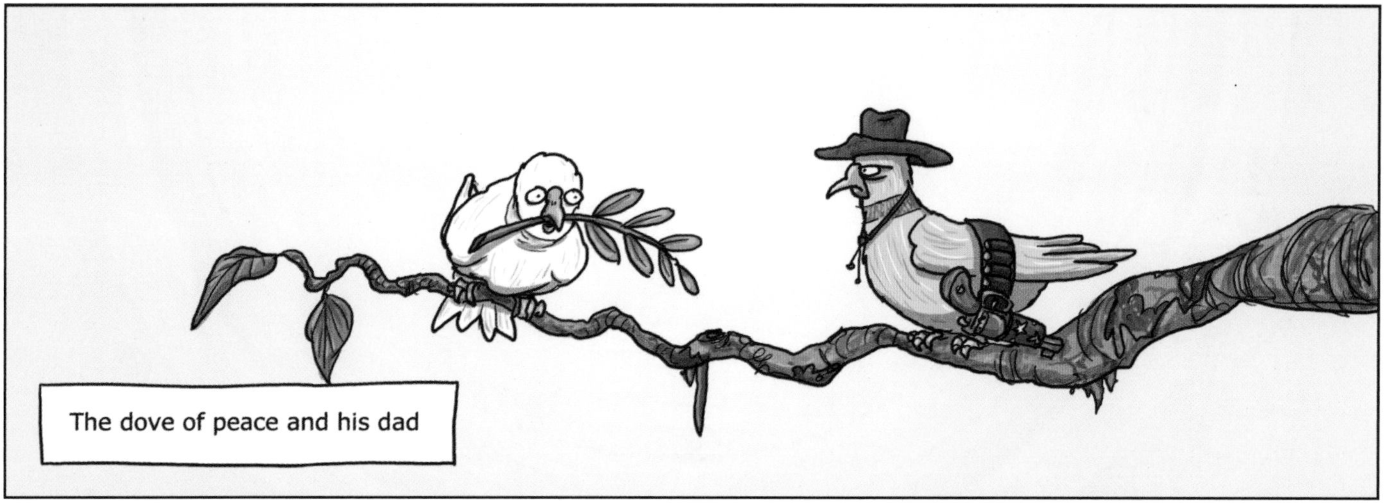
The dove of peace and his dad

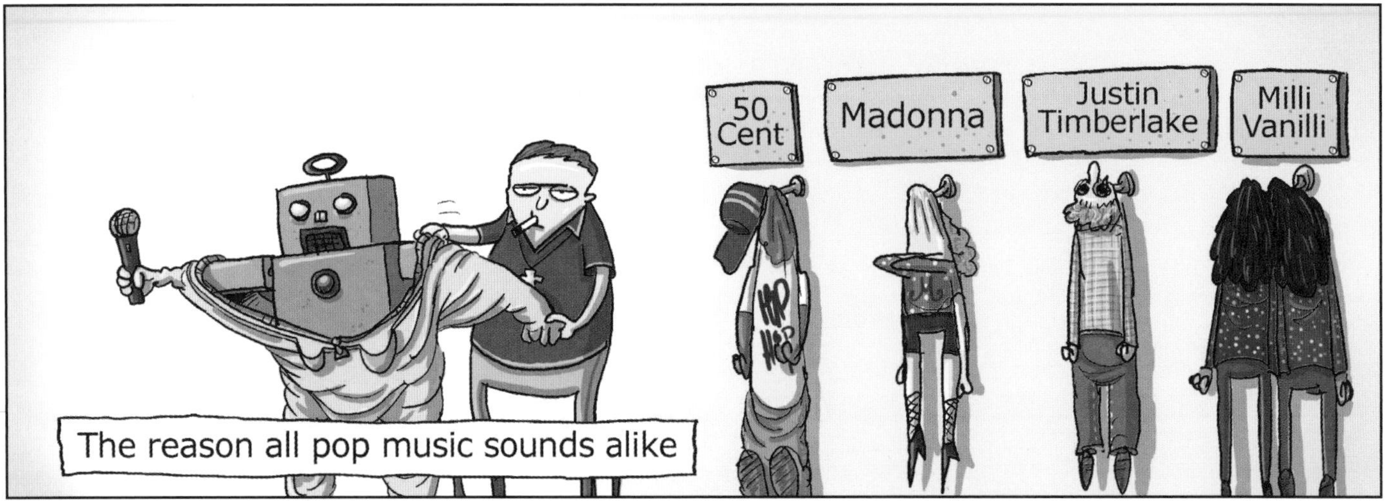
50 Cent
Madonna
Justin Timberlake
Milli Vanilli
The reason all pop music sounds alike

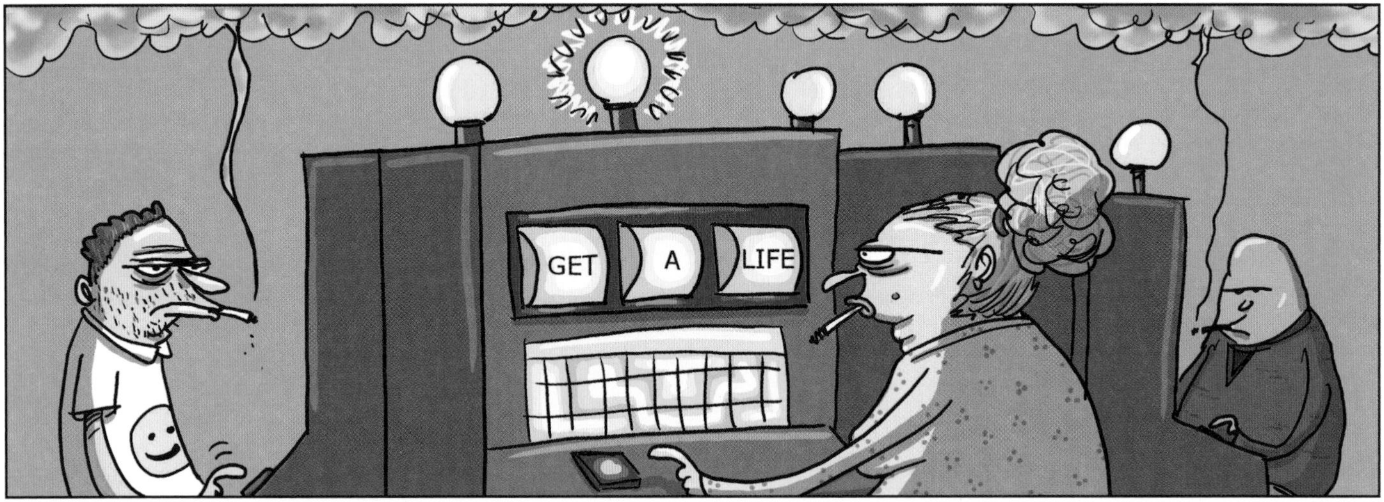
GET
A
LIFE

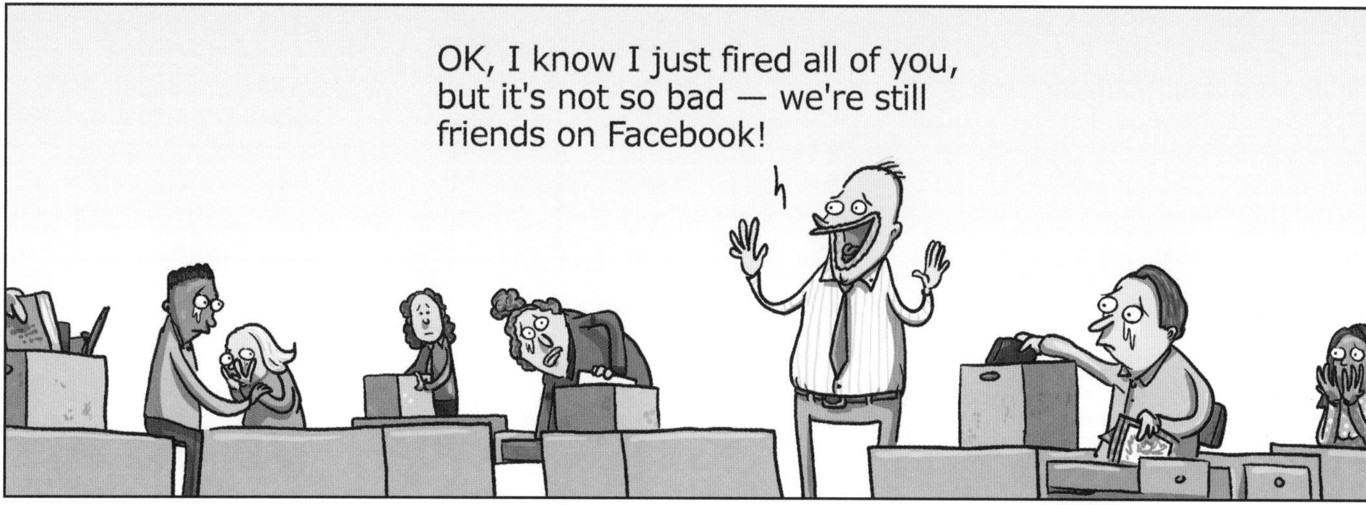
OK, I know I just fired all of you, but it's not so bad — we're still friends on Facebook!

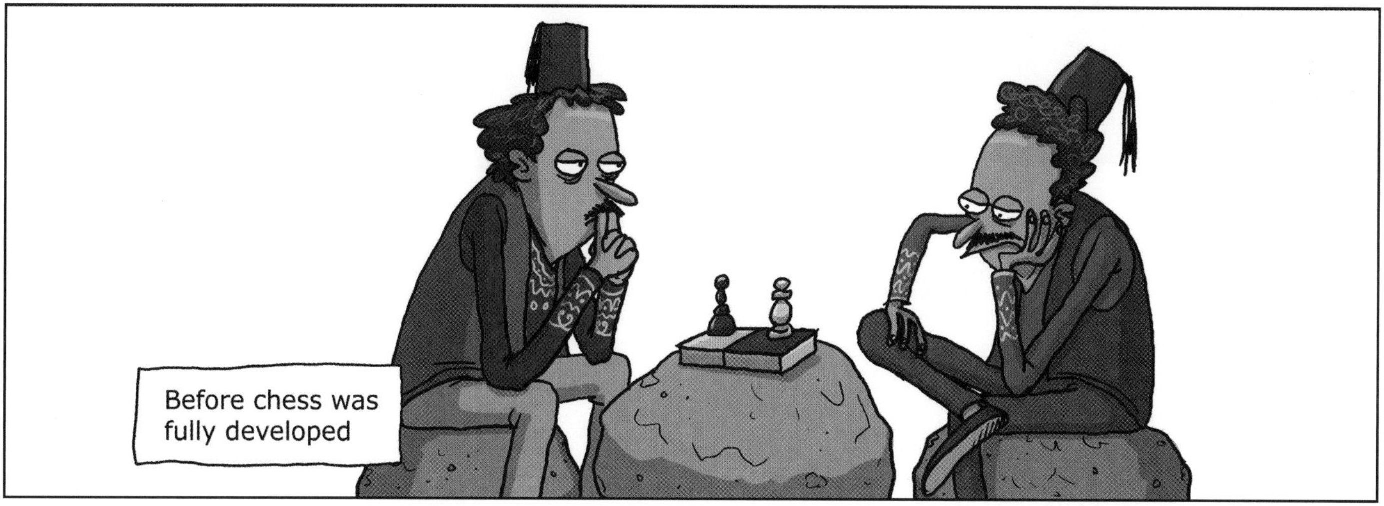
Before chess was fully developed

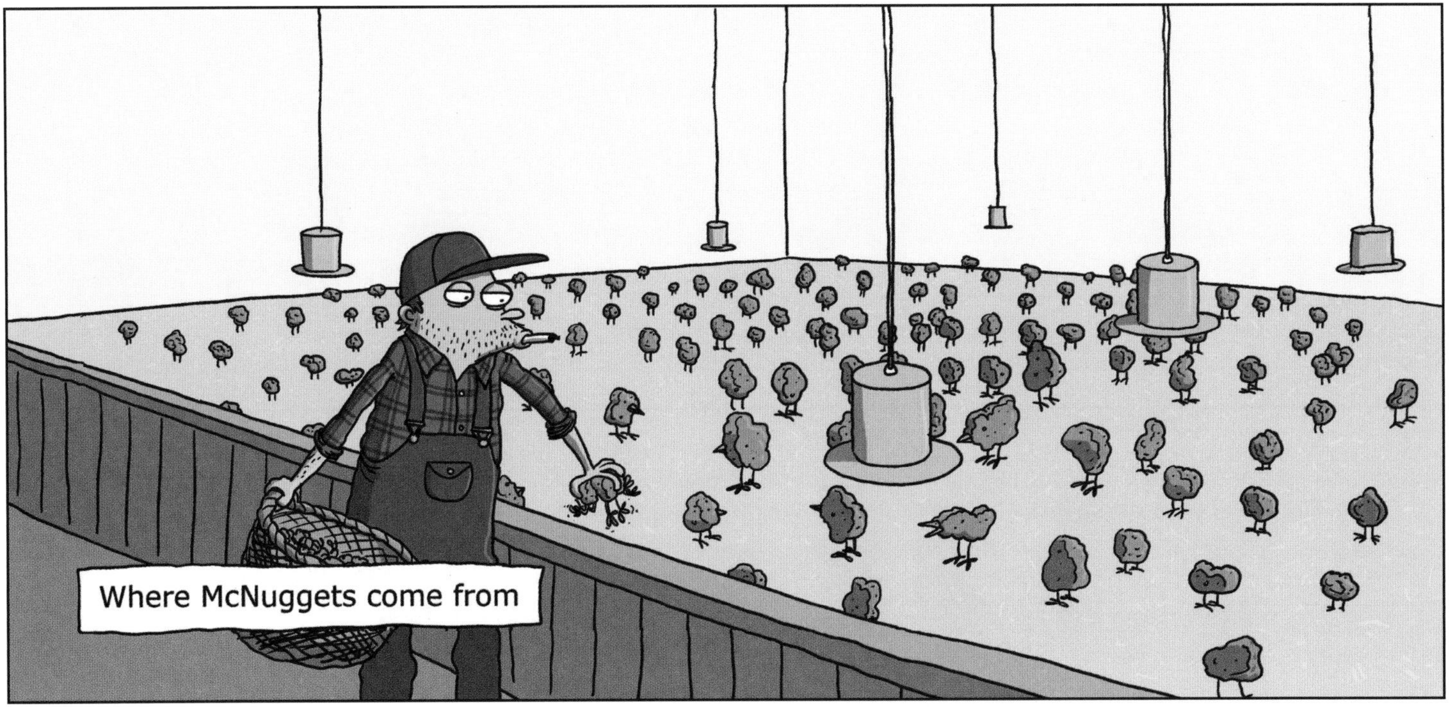
Where McNuggets come from

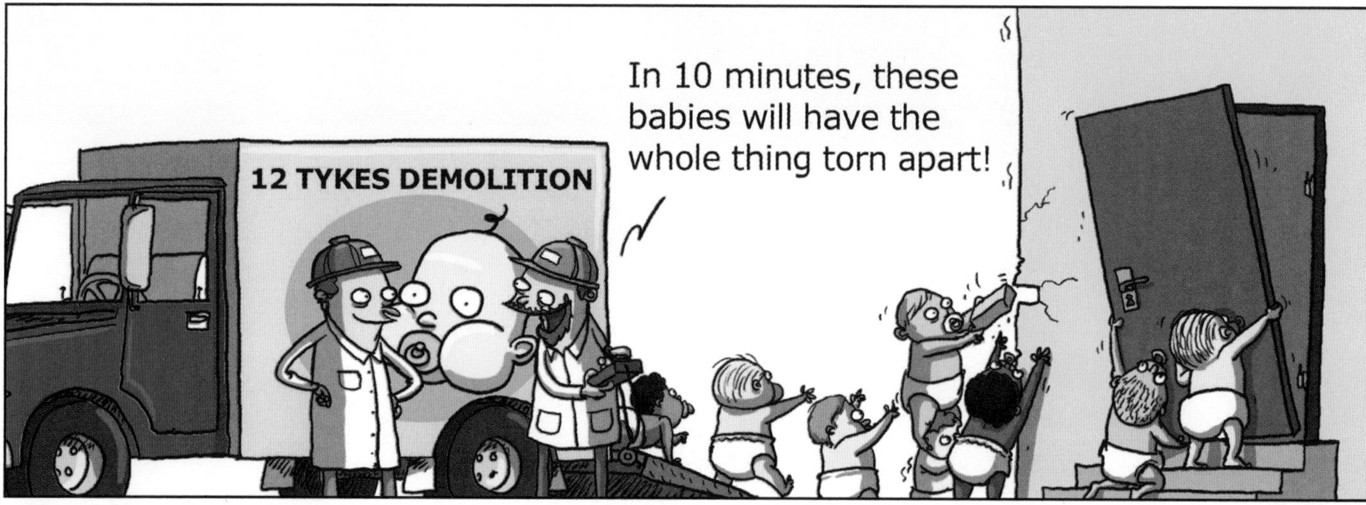
12 TYKES DEMOLITION
In 10 minutes, these babies will have the whole thing torn apart!

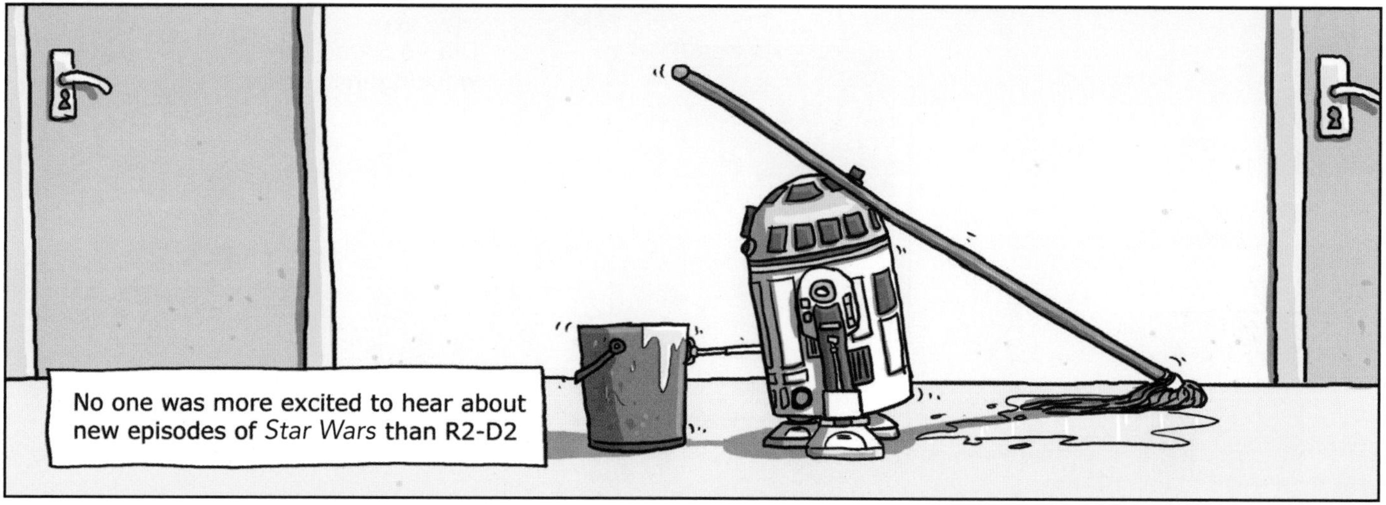
No one was more excited to hear about new episodes of *Star Wars* than R2-D2

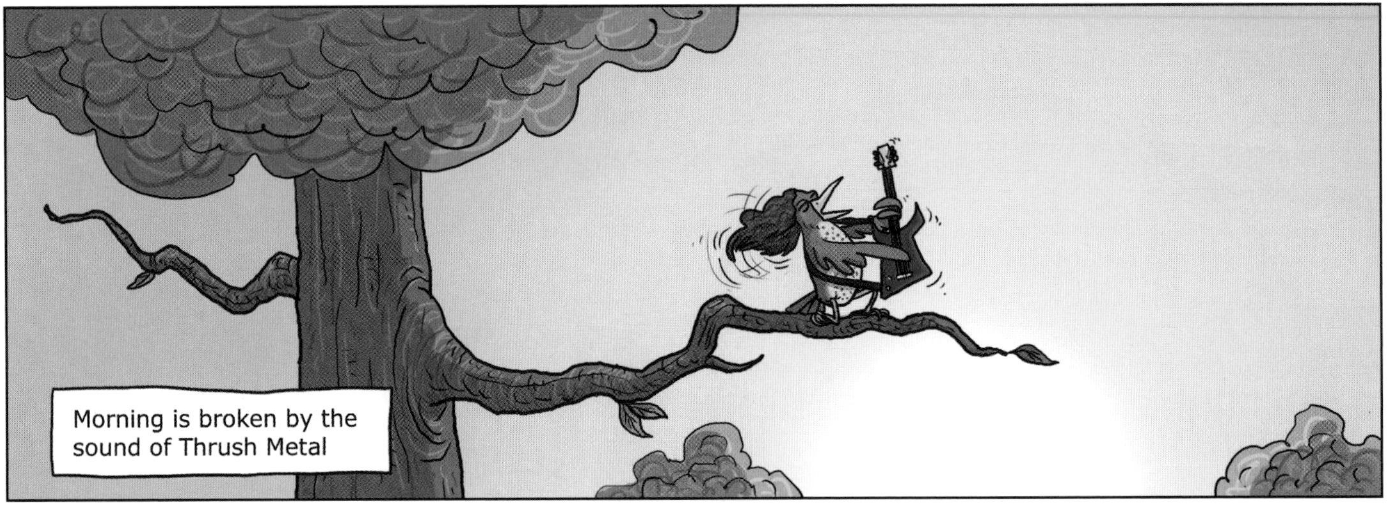
Morning is broken by the sound of Thrush Metal

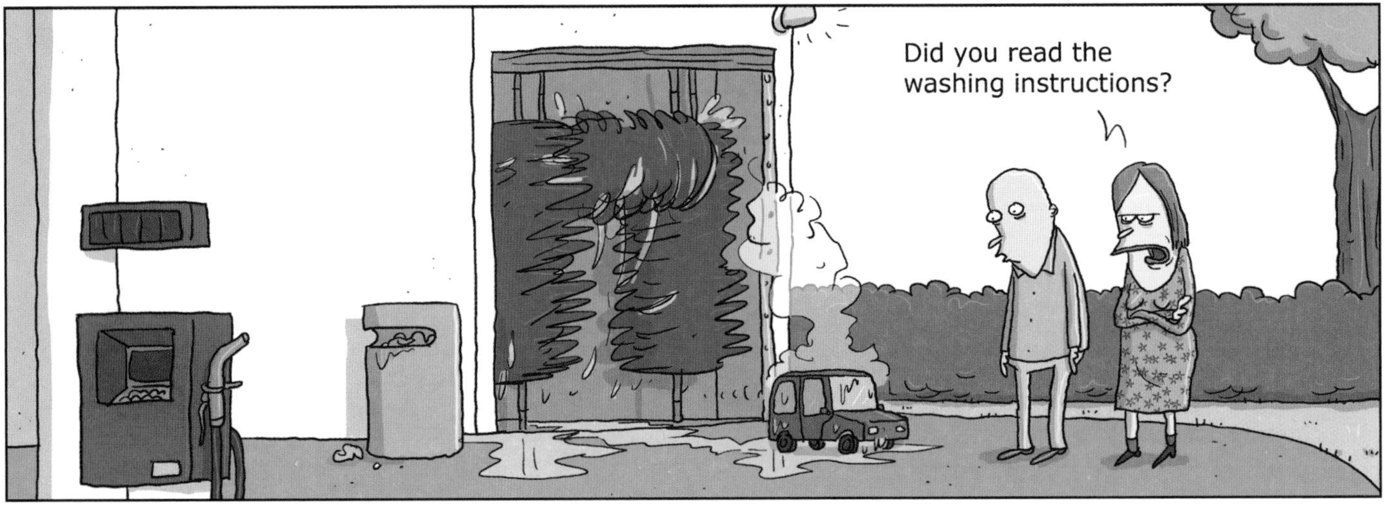
Did you read the washing instructions?

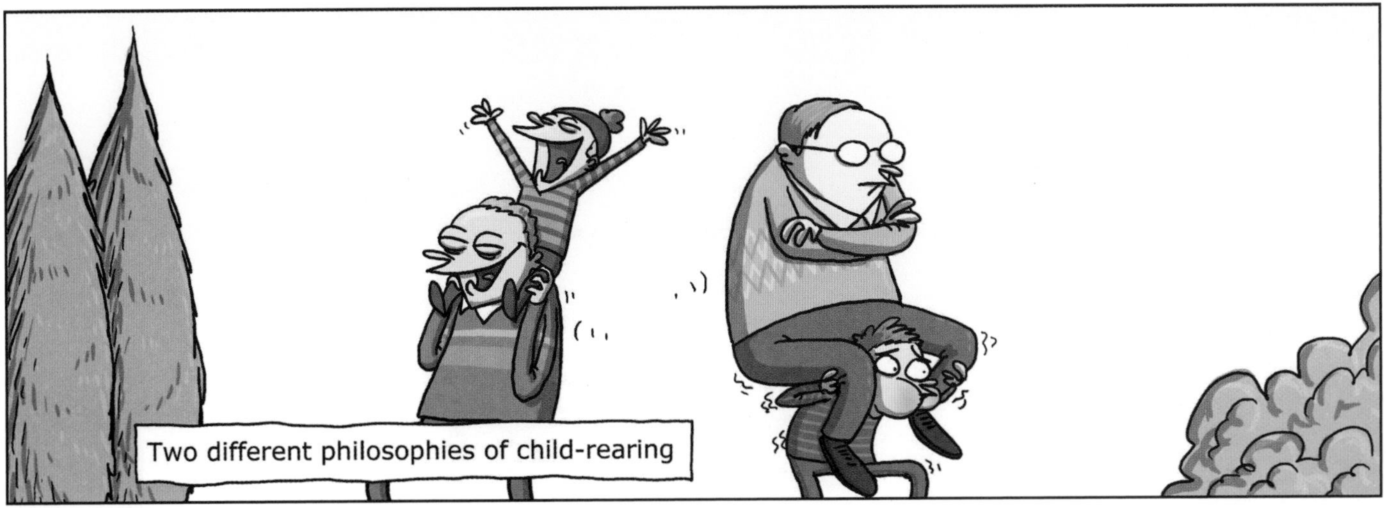
Two different philosophies of child-rearing

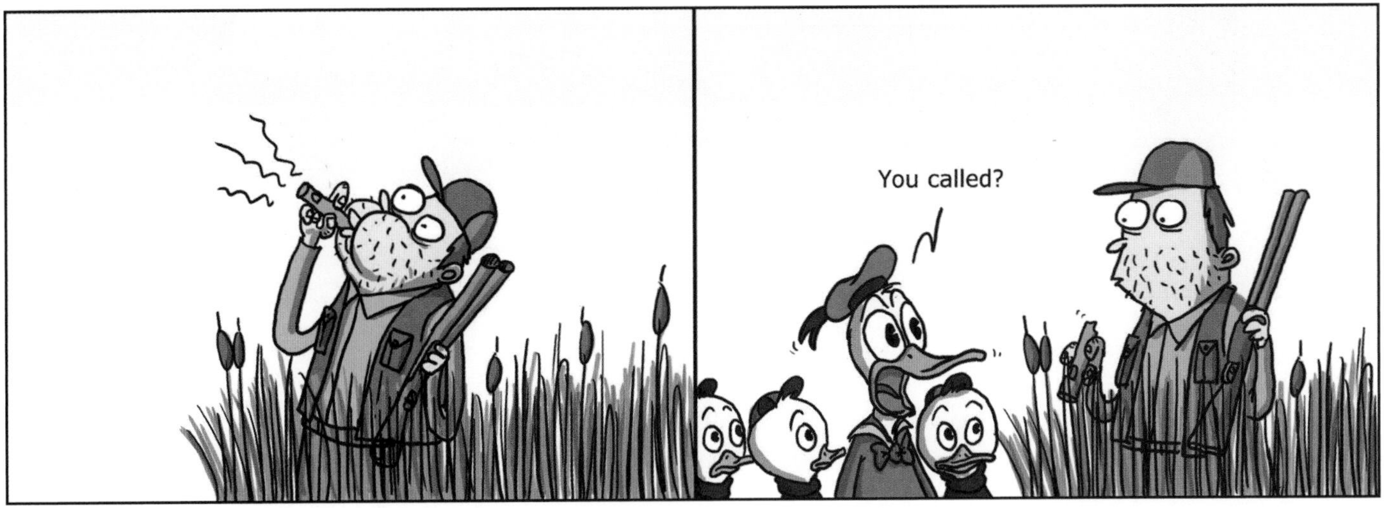
You called?

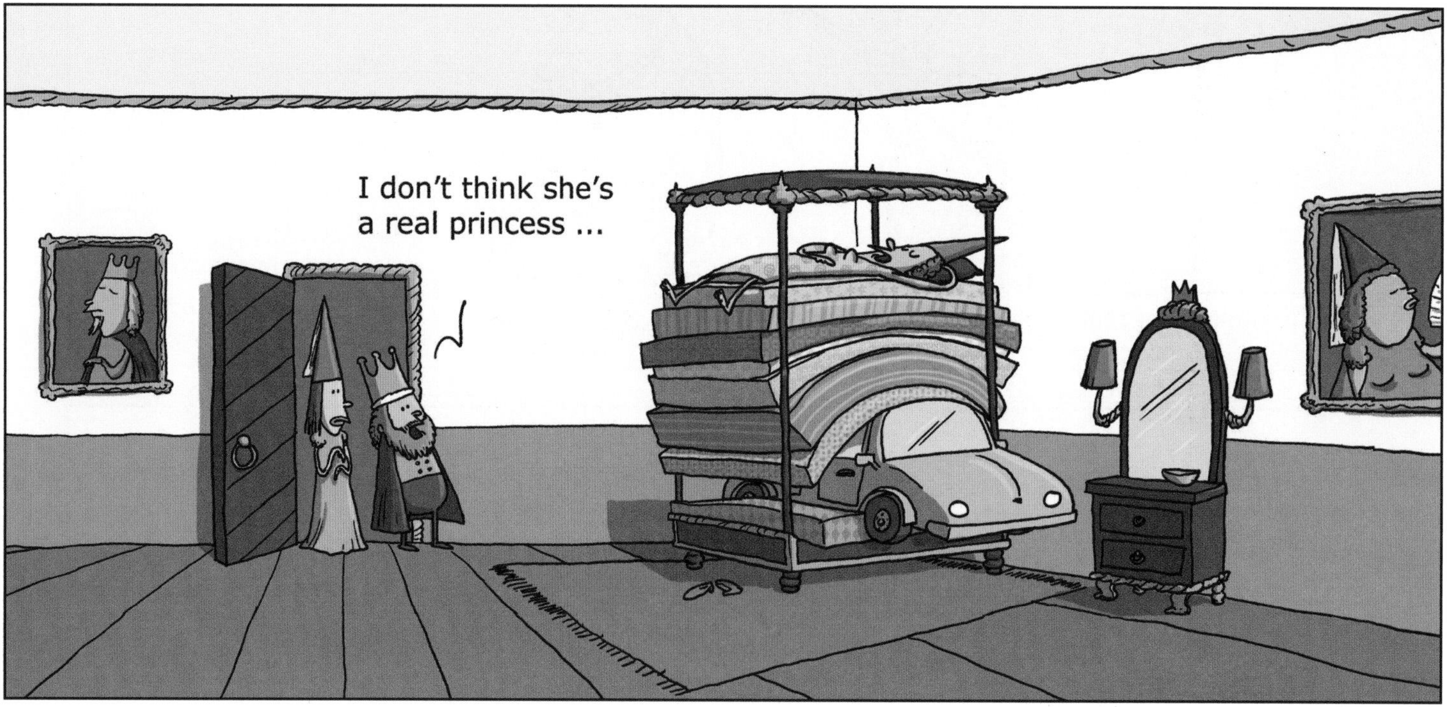
I don't think she's a real princess ...

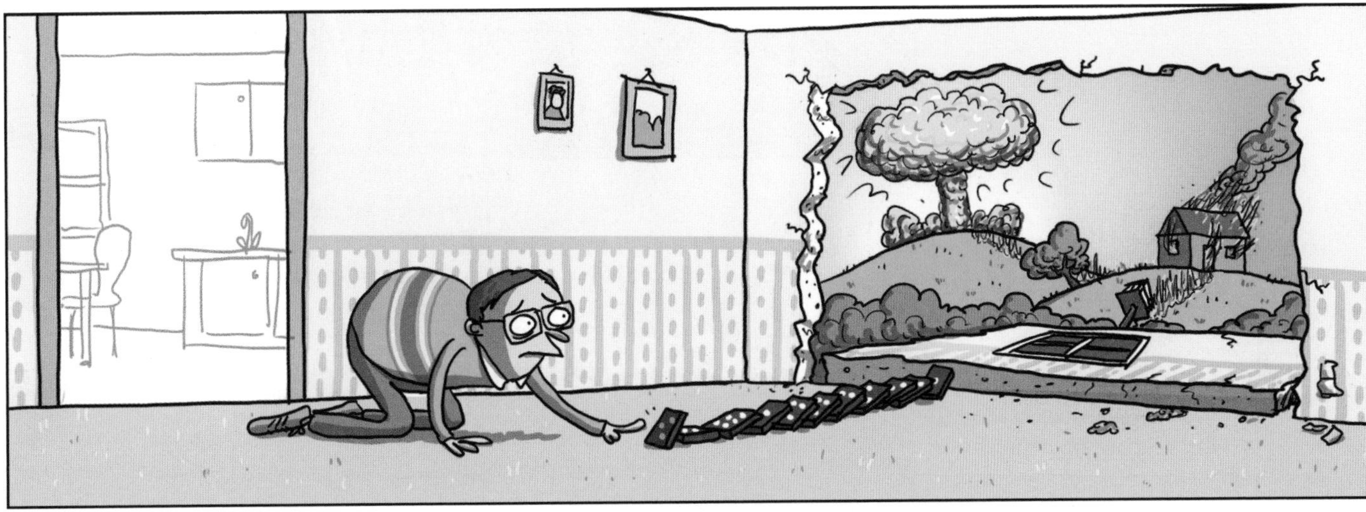

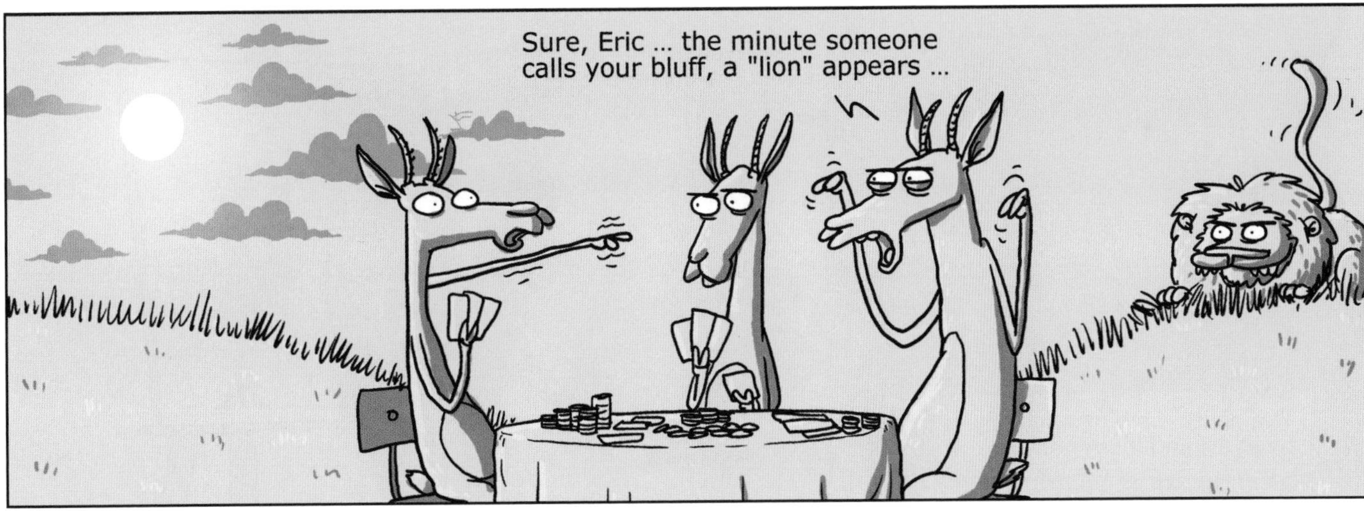
Sure, Eric ... the minute someone calls your bluff, a "lion" appears ...

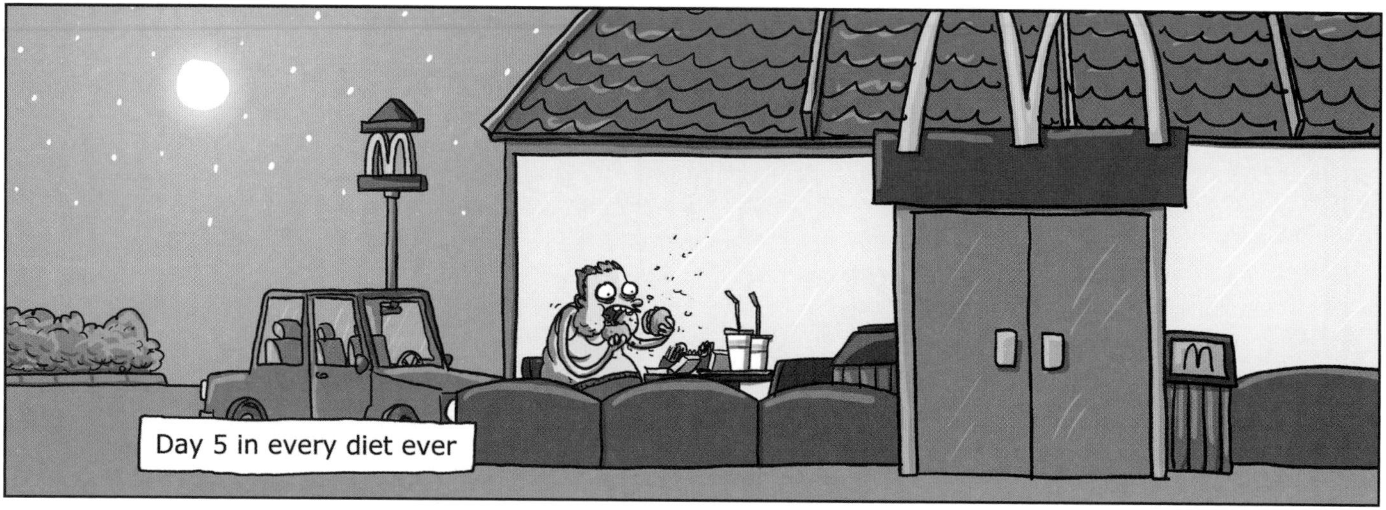
Day 5 in every diet ever

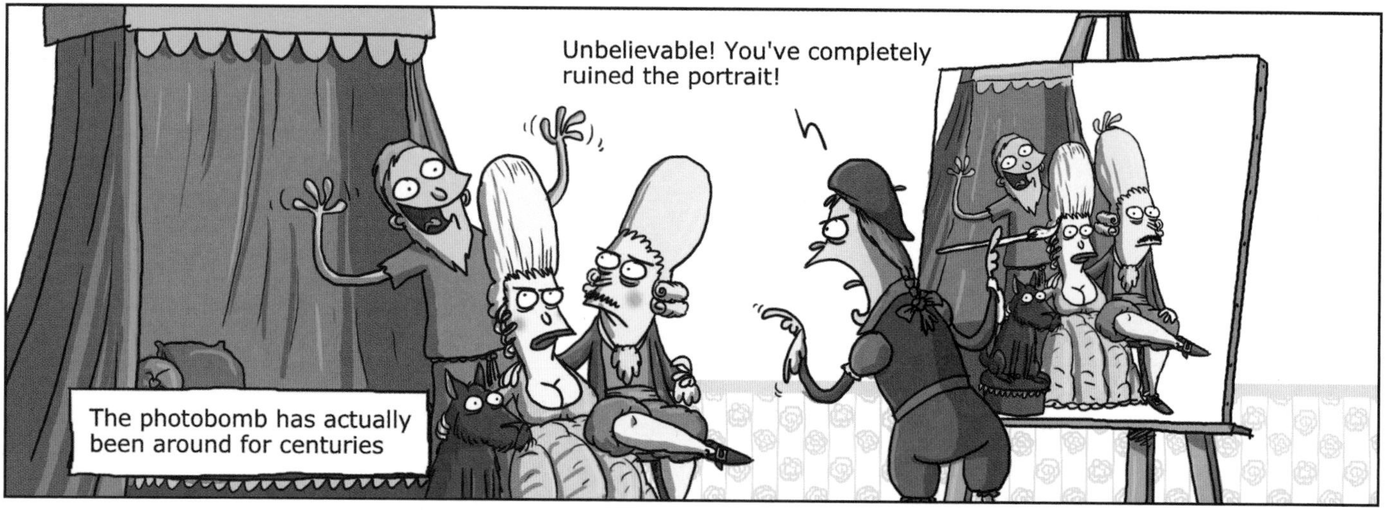
Unbelievable! You've completely ruined the portrait!
The photobomb has actually been around for centuries

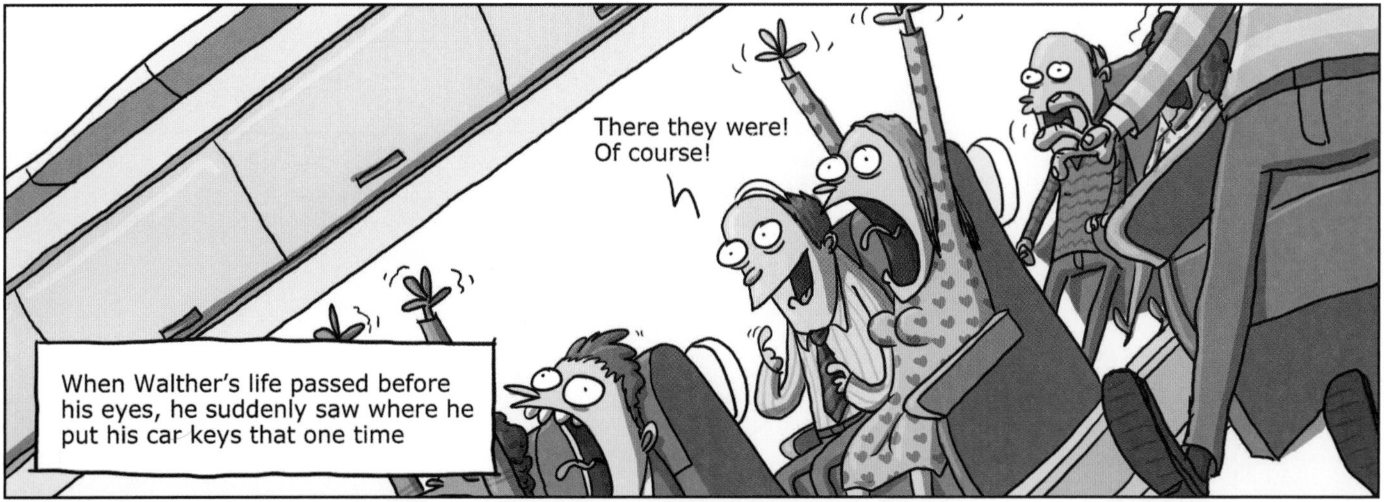
When Walther's life passed before his eyes, he suddenly saw where he put his car keys that one time
There they were! Of course!

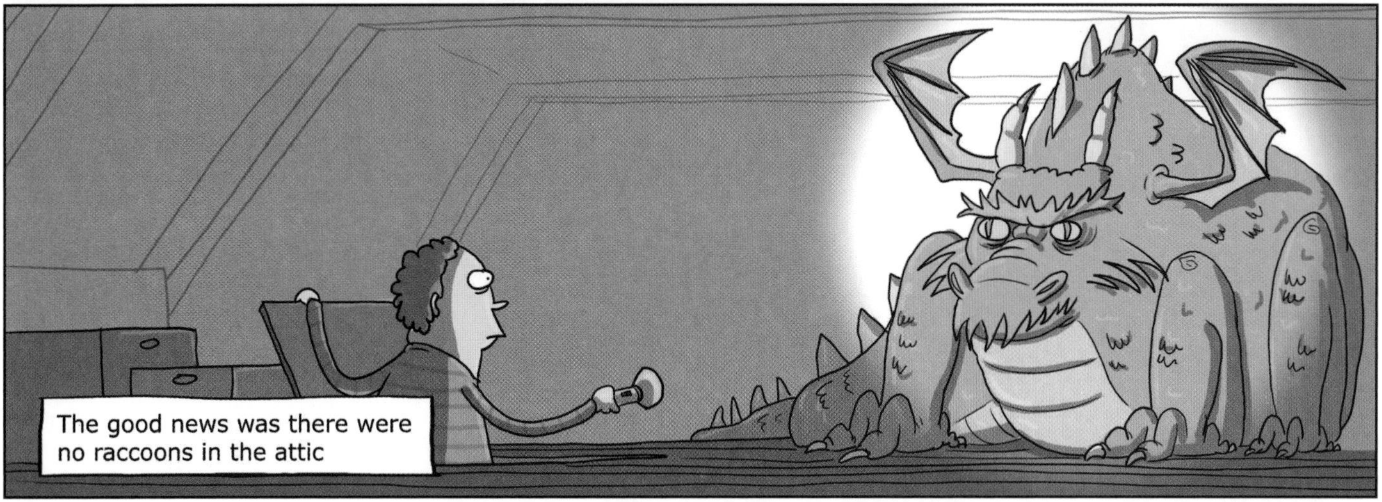
The good news was there were no raccoons in the attic

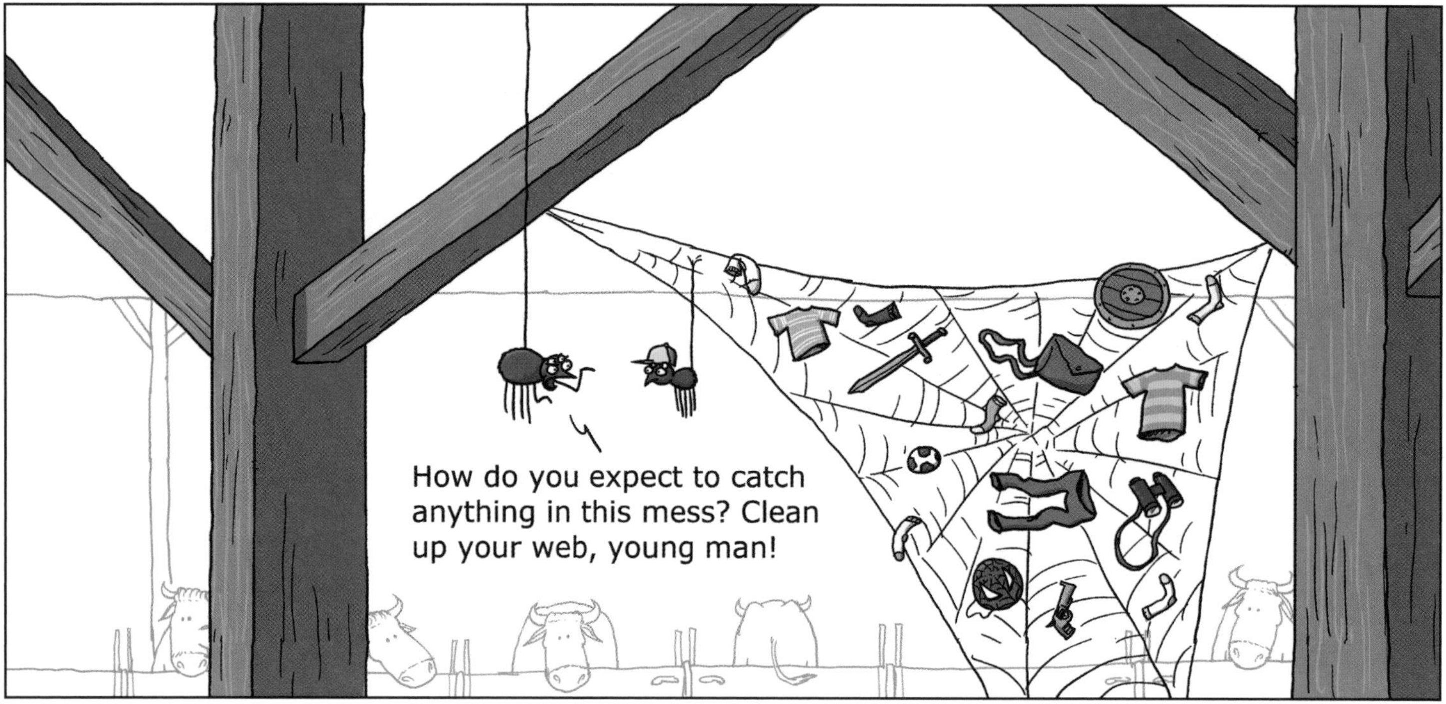
How do you expect to catch anything in this mess? Clean up your web, young man!

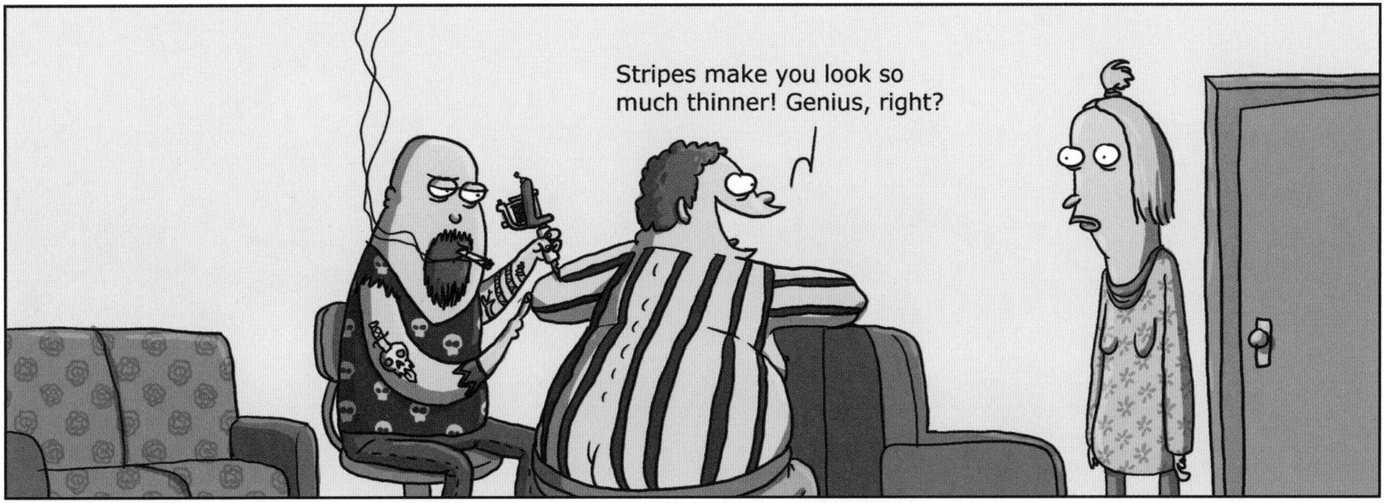
Stripes make you look so much thinner! Genius, right?

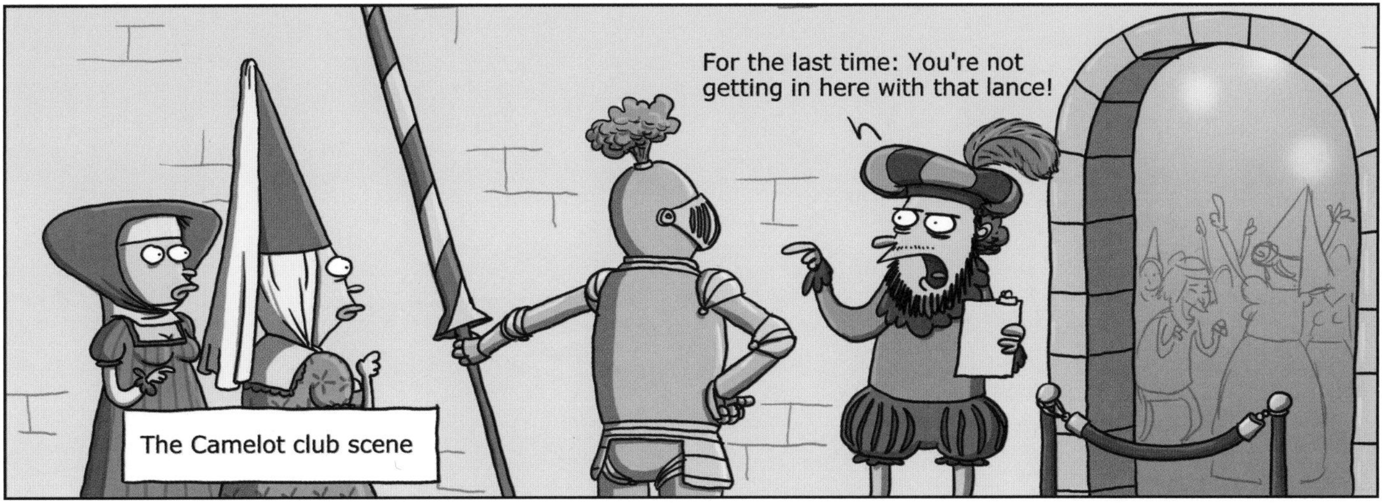
For the last time: You're not getting in here with that lance!
The Camelot club scene

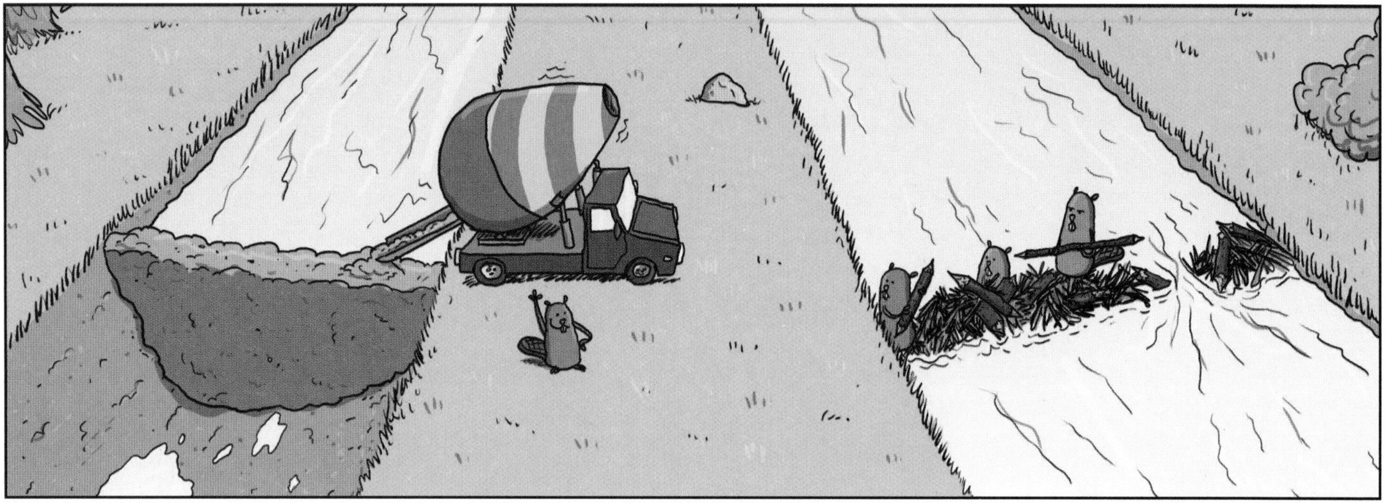

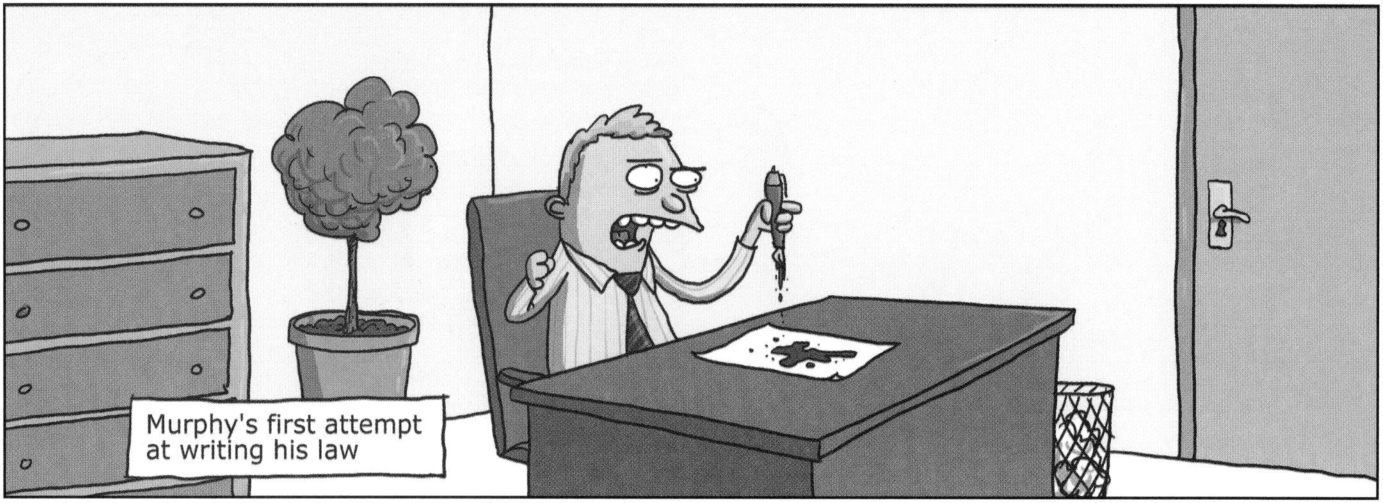
Murphy's first attempt at writing his law

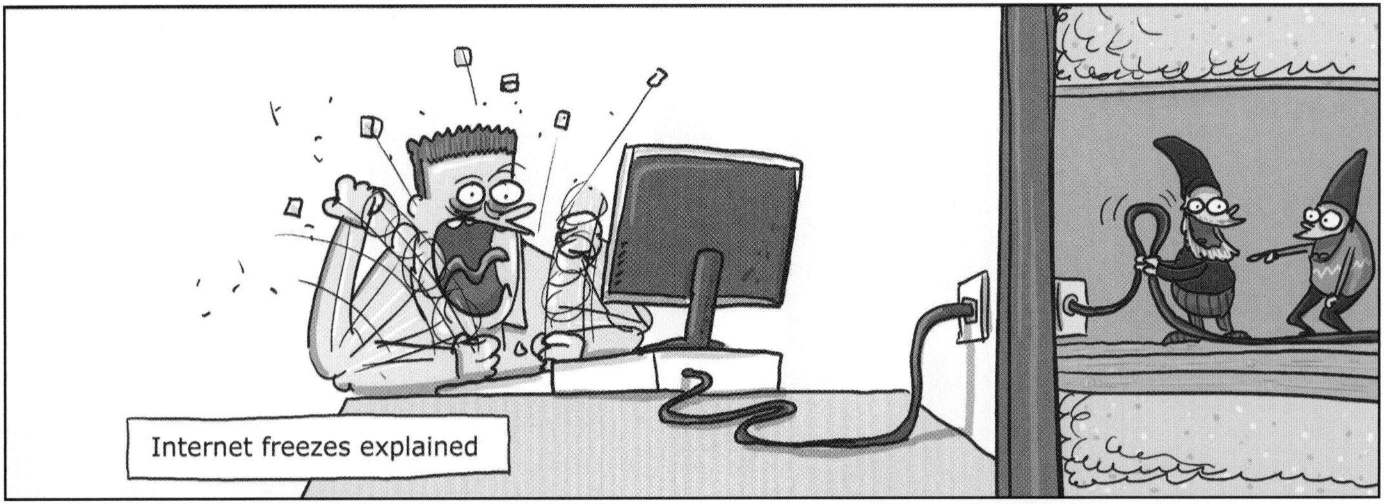
Internet freezes explained

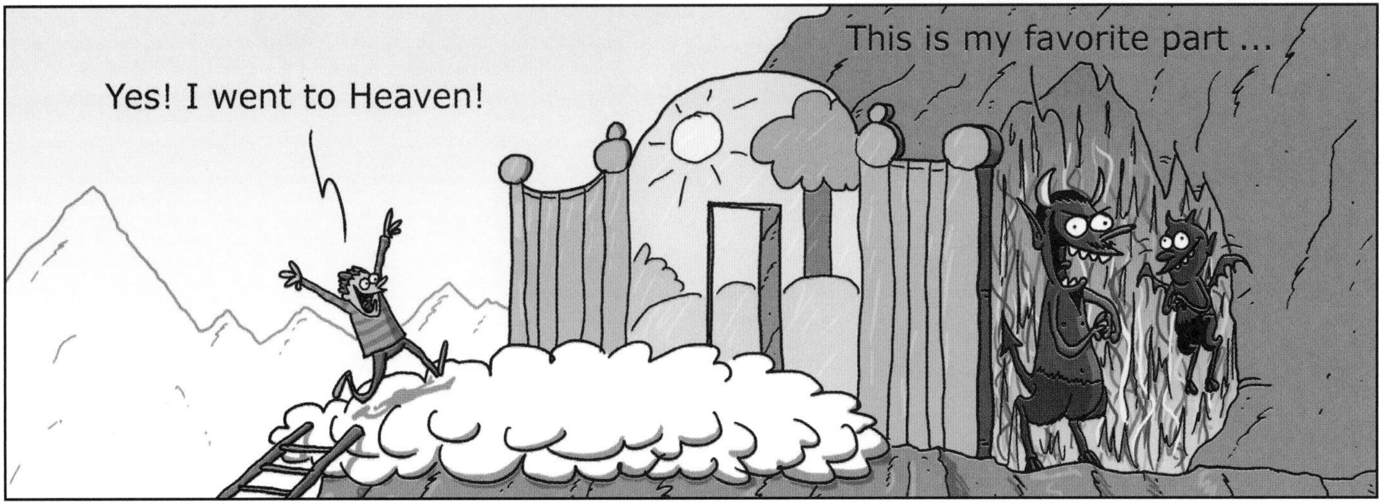
This is my favorite part ...
Yes! I went to Heaven!

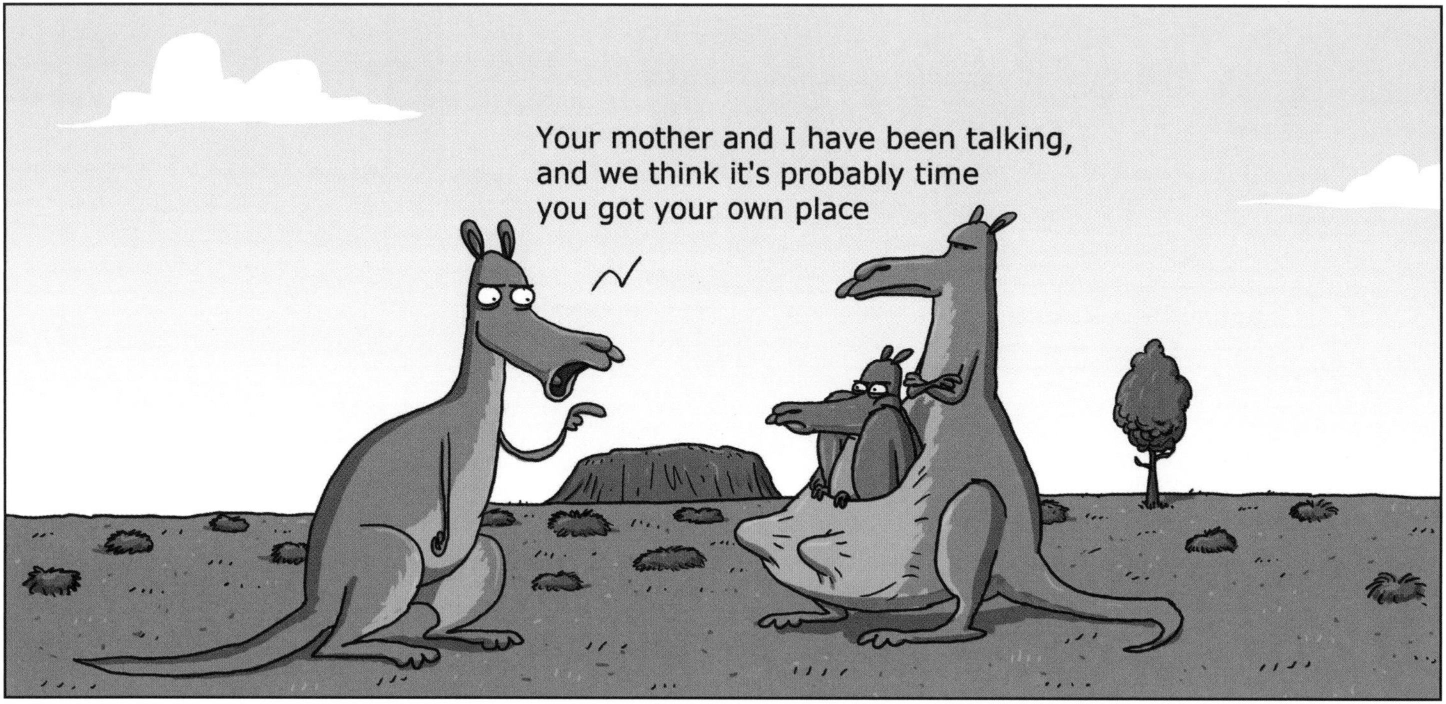
Your mother and I have been talking,
and we think it's probably time
you got your own place

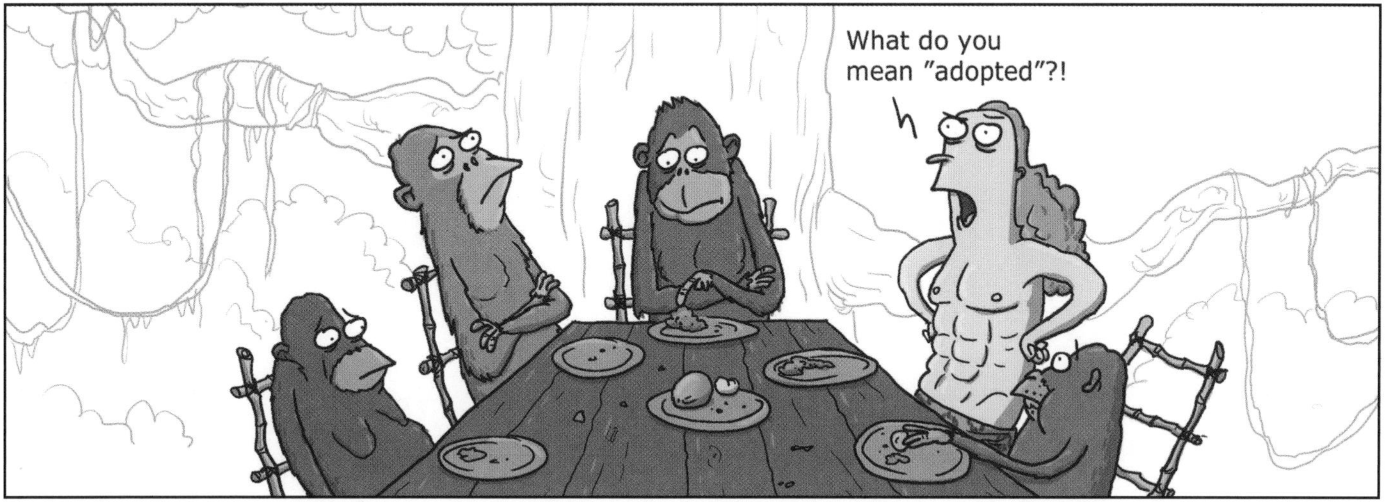
What do you
mean "adopted"?!

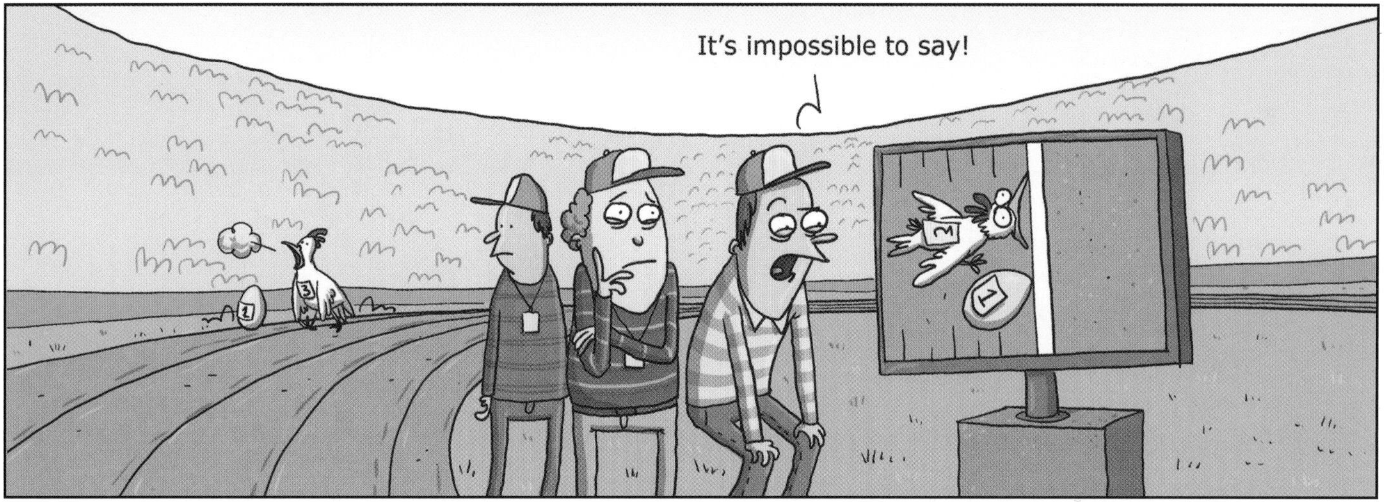
It's impossible to say!

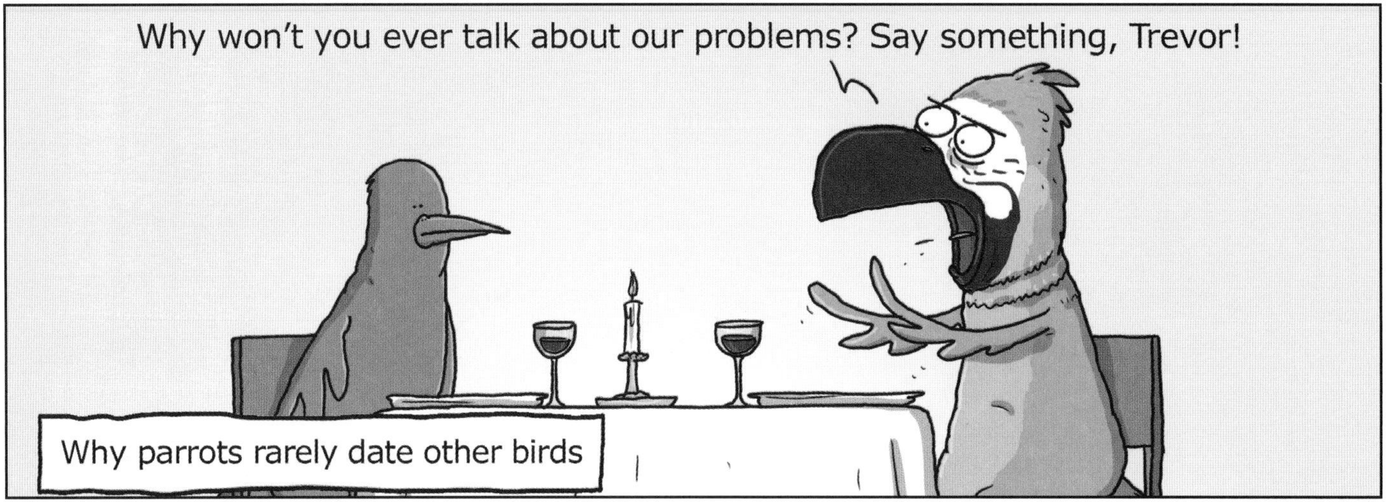
Why won't you ever talk about our problems? Say something, Trevor!
Why parrots rarely date other birds

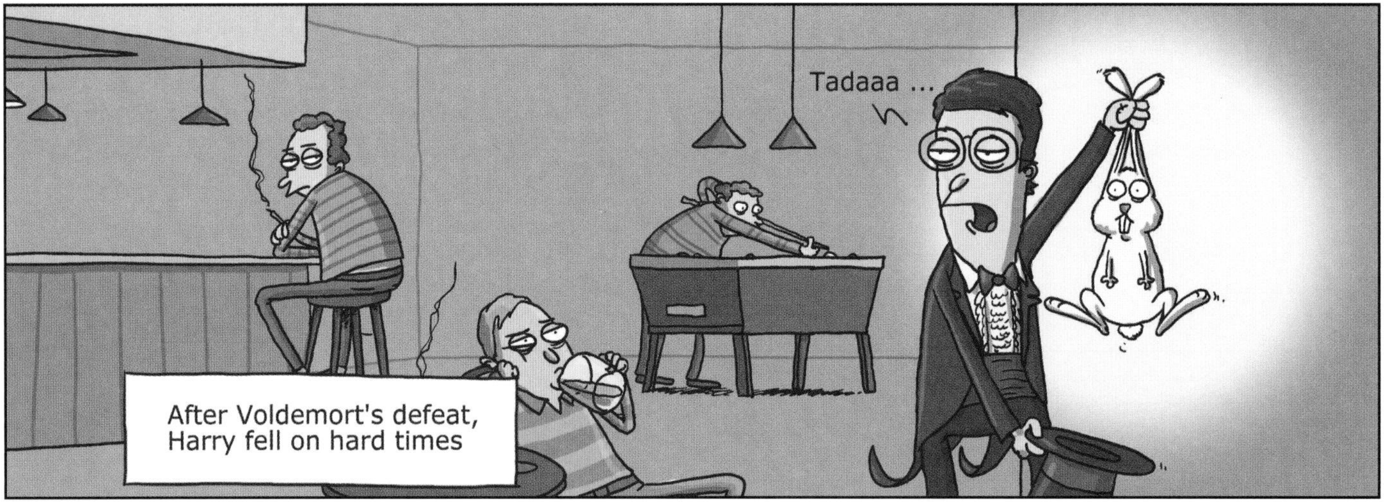
After Voldemort's defeat, Harry fell on hard times
Tadaaa ...

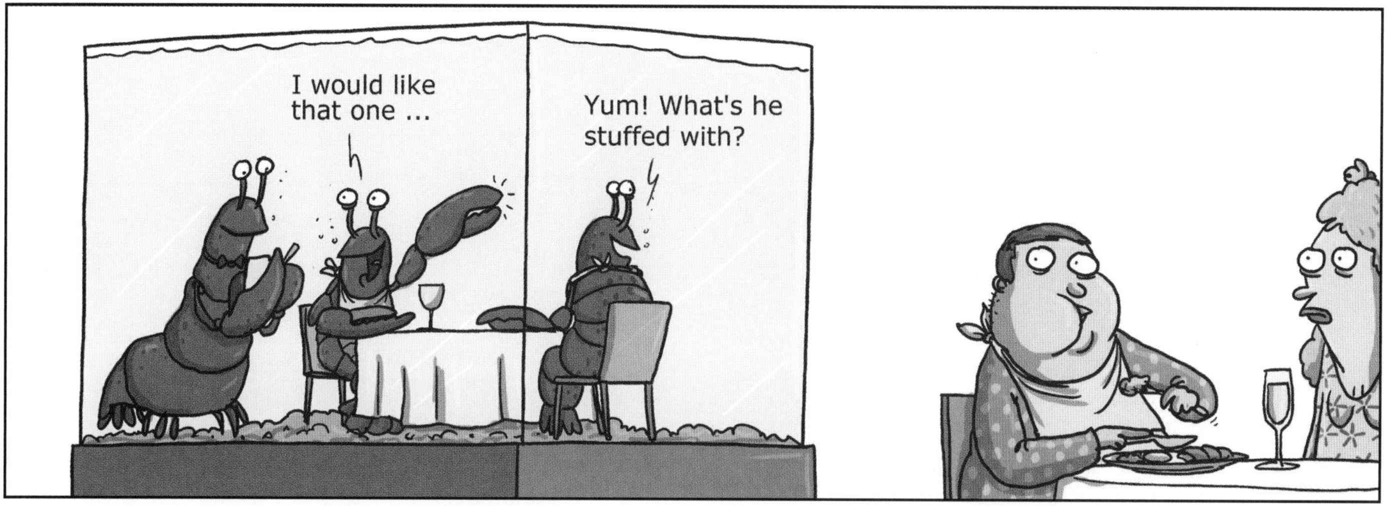

I would like that one ...
Yum! What's he stuffed with?

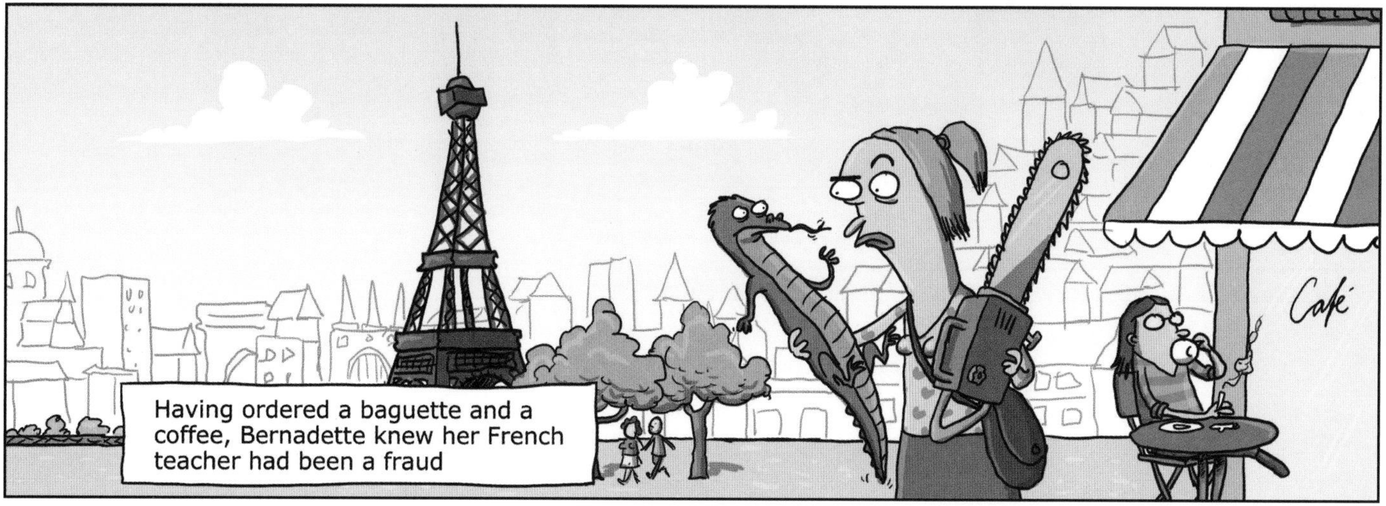

Café
Having ordered a baguette and a coffee, Bernadette knew her French teacher had been a fraud

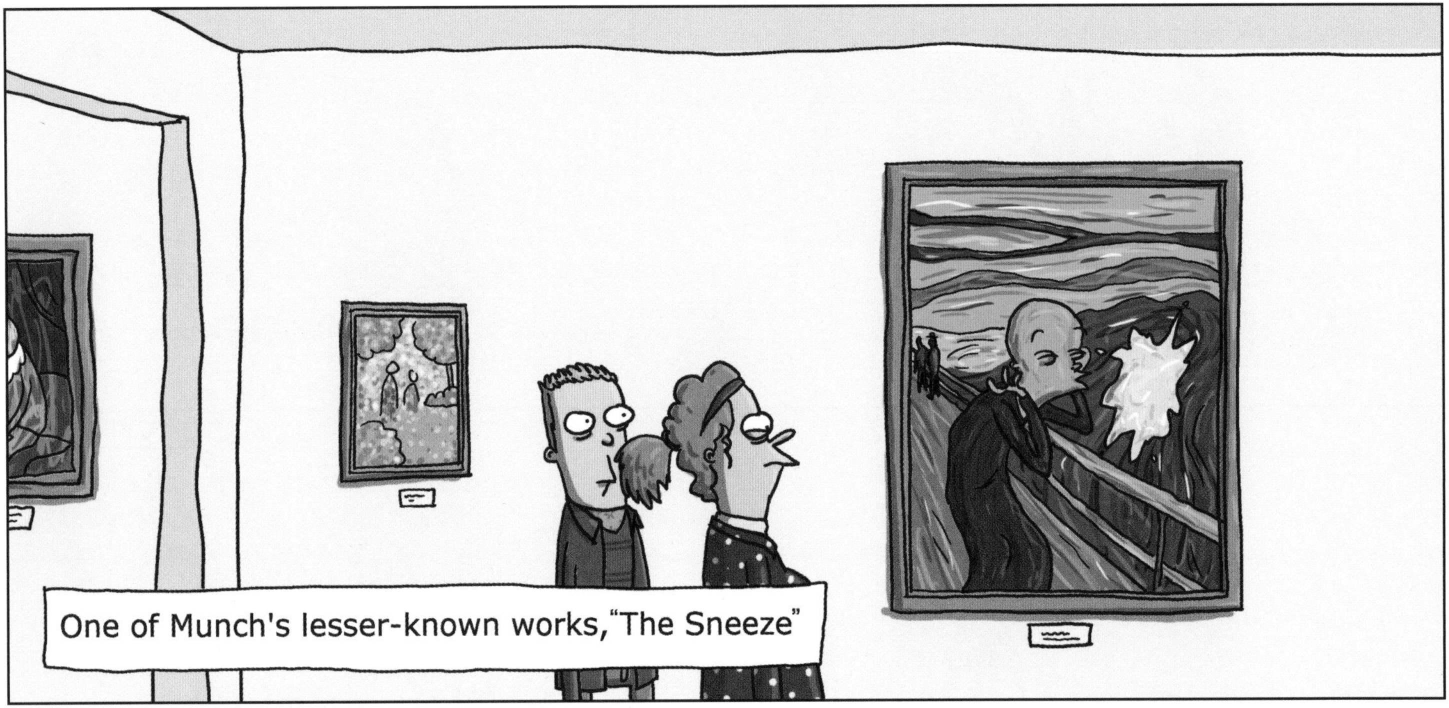
One of Munch's lesser-known works,"The Sneeze"

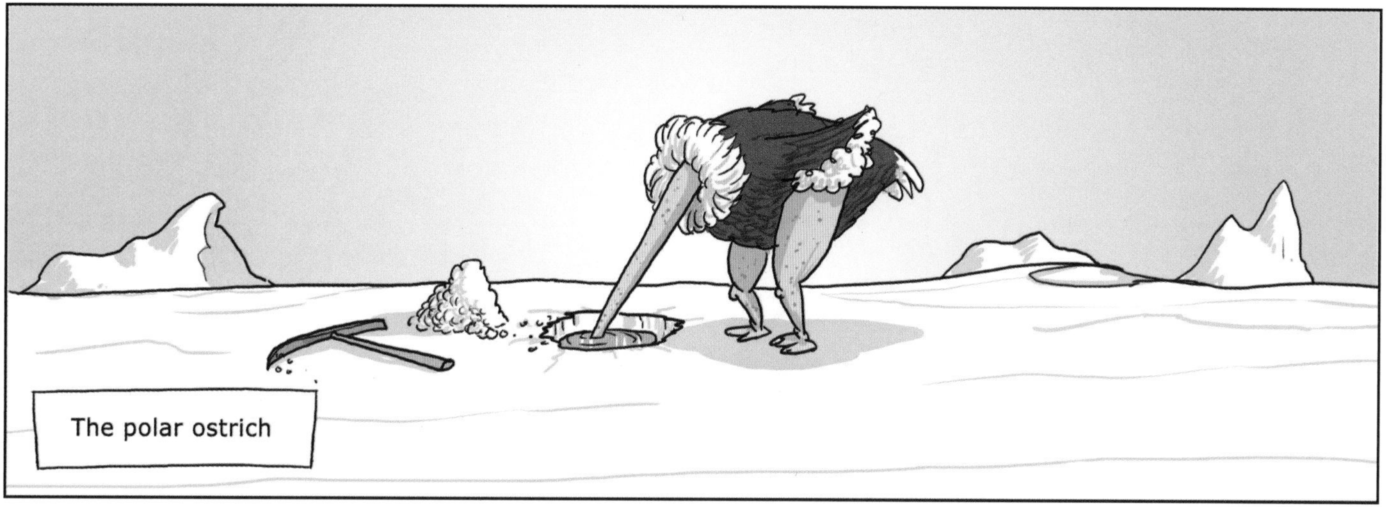
The polar ostrich

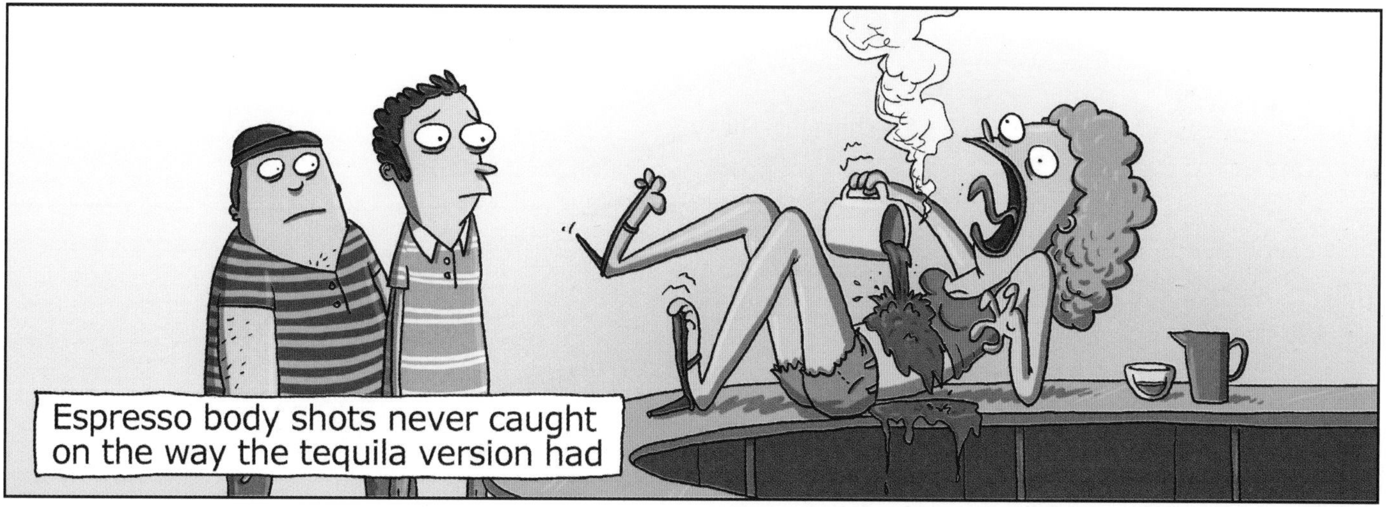
Espresso body shots never caught on the way the tequila version had

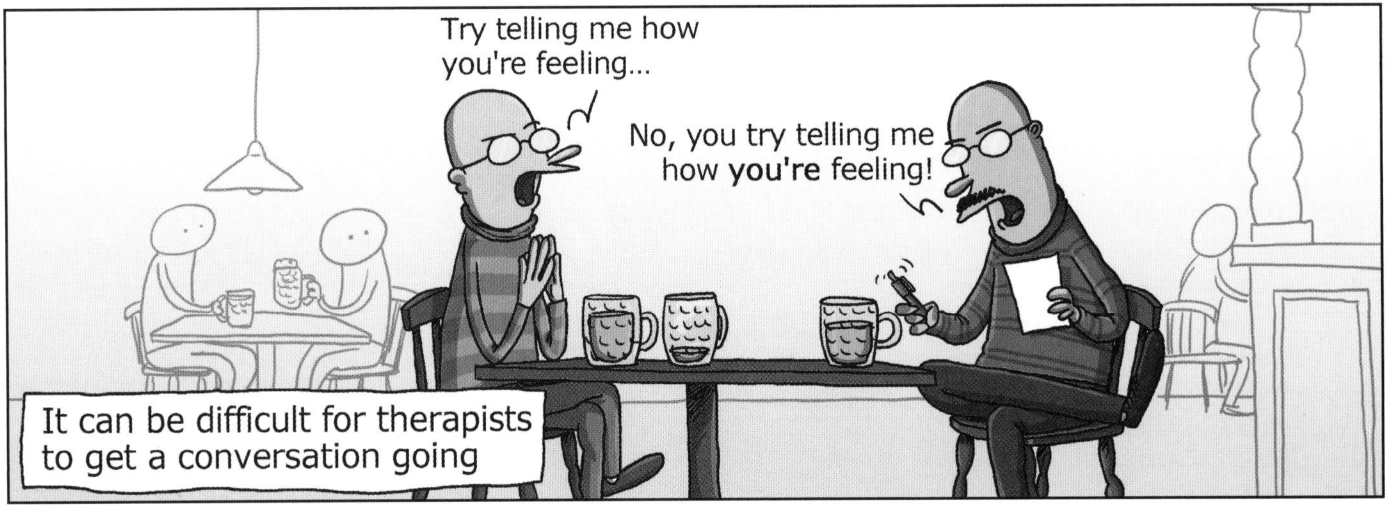
Try telling me how you're feeling...
No, you try telling me how **you're** feeling!
It can be difficult for therapists to get a conversation going

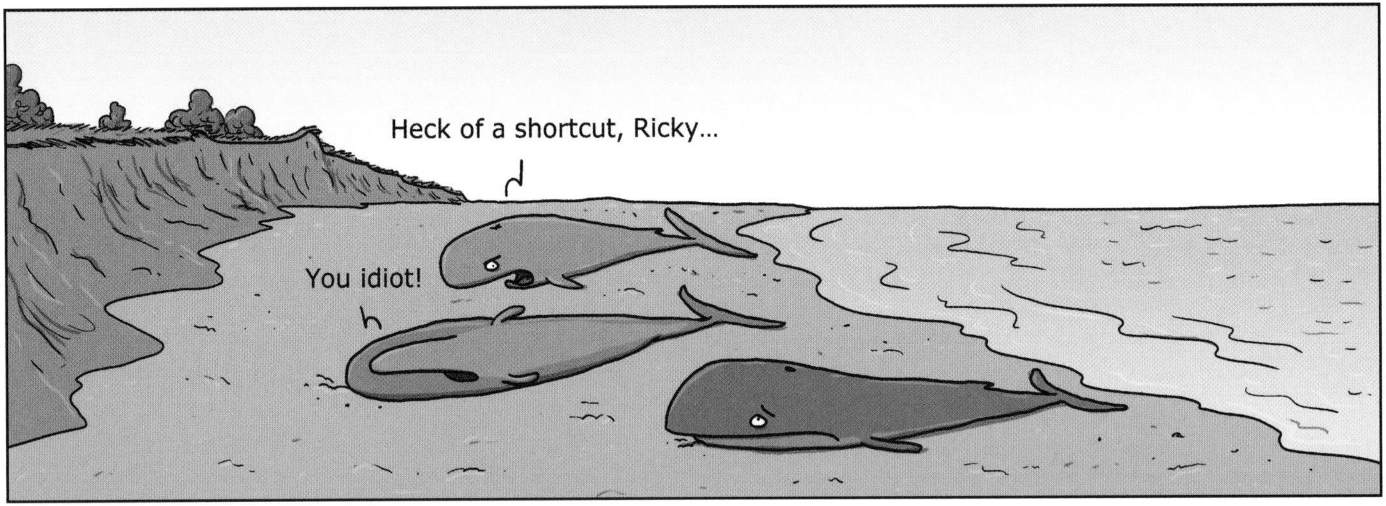
Heck of a shortcut, Ricky...
You idiot!

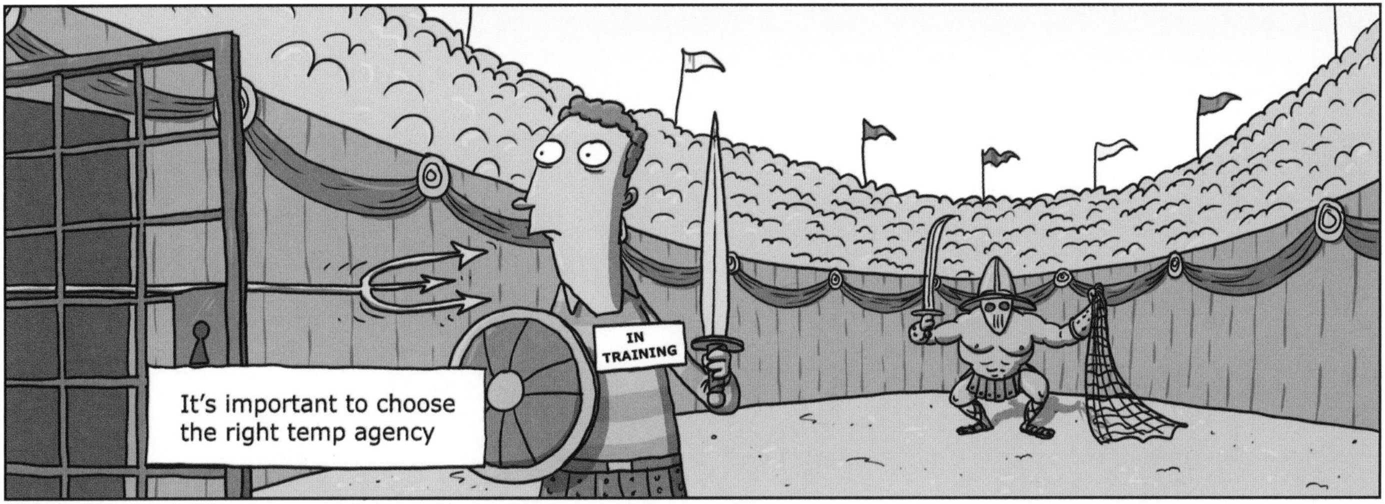
IN TRAINING
It's important to choose the right temp agency

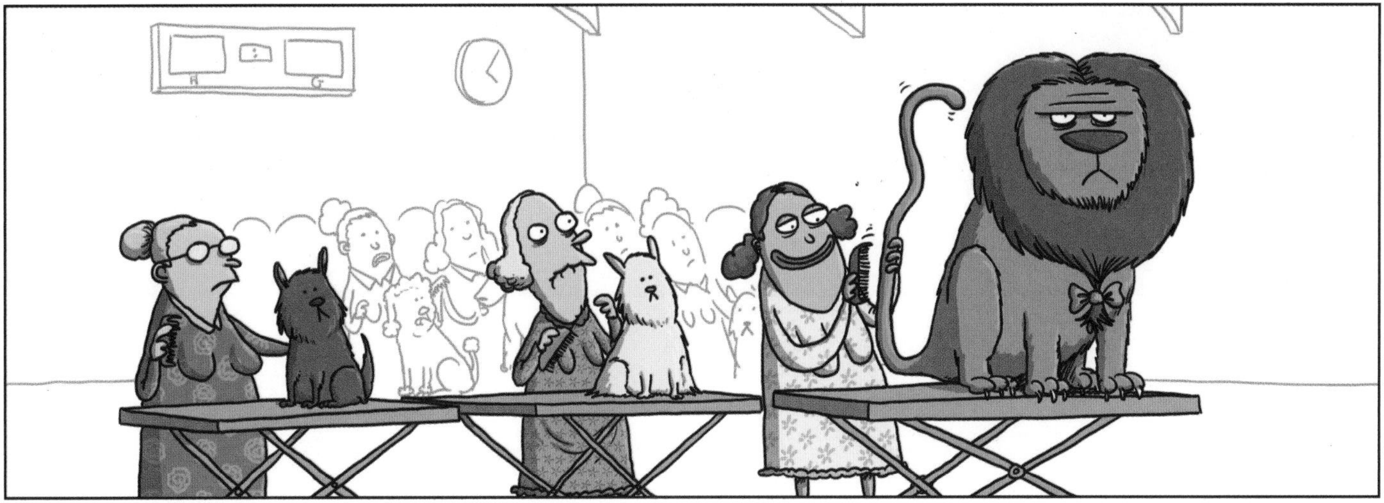

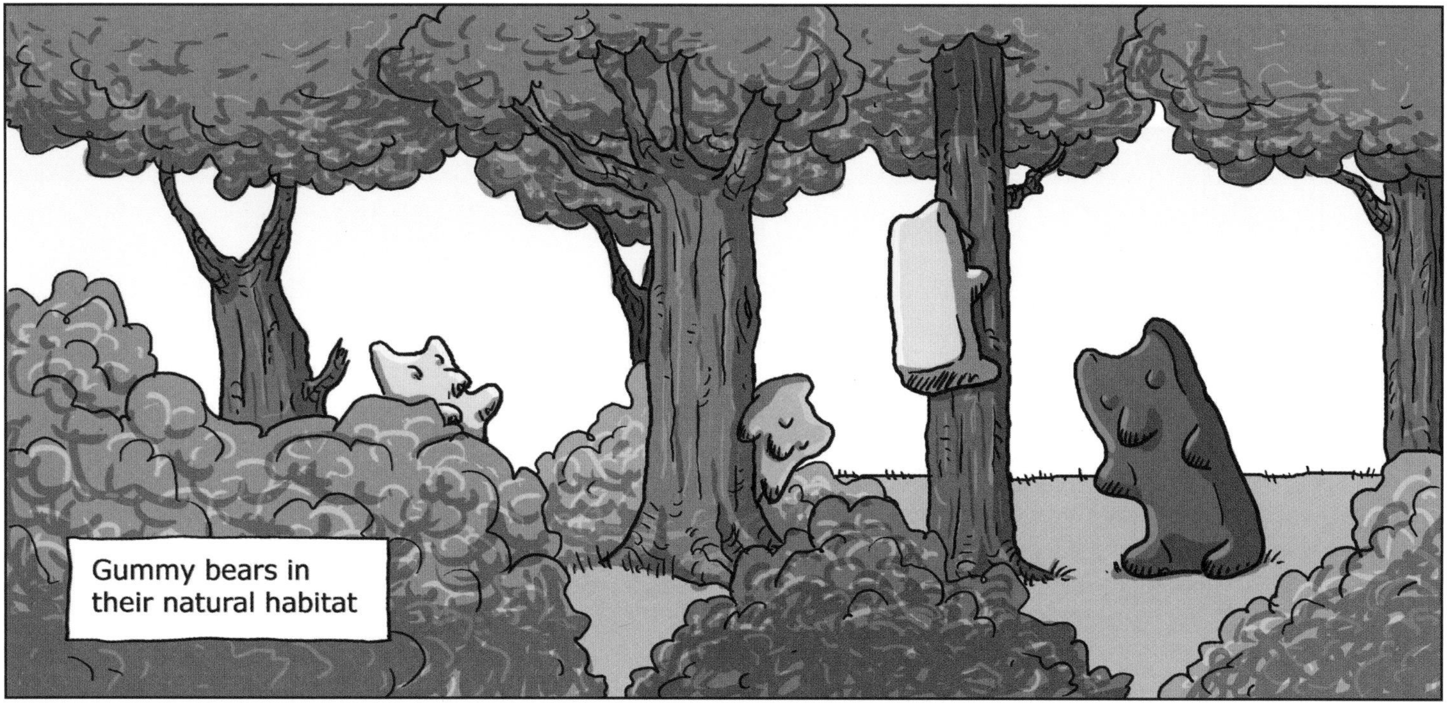
Gummy bears in
their natural habitat

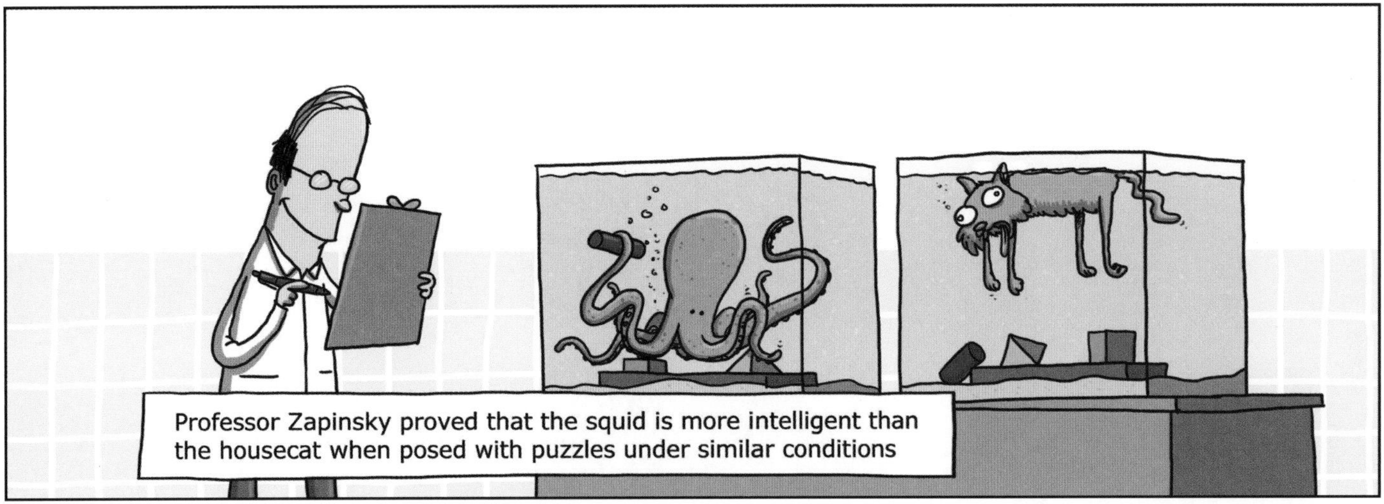
Professor Zapinsky proved that the squid is more intelligent than the housecat when posed with puzzles under similar conditions

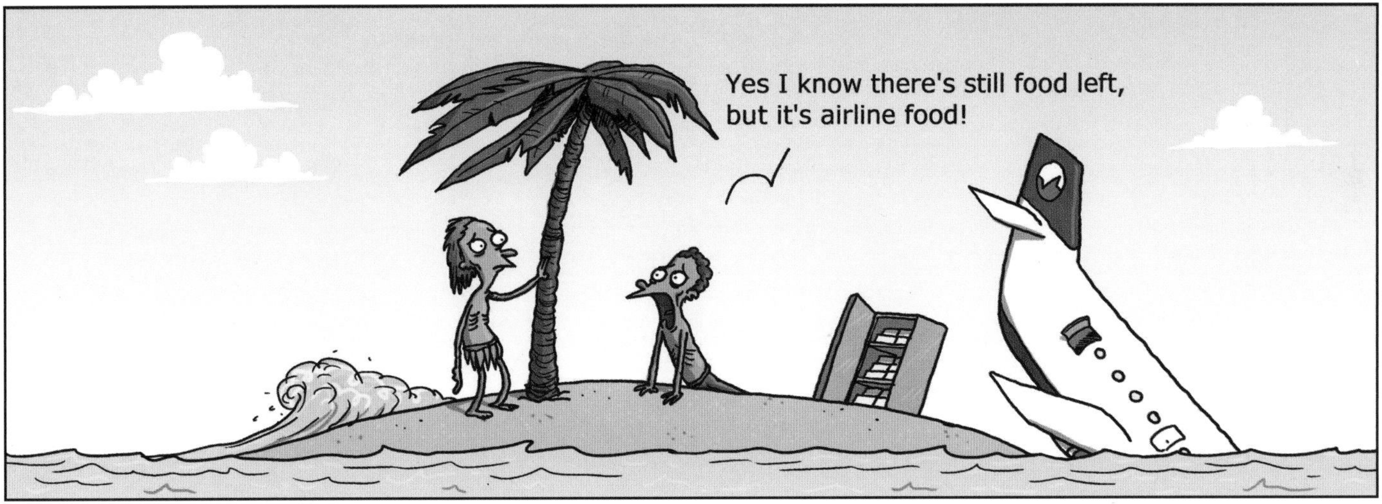
Yes I know there's still food left, but it's airline food!

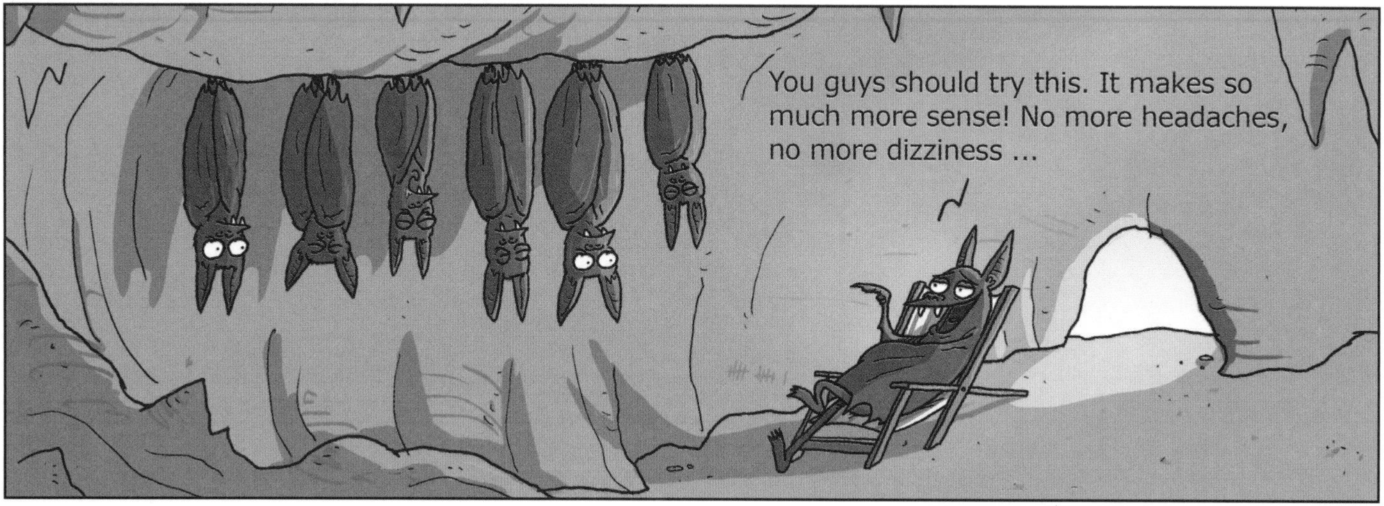
You guys should try this. It makes so much more sense! No more headaches, no more dizziness ...

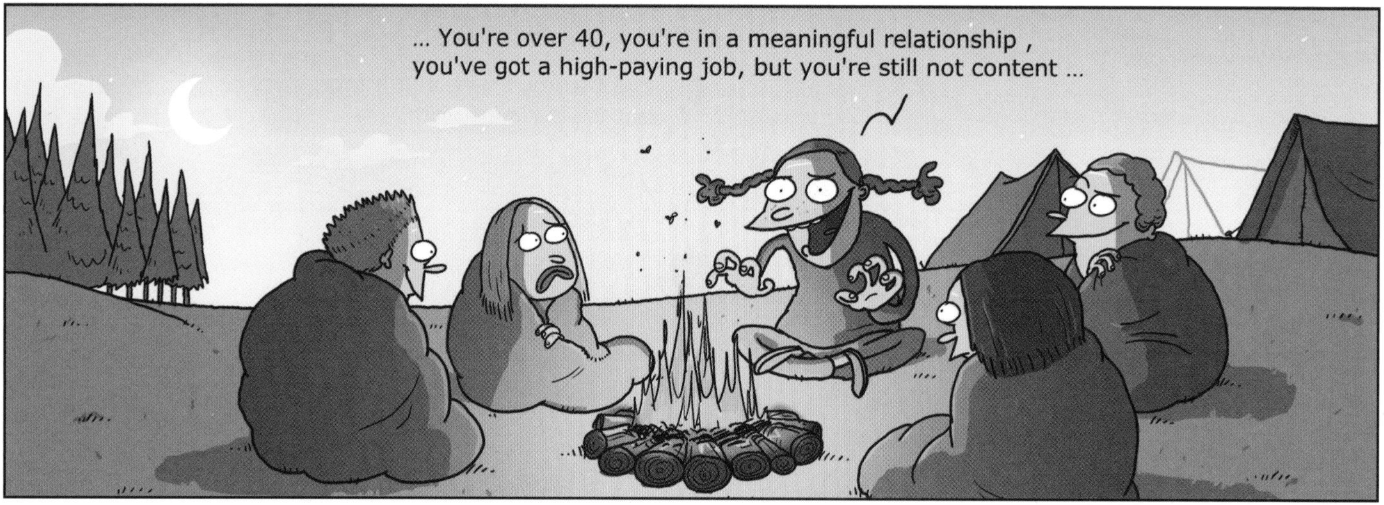
... You're over 40, you're in a meaningful relationship ,
you've got a high-paying job, but you're still not content ...

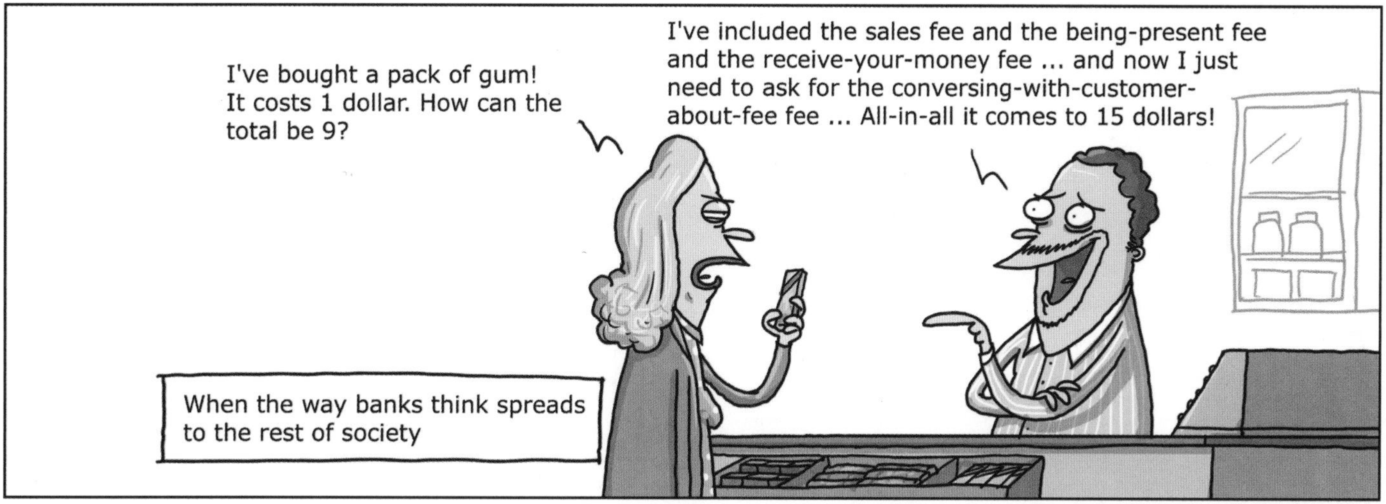
When the way banks think spreads to the rest of society
I've bought a pack of gum! It costs 1 dollar. How can the total be 9?
I've included the sales fee and the being-present fee and the receive-your-money fee ... and now I just need to ask for the conversing-with-customer-about-fee fee ... All-in-all it comes to 15 dollars!

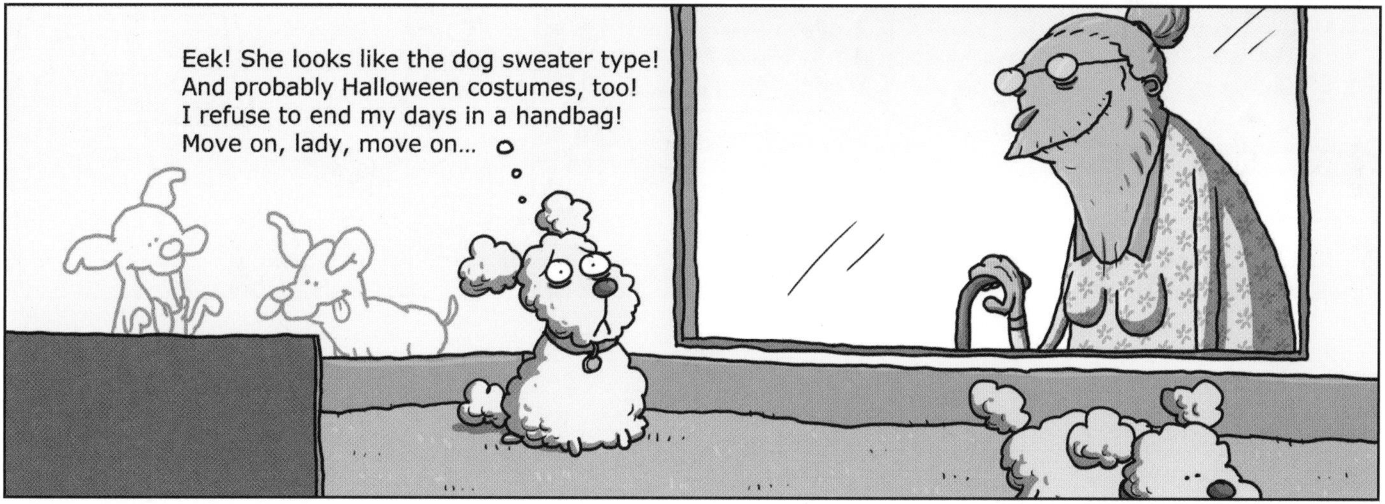
Eek! She looks like the dog sweater type!
And probably Halloween costumes, too!
I refuse to end my days in a handbag!
Move on, lady, move on...

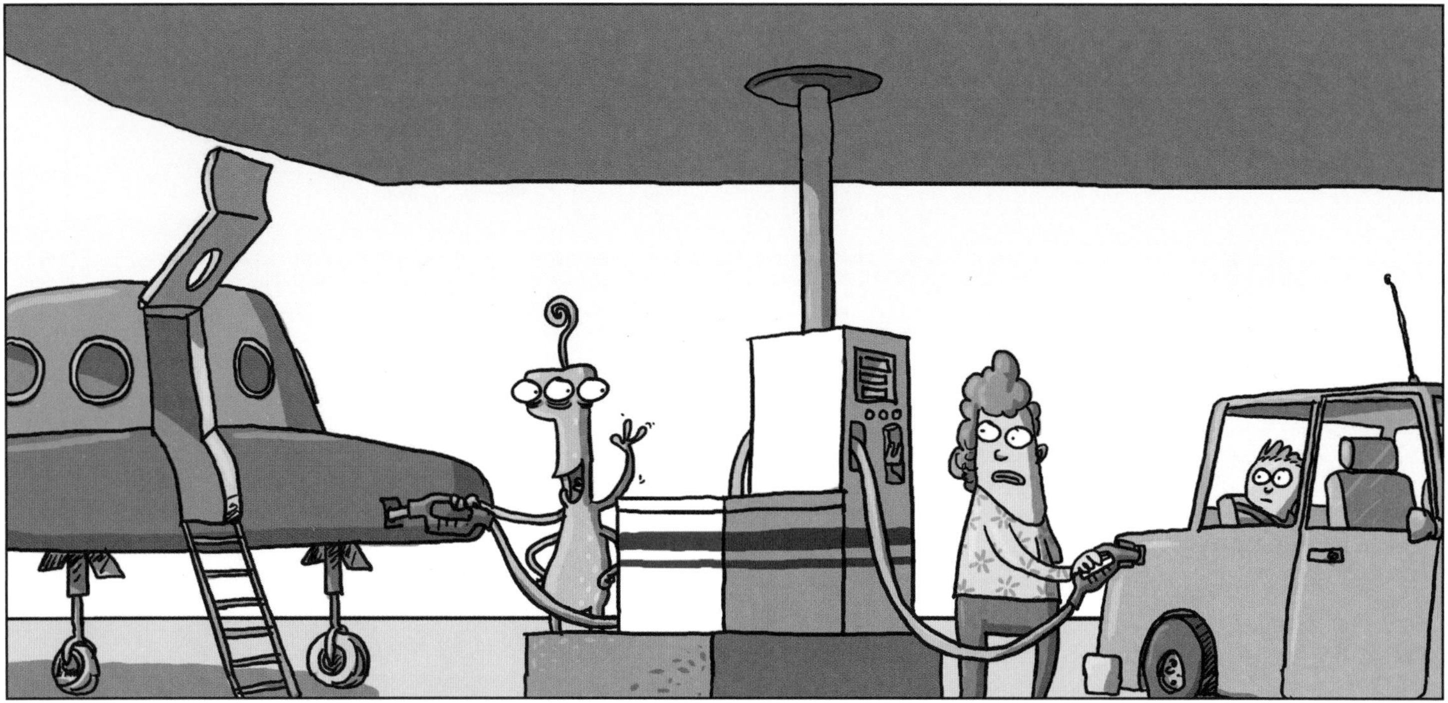

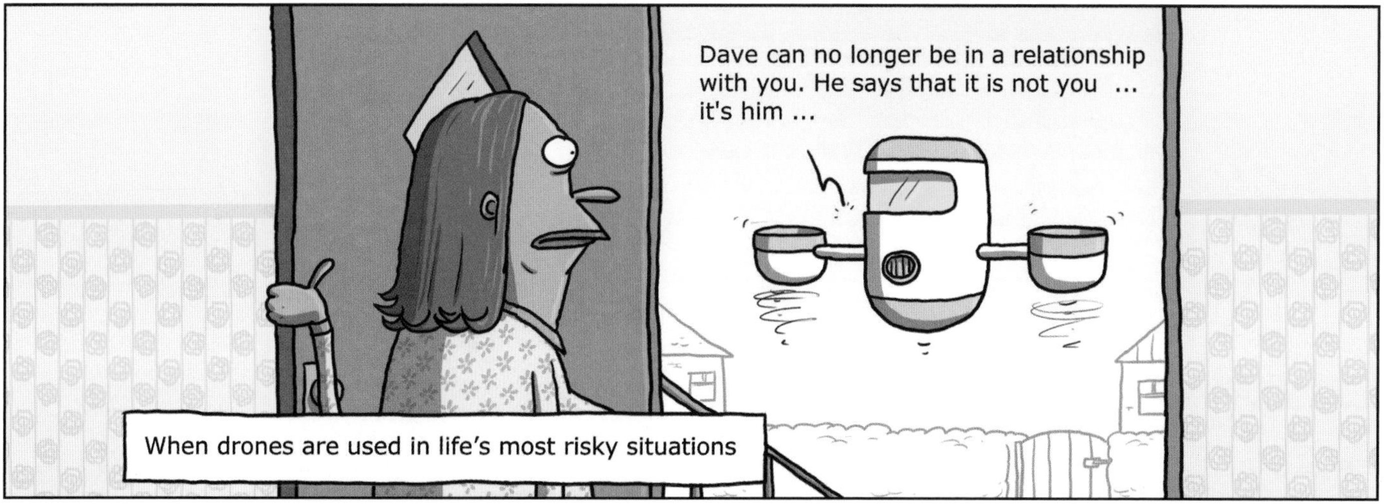
Dave can no longer be in a relationship with you. He says that it is not you ... it's him ...
When drones are used in life's most risky situations

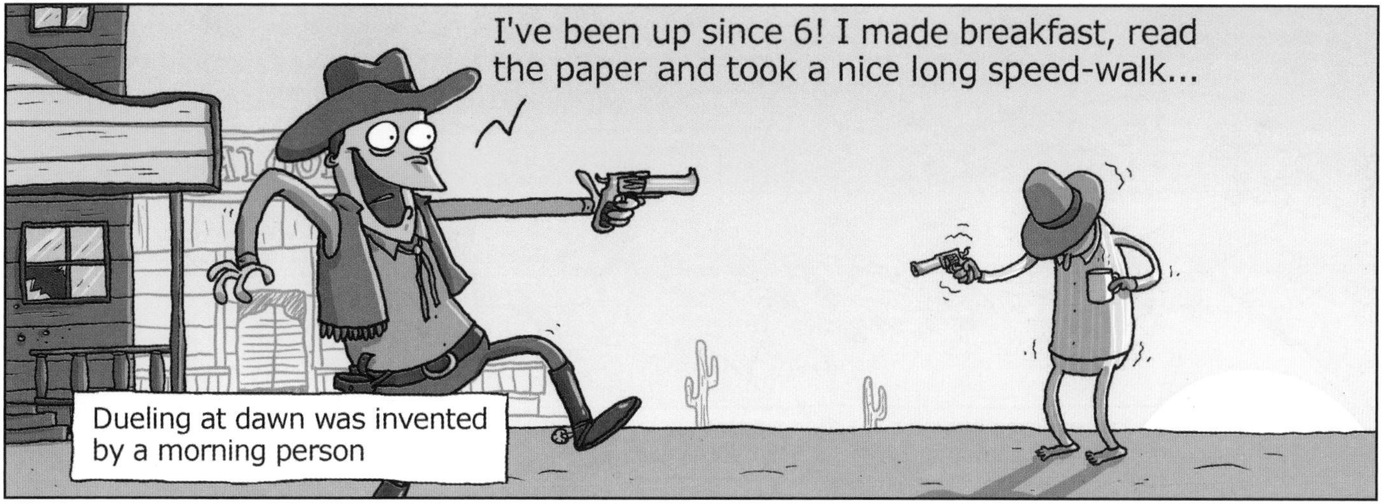
I've been up since 6! I made breakfast, read the paper and took a nice long speed-walk...
Dueling at dawn was invented by a morning person

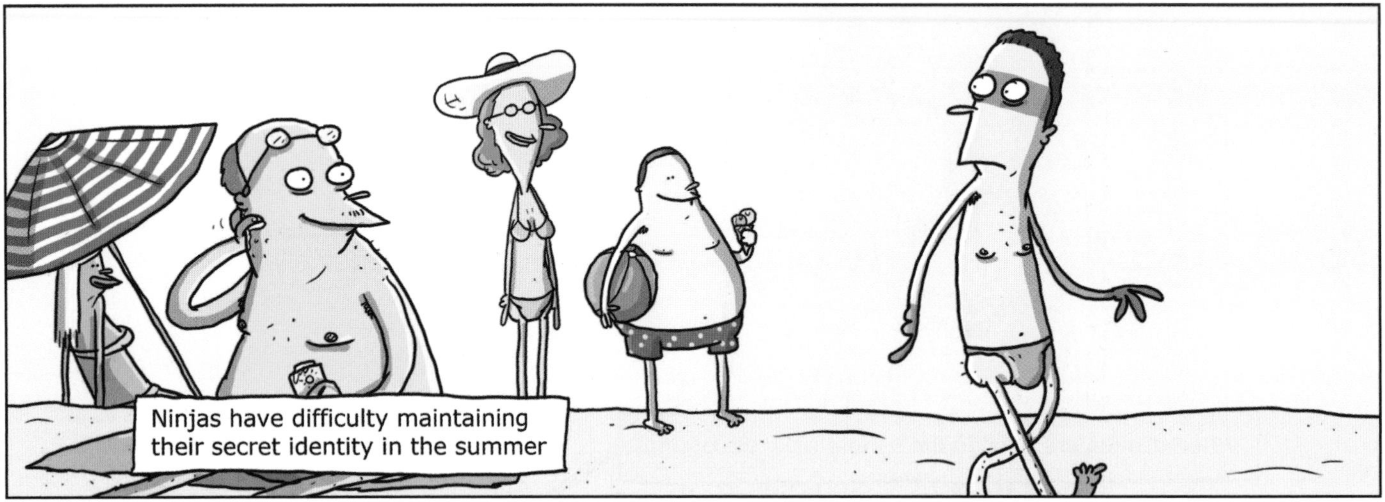
Ninjas have difficulty maintaining
their secret identity in the summer

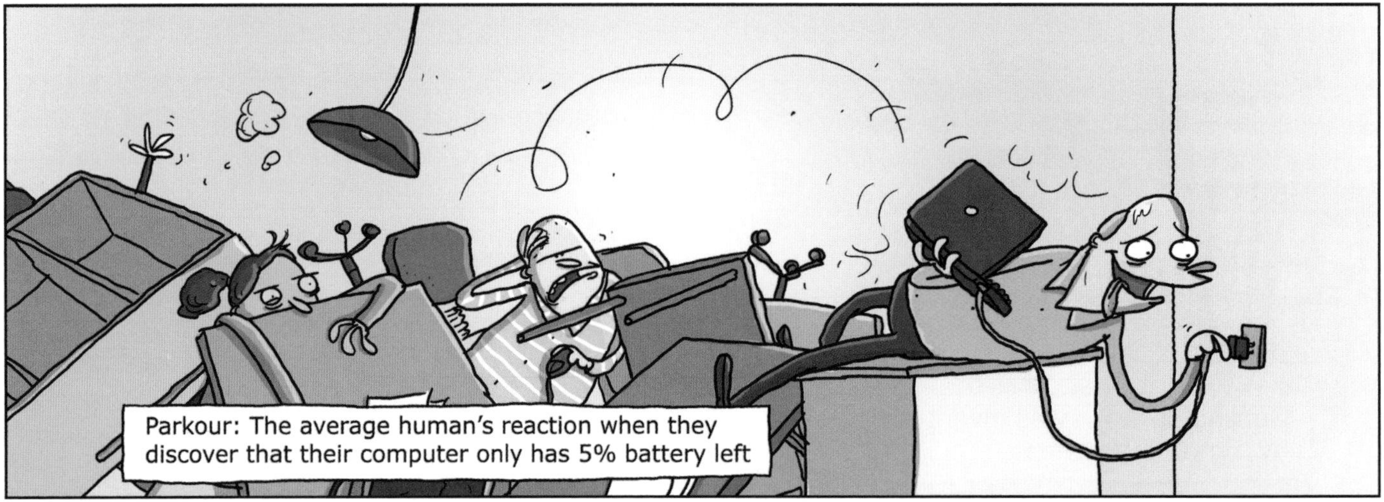
Parkour: The average human's reaction when they
discover that their computer only has 5% battery left

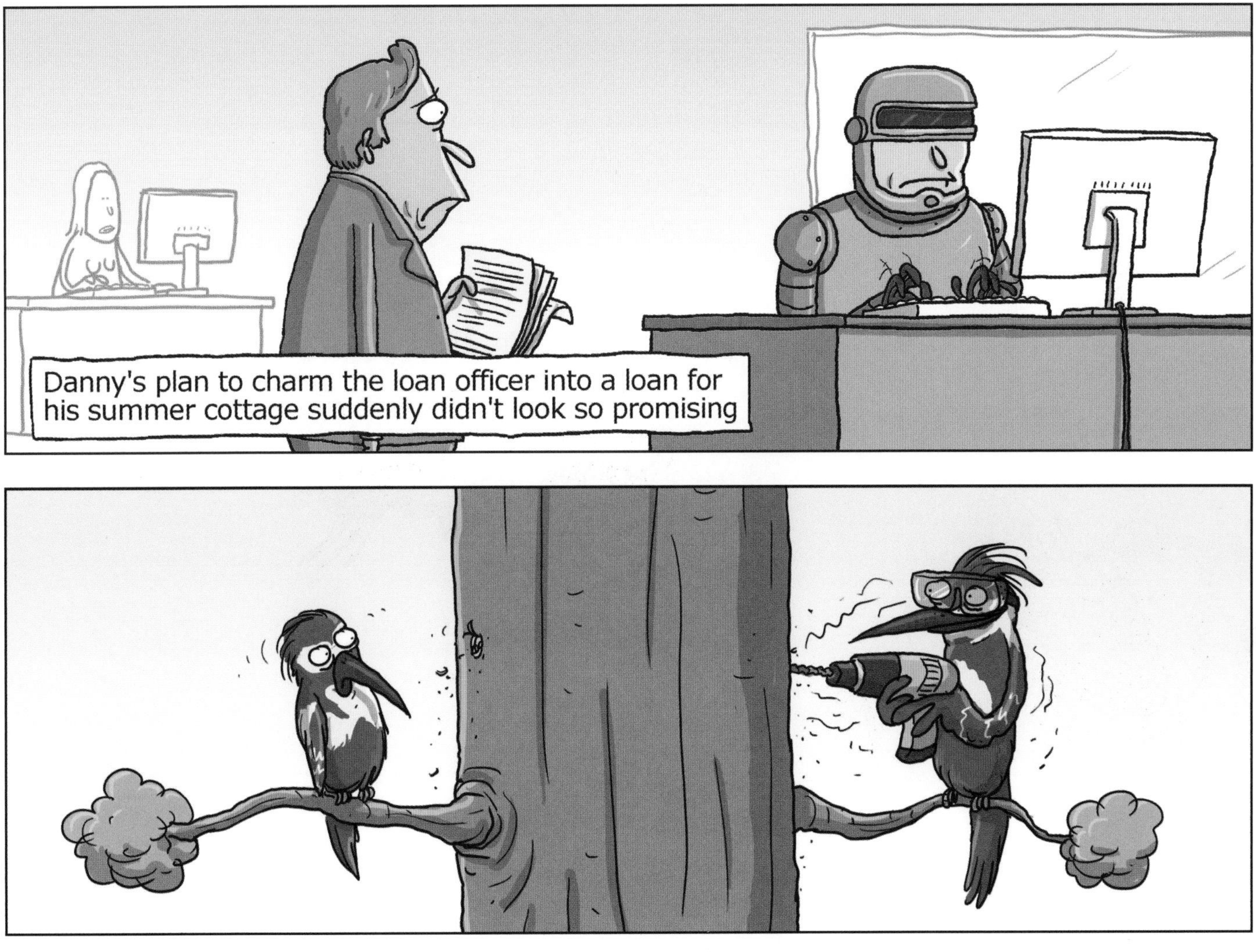
Danny's plan to charm the loan officer into a loan for his summer cottage suddenly didn't look so promising

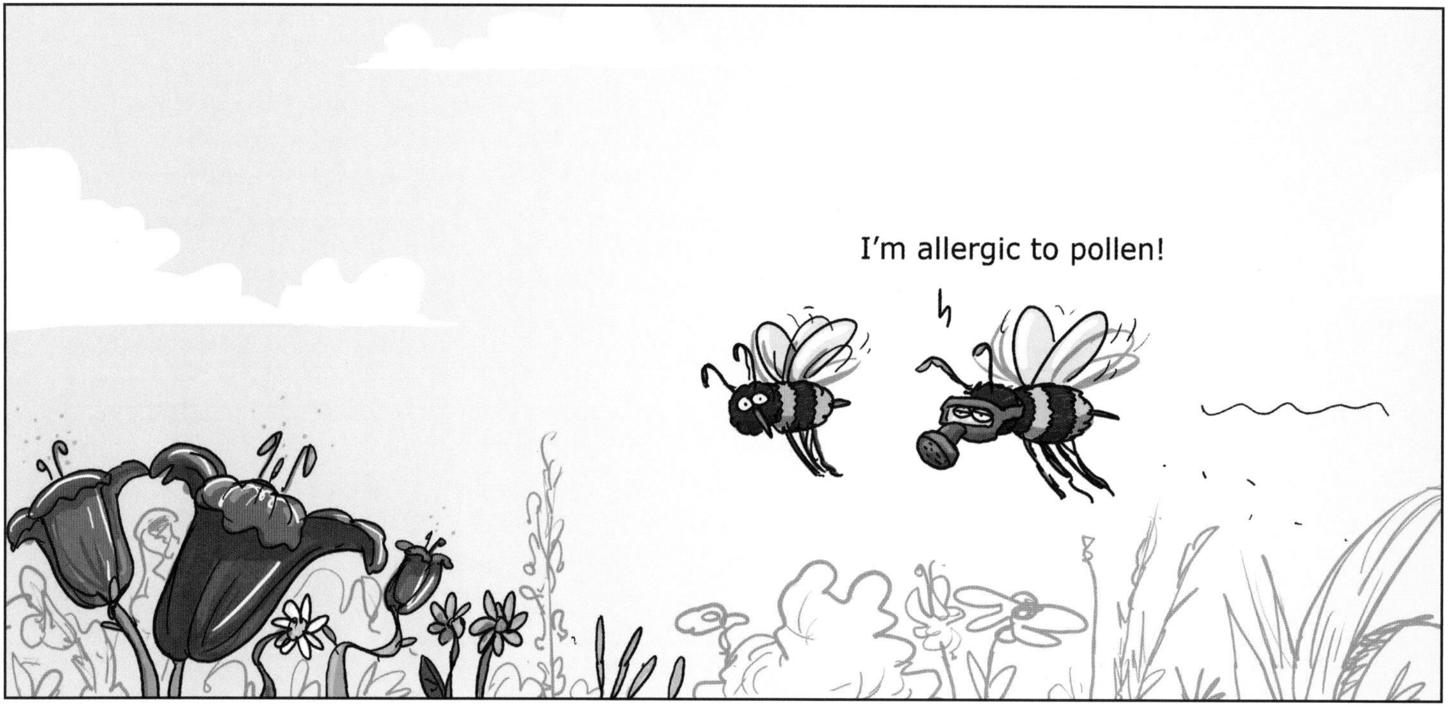
I'm allergic to pollen!

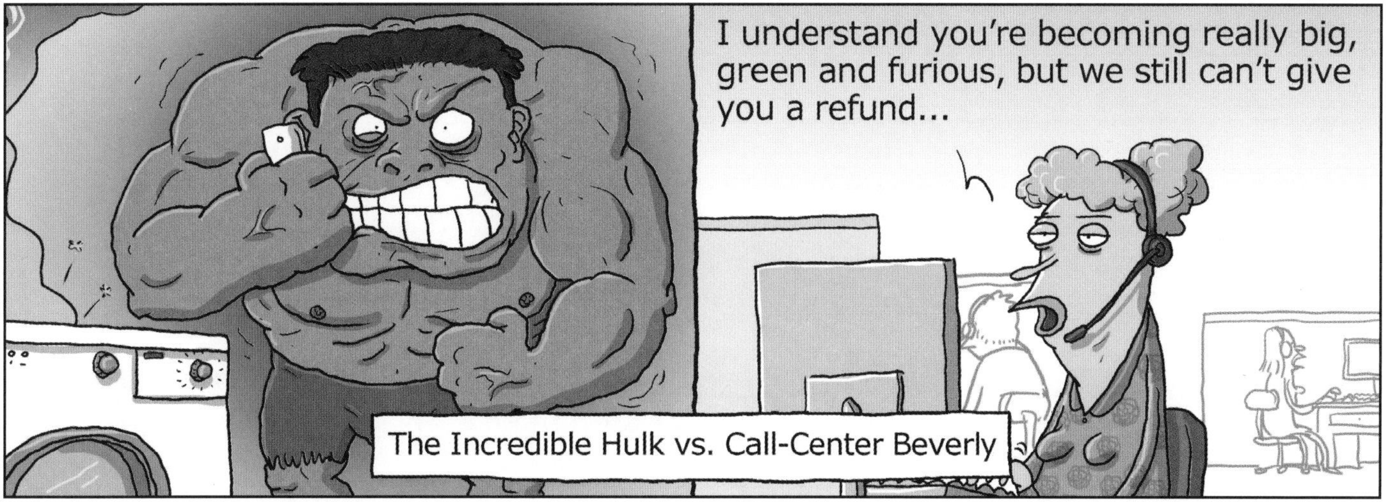

I understand you're becoming really big, green and furious, but we still can't give you a refund...
The Incredible Hulk vs. Call-Center Beverly

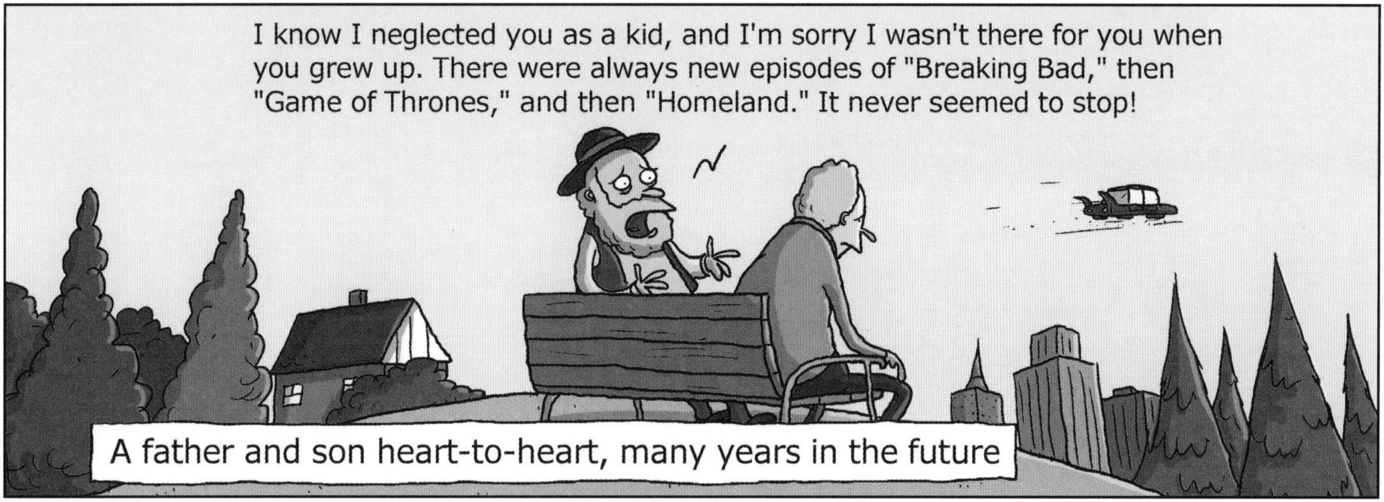

I know I neglected you as a kid, and I'm sorry I wasn't there for you when you grew up. There were always new episodes of "Breaking Bad," then "Game of Thrones," and then "Homeland." It never seemed to stop!
A father and son heart-to-heart, many years in the future

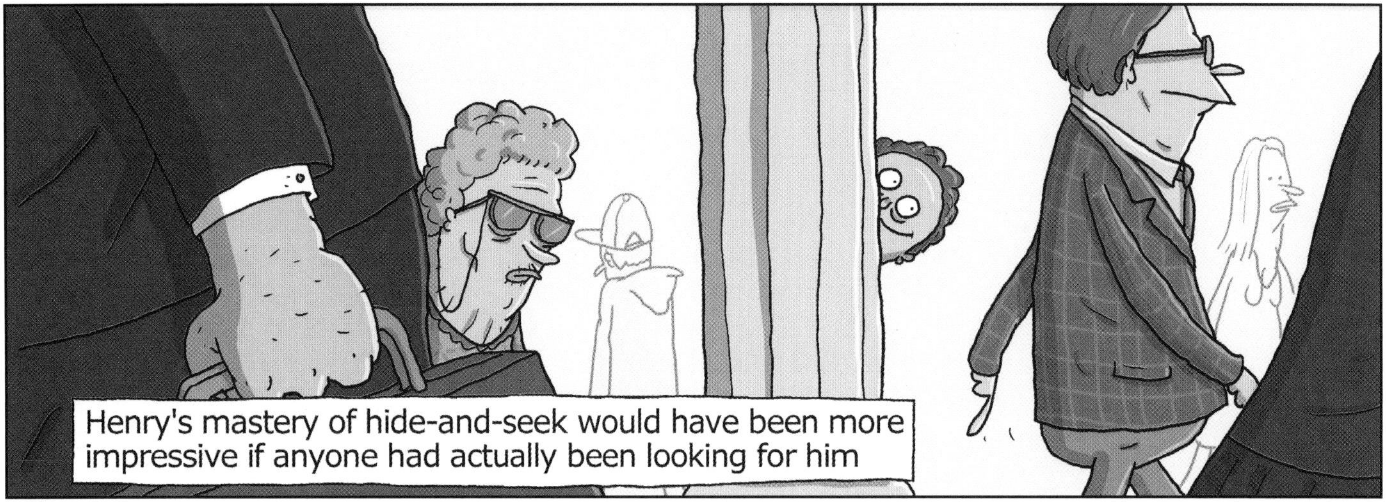
Henry's mastery of hide-and-seek would have been more impressive if anyone had actually been looking for him

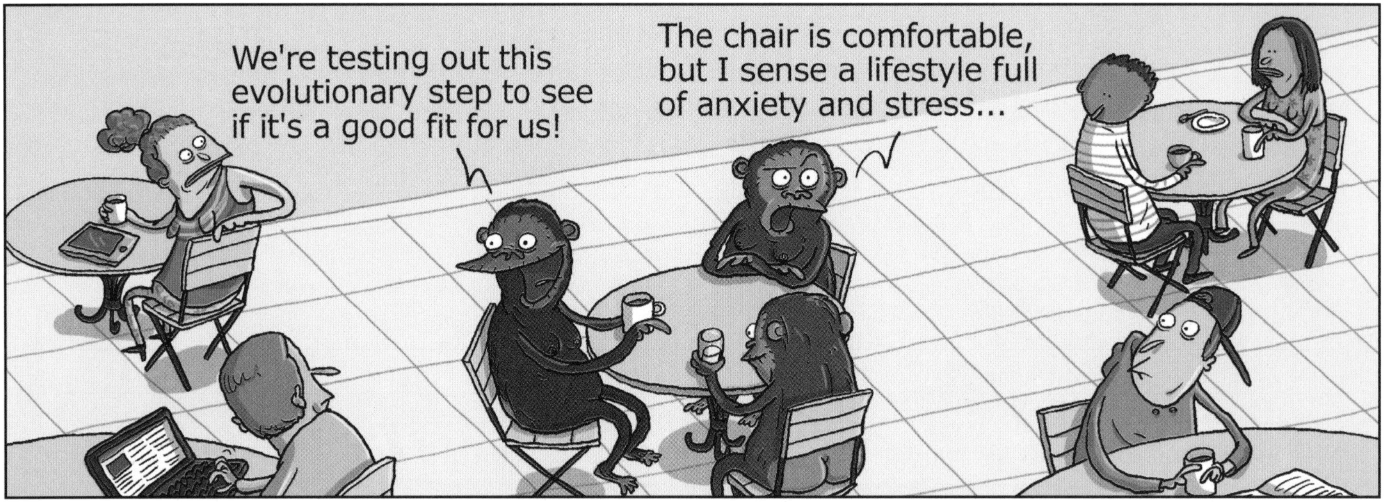
We're testing out this evolutionary step to see if it's a good fit for us!
The chair is comfortable, but I sense a lifestyle full of anxiety and stress...

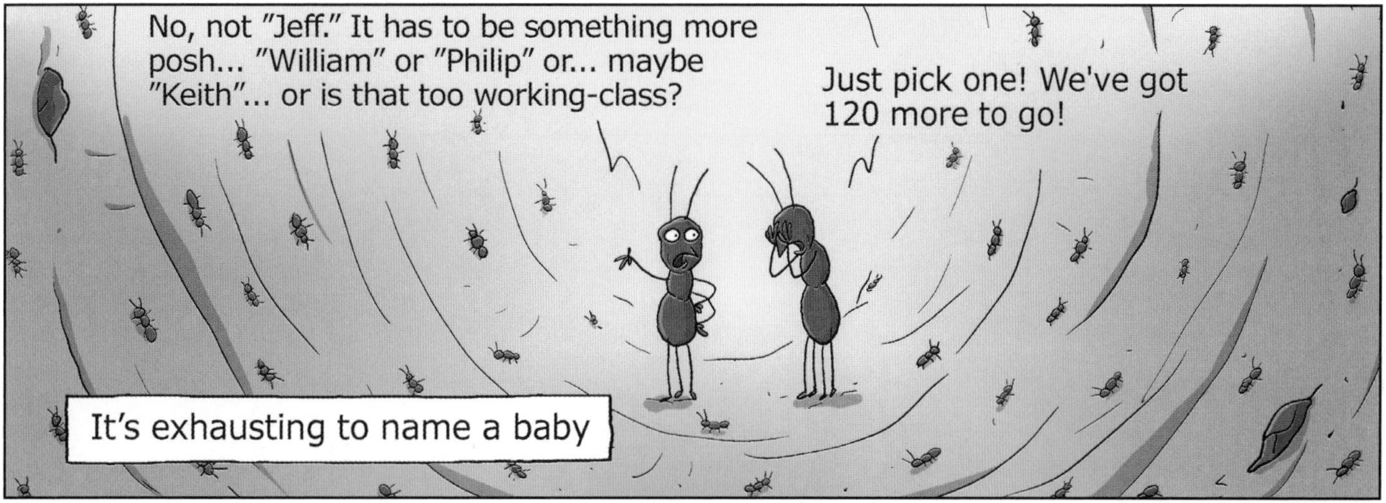
No, not "Jeff." It has to be something more posh... "William" or "Philip" or... maybe "Keith"... or is that too working-class?
Just pick one! We've got 120 more to go!
It's exhausting to name a baby

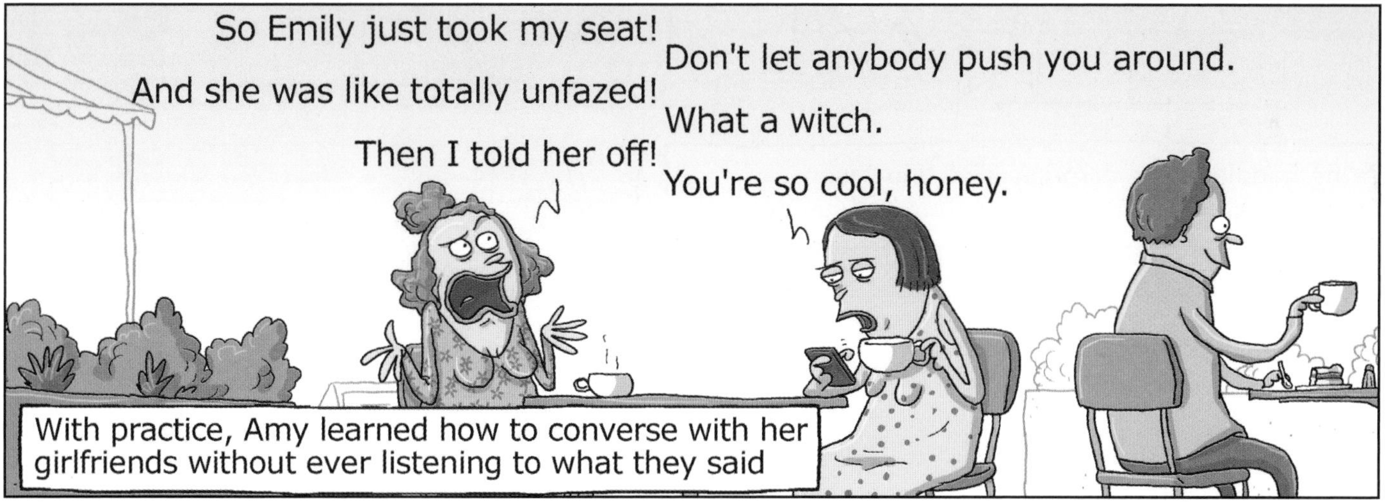
So Emily just took my seat!
And she was like totally unfazed!
Then I told her off!
Don't let anybody push you around.
What a witch.
You're so cool, honey.
With practice, Amy learned how to converse with her girlfriends without ever listening to what they said

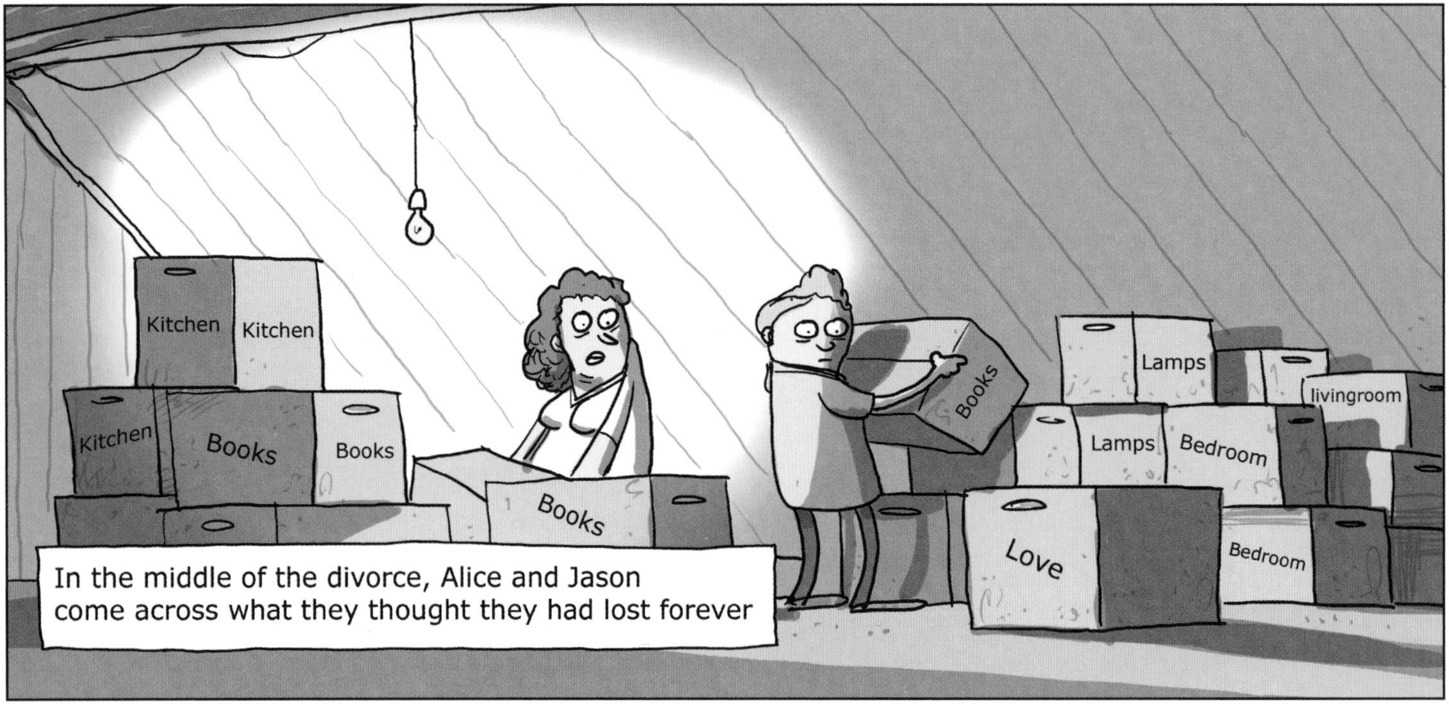
Kitchen
Kitchen
Kitchen
Books
Books
Books
Books
Lamps
livingroom
Lamps
Bedroom
Love
Bedroom
In the middle of the divorce, Alice and Jason come across what they thought they had lost forever

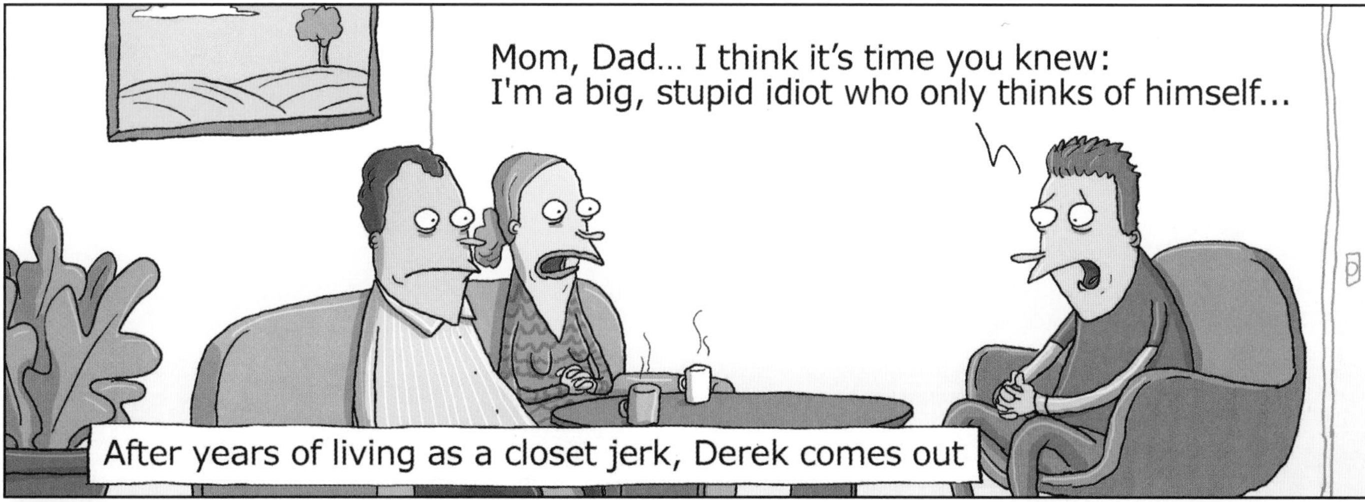
Mom, Dad... I think it's time you knew:
I'm a big, stupid idiot who only thinks of himself...
After years of living as a closet jerk, Derek comes out

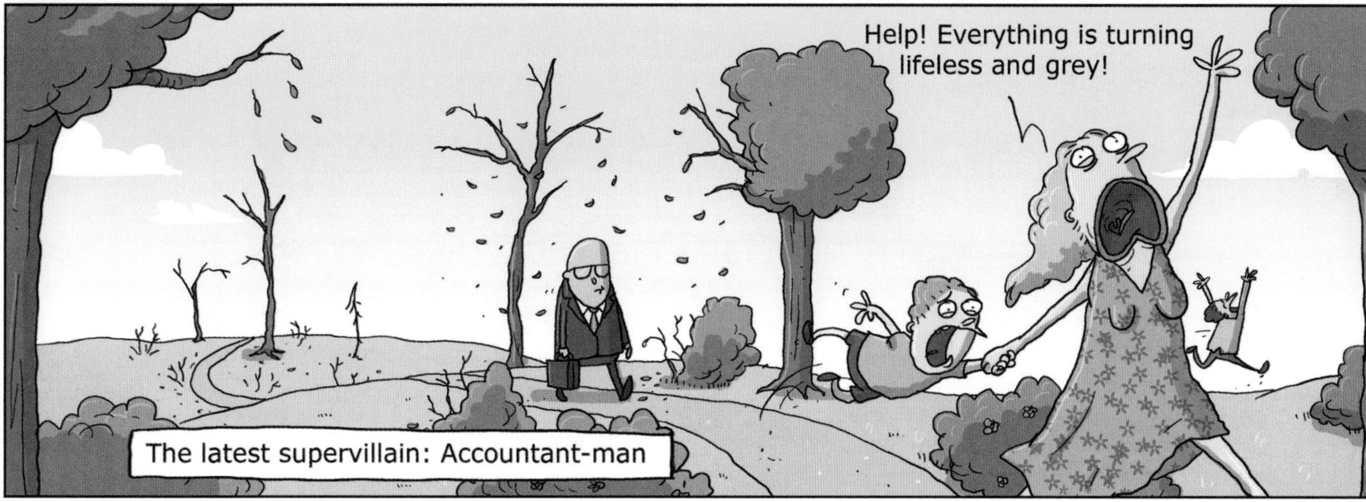
Help! Everything is turning lifeless and grey!
The latest supervillain: Accountant-man

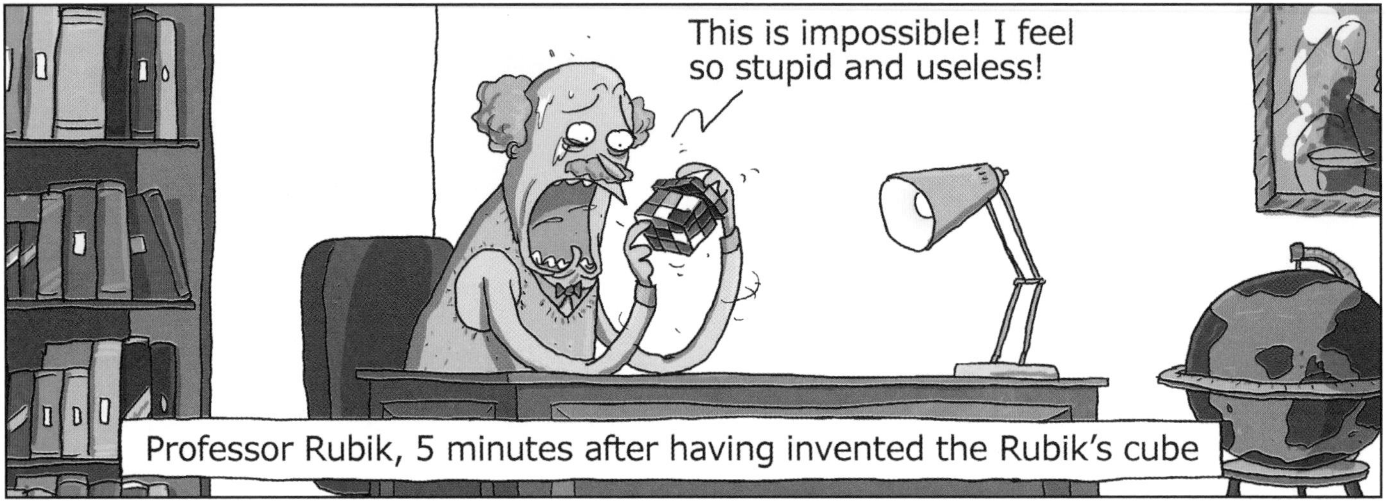
This is impossible! I feel so stupid and useless!
Professor Rubik, 5 minutes after having invented the Rubik's cube

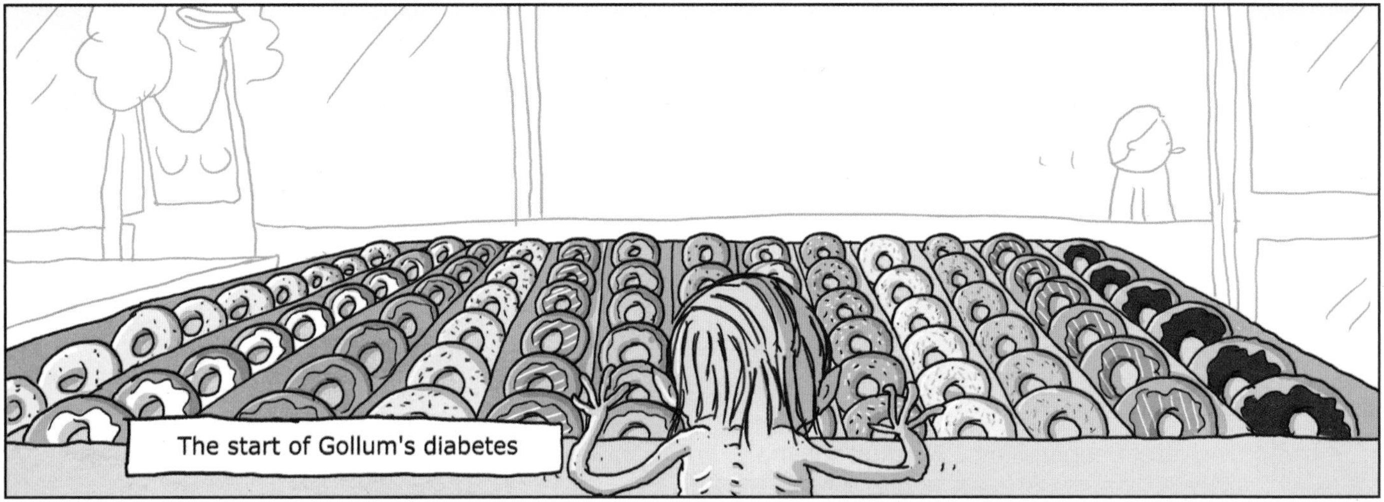
The start of Gollum's diabetes

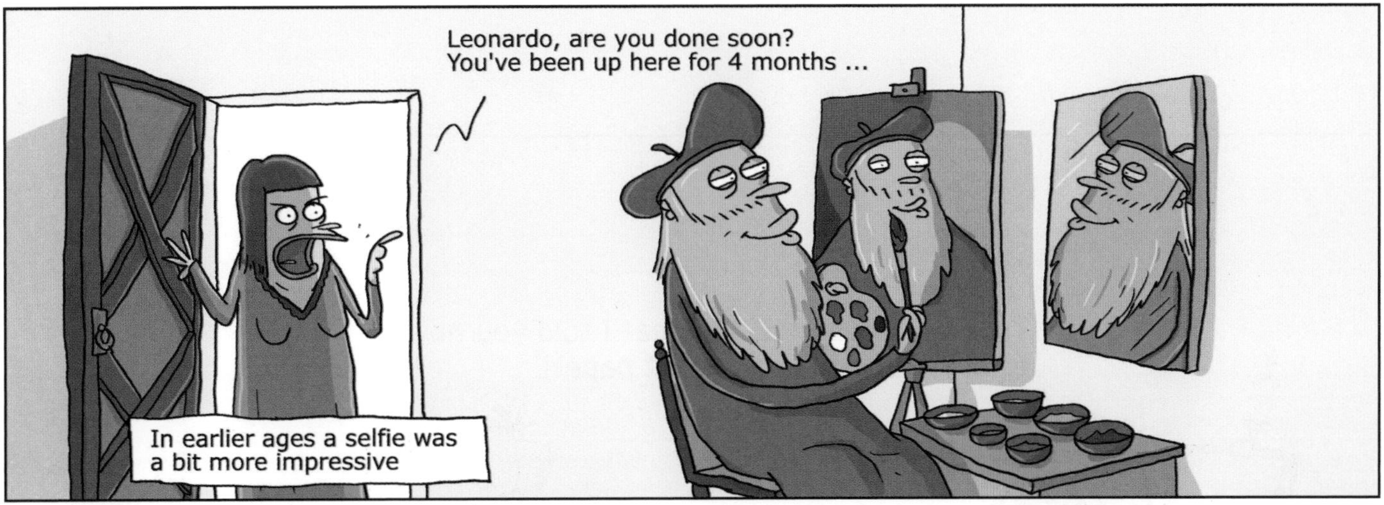
Leonardo, are you done soon?
You've been up here for 4 months ...
In earlier ages a selfie was a bit more impressive

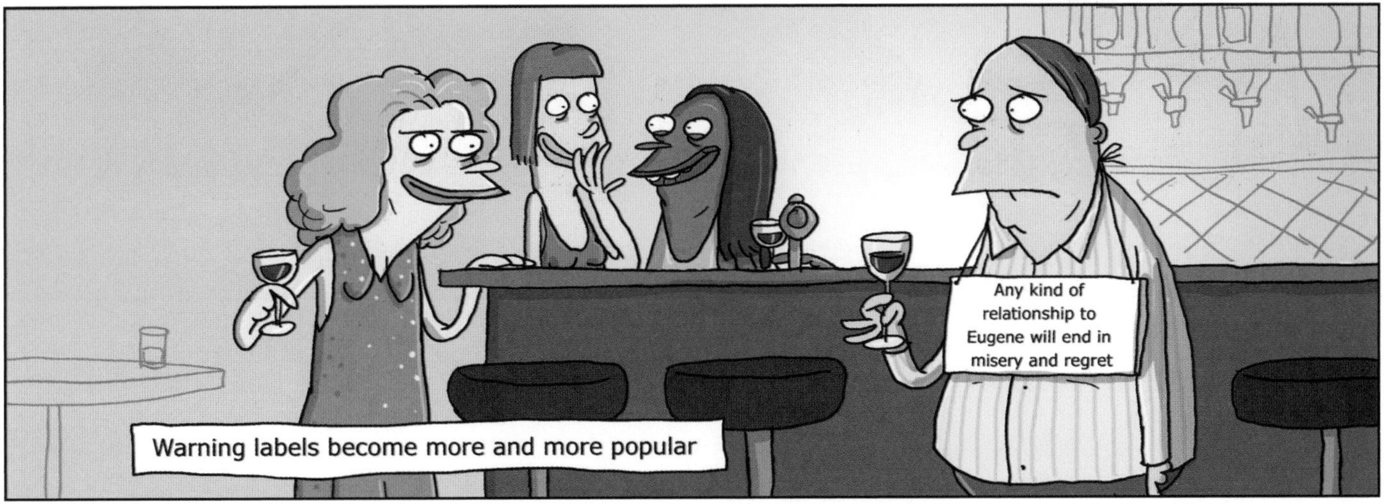
Any kind of relationship to Eugene will end in misery and regret
Warning labels become more and more popular

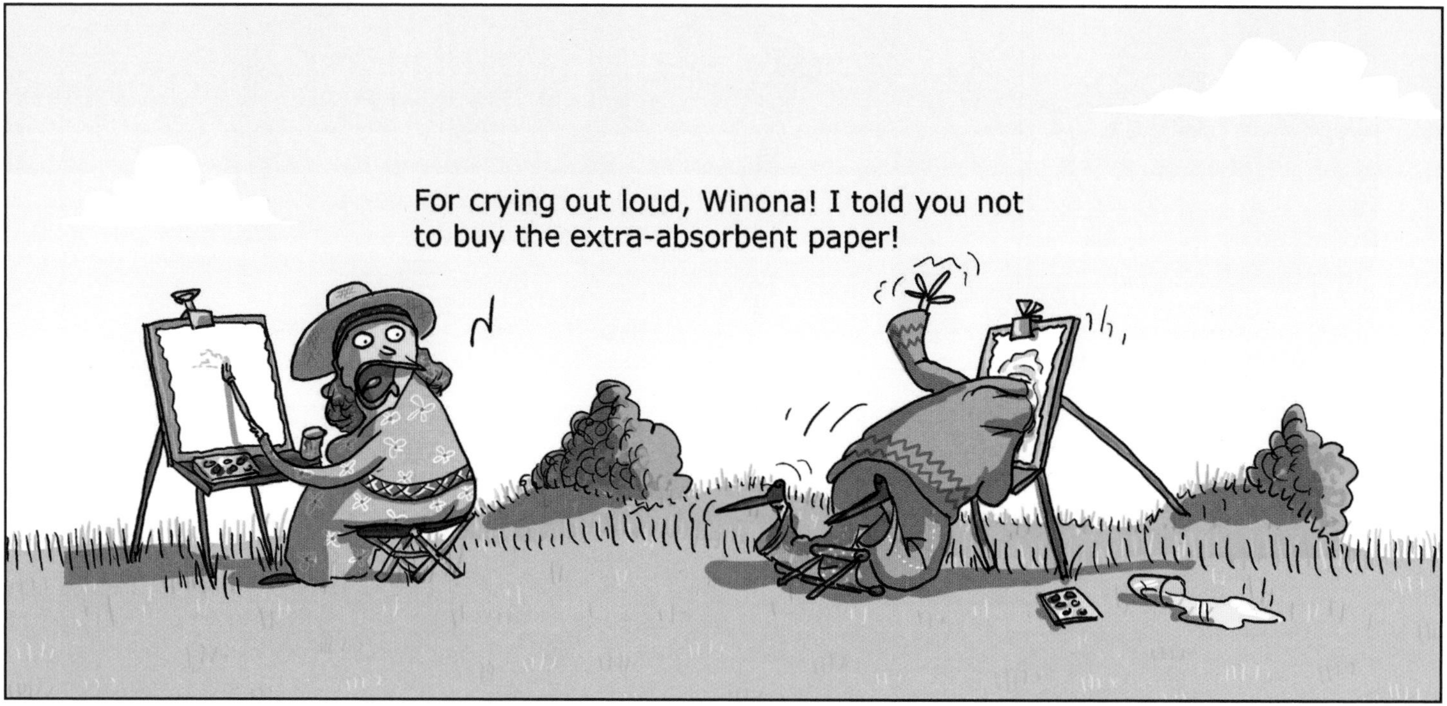
For crying out loud, Winona! I told you not to buy the extra-absorbent paper!

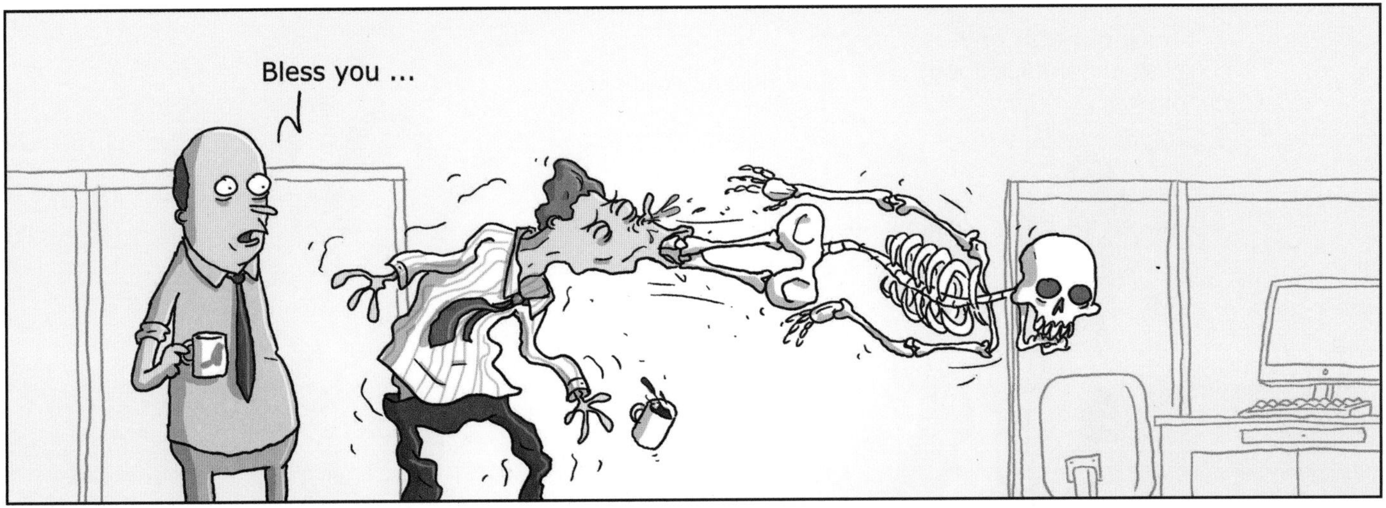
Bless you ...

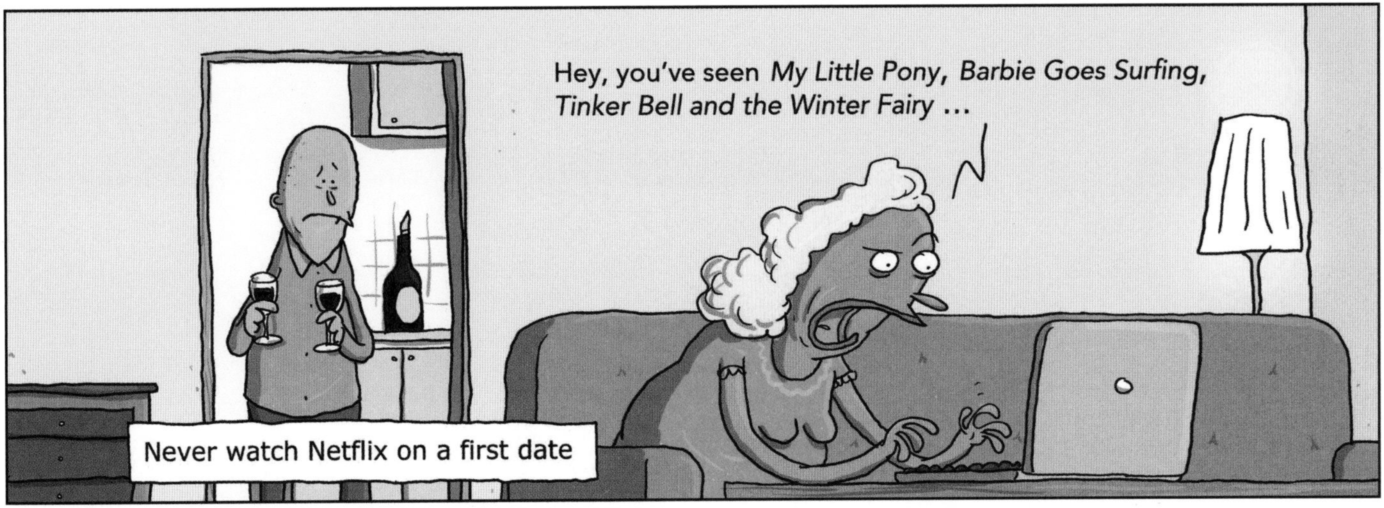
Hey, you've seen *My Little Pony*, *Barbie Goes Surfing*, *Tinker Bell and the Winter Fairy* ...
Never watch Netflix on a first date

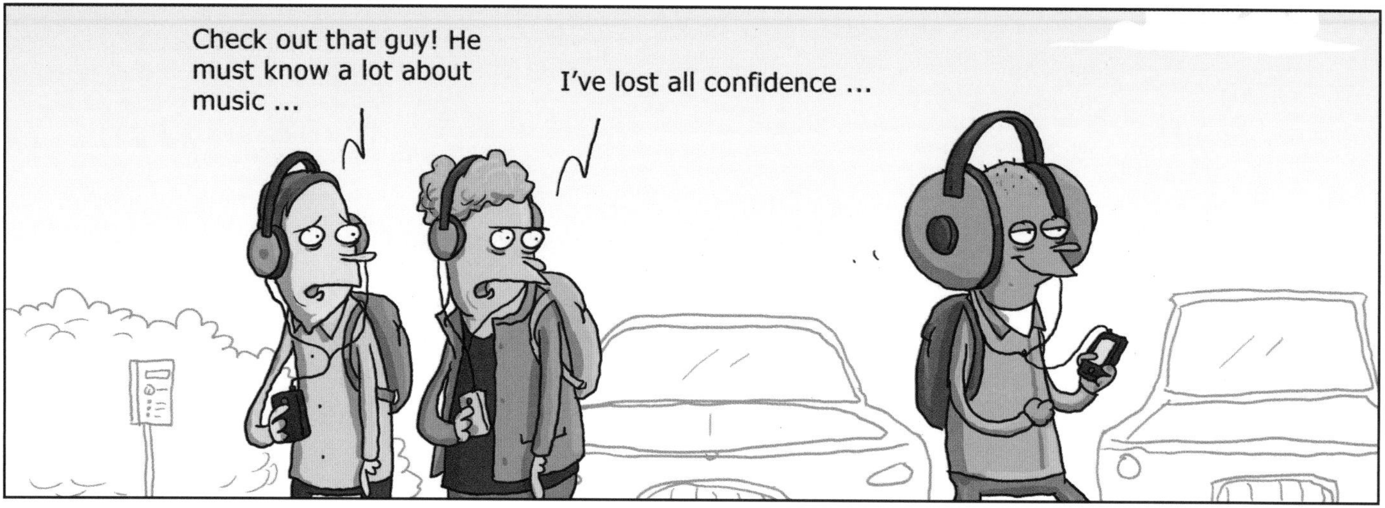
Check out that guy! He must know a lot about music ...
I've lost all confidence ...

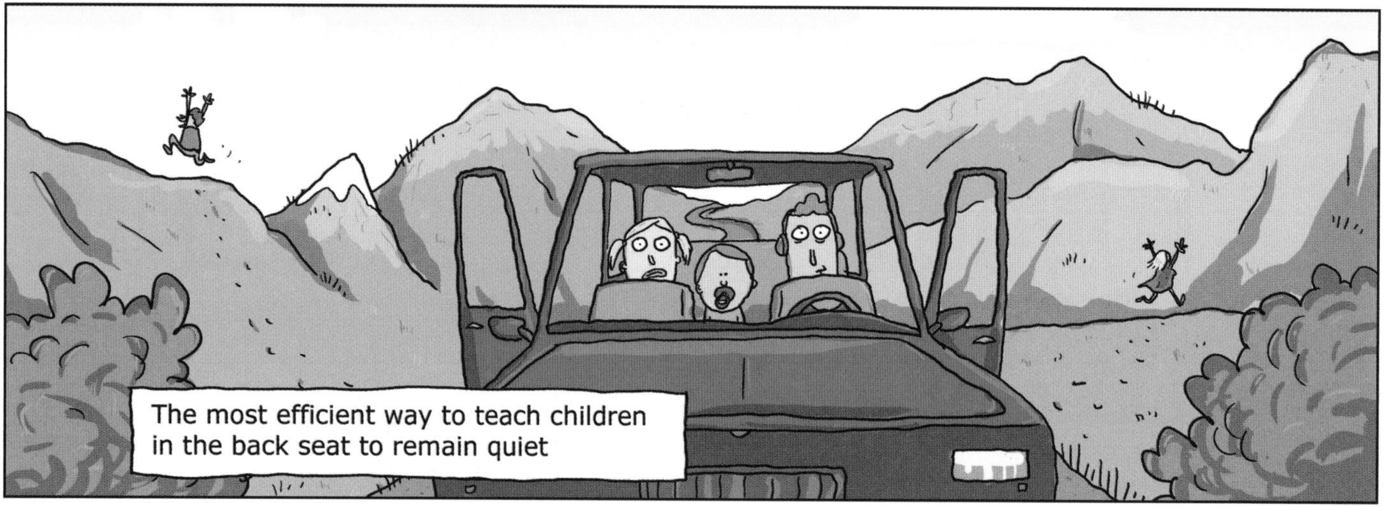
The most efficient way to teach children in the back seat to remain quiet

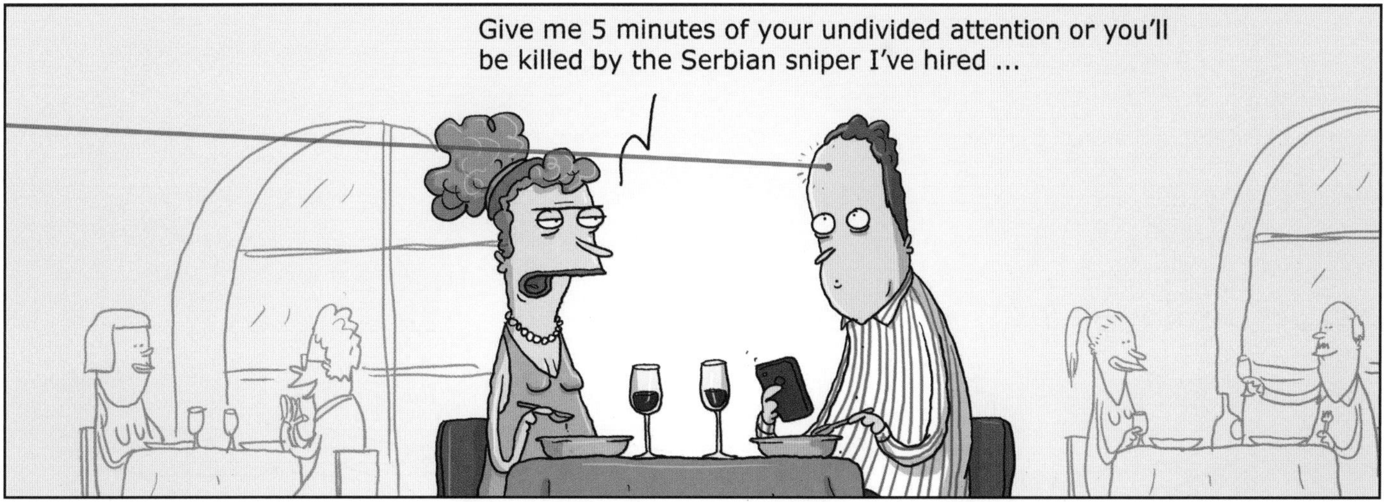
Give me 5 minutes of your undivided attention or you'll be killed by the Serbian sniper I've hired ...

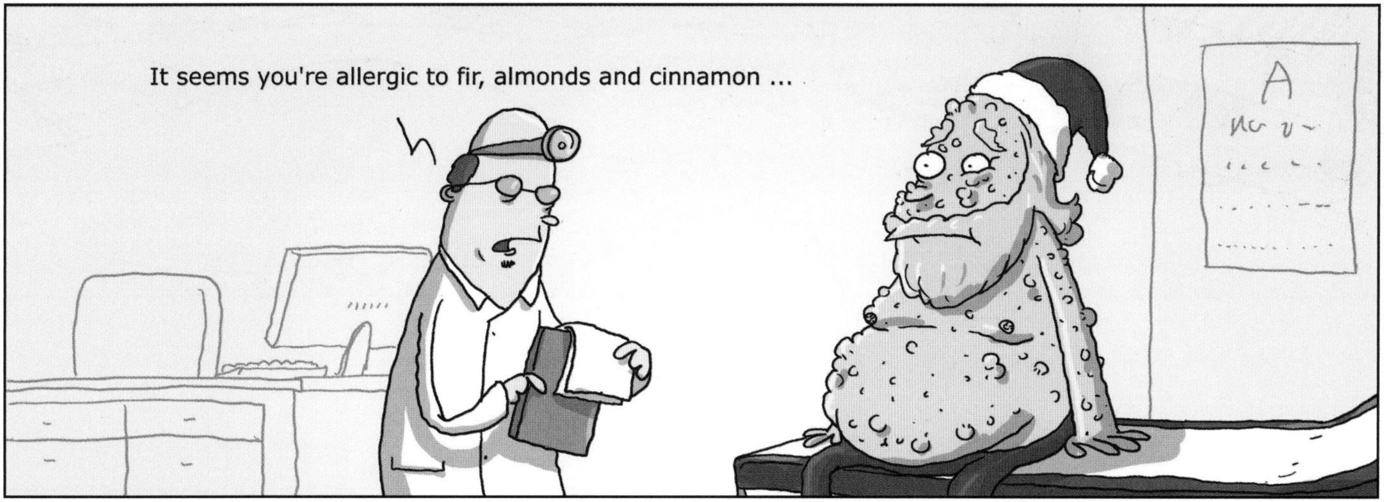
It seems you're allergic to fir, almonds and cinnamon ...
A

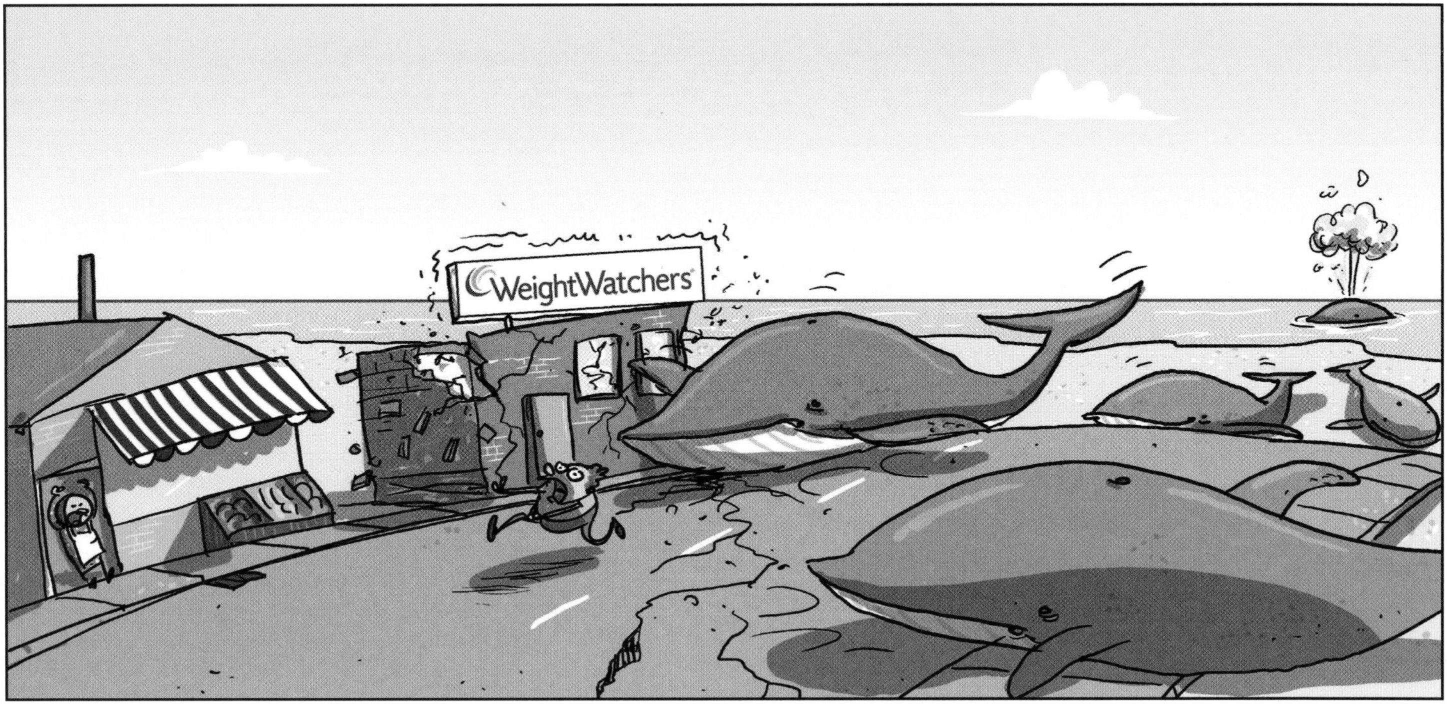
WeightWatchers

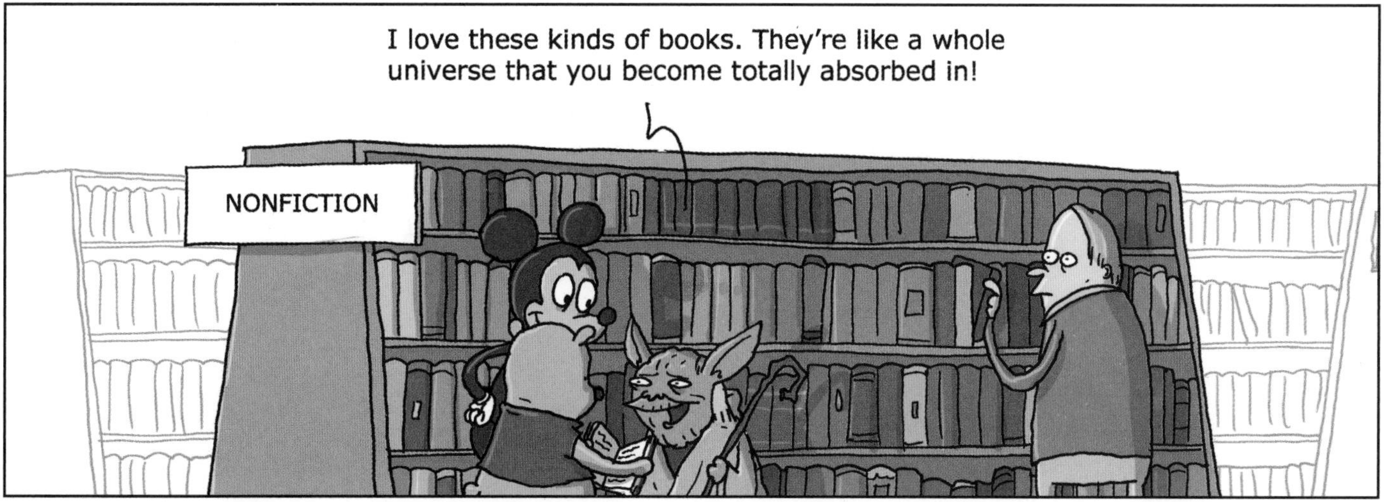
I love these kinds of books. They're like a whole universe that you become totally absorbed in!
NONFICTION

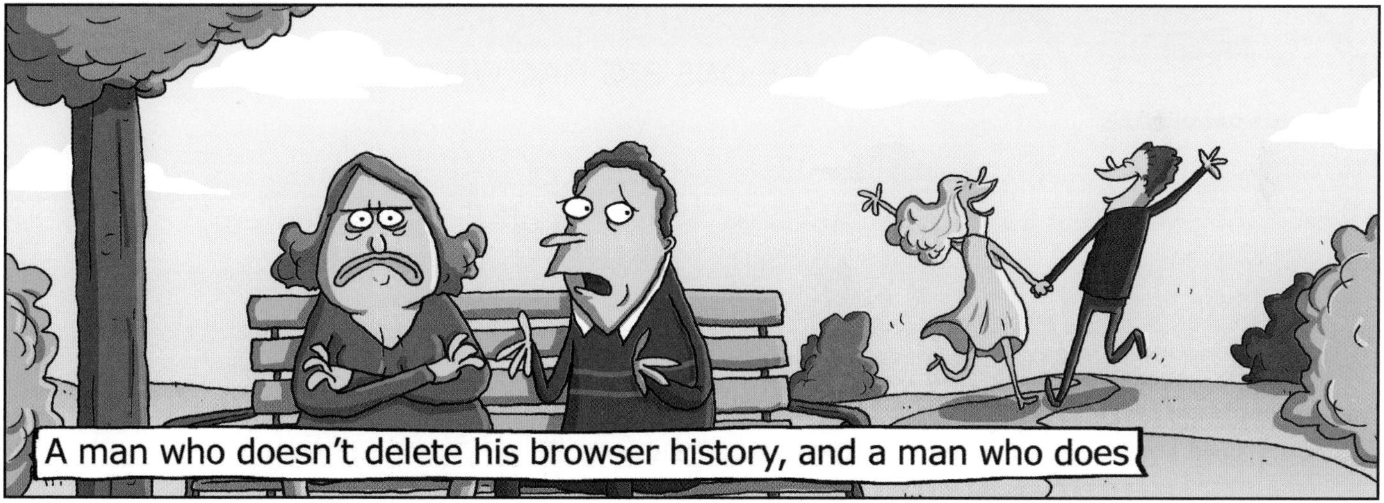
A man who doesn't delete his browser history, and a man who does

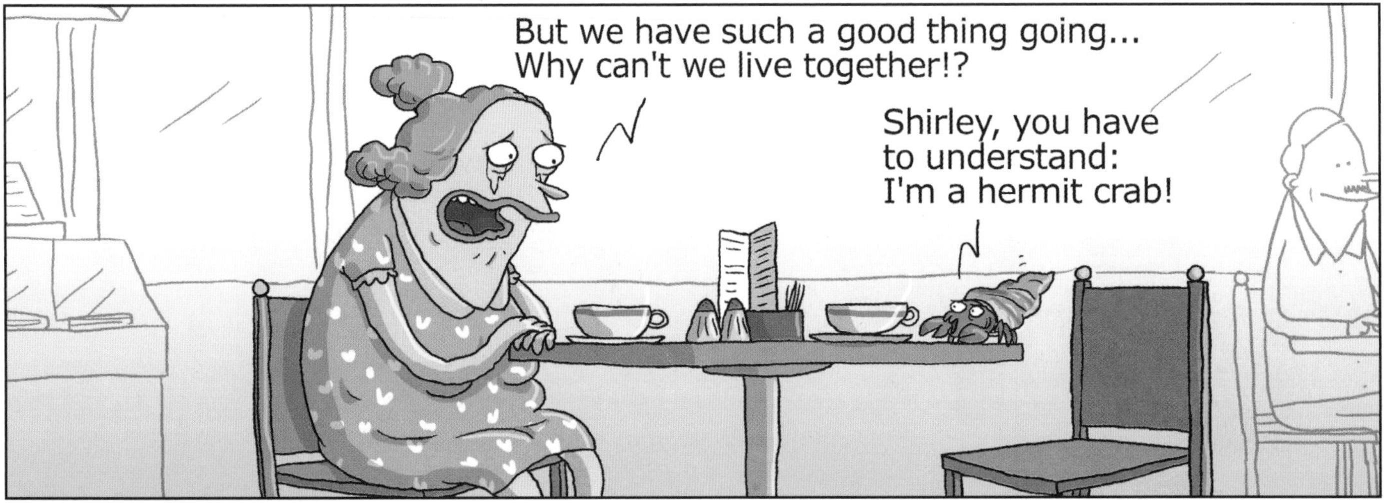
But we have such a good thing going...
Why can't we live together!?
Shirley, you have to understand: I'm a hermit crab!

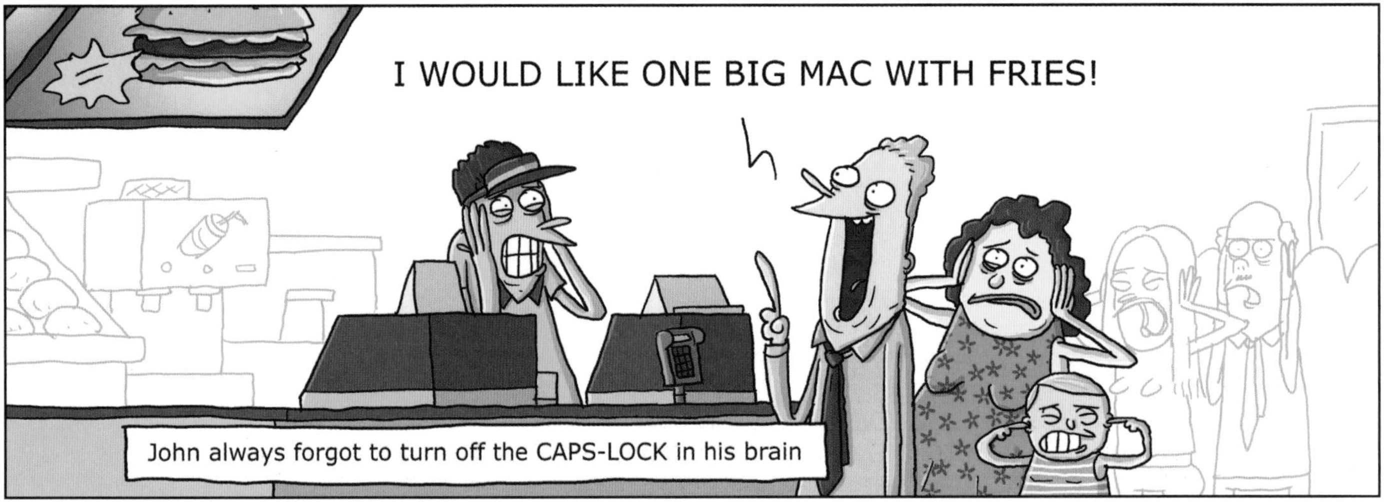
I WOULD LIKE ONE BIG MAC WITH FRIES!
John always forgot to turn off the CAPS-LOCK in his brain

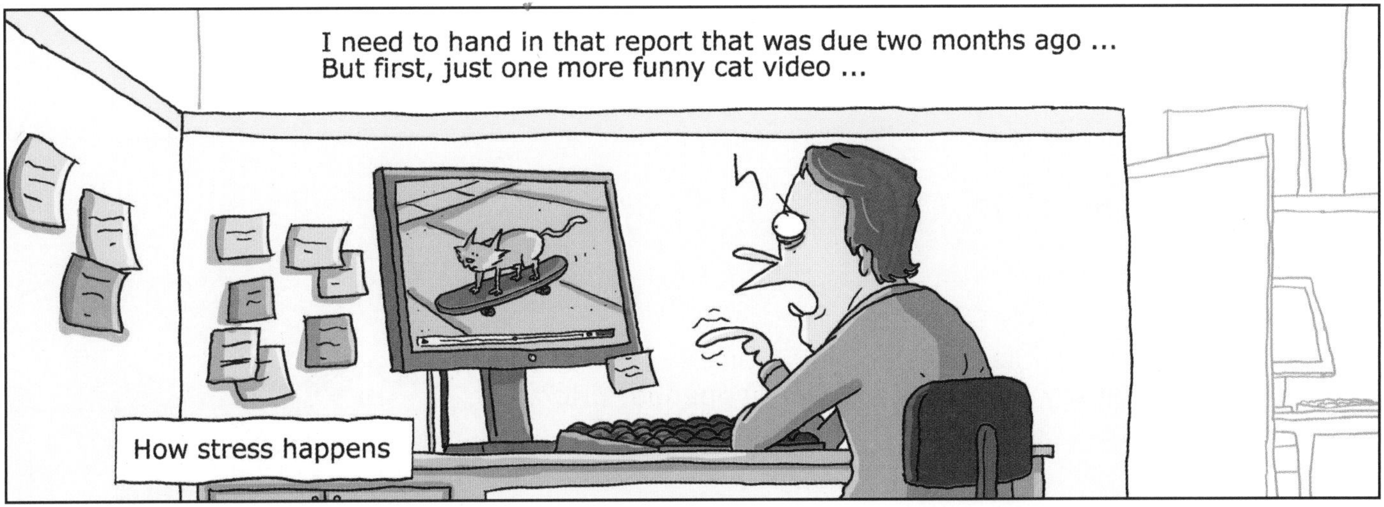
I need to hand in that report that was due two months ago ...
But first, just one more funny cat video ...
How stress happens

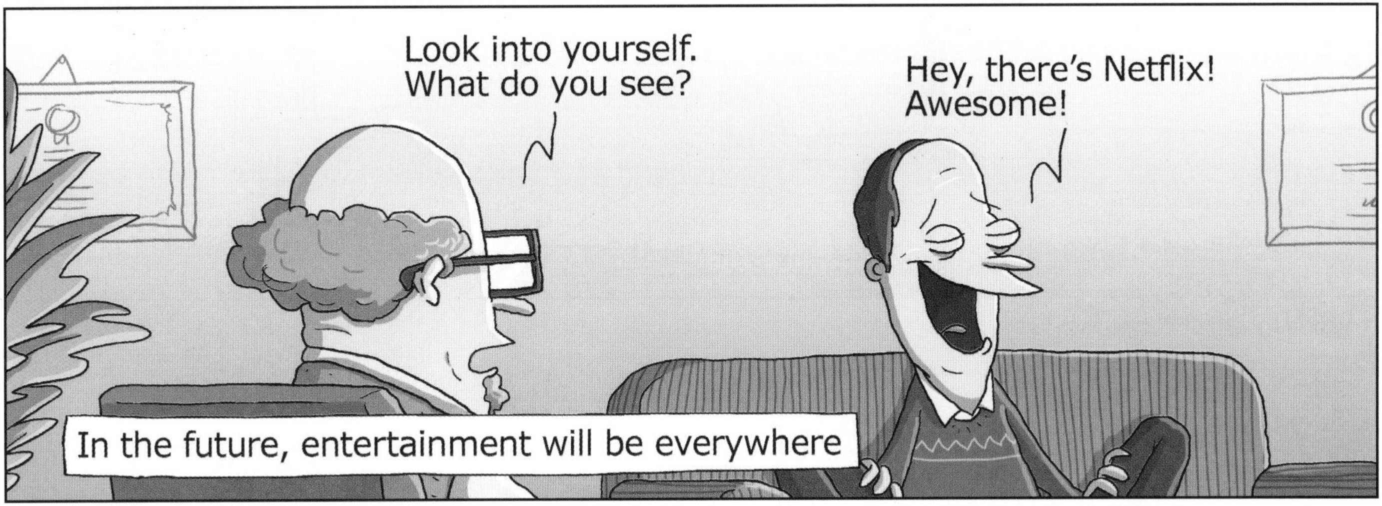
Look into yourself. What do you see?
Hey, there's Netflix! Awesome!
In the future, entertainment will be everywhere

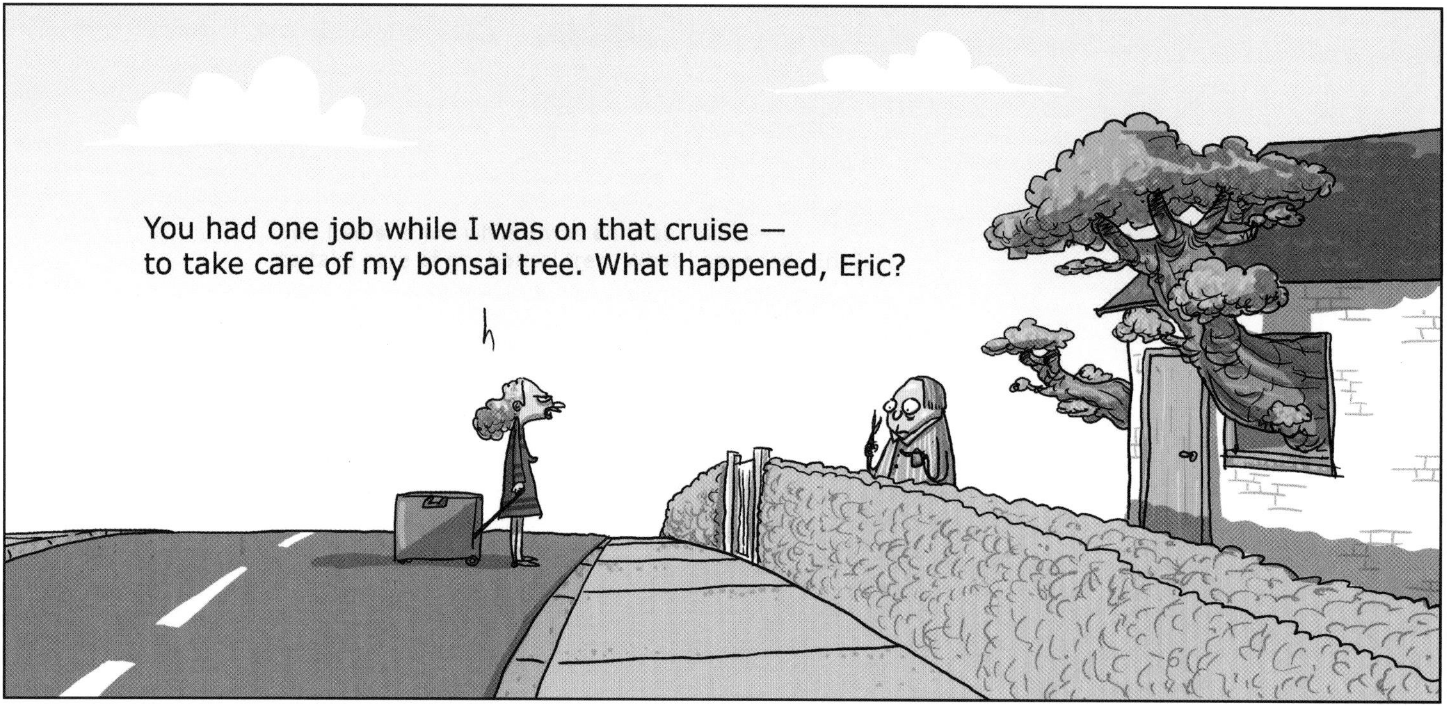
You had one job while I was on that cruise —
to take care of my bonsai tree. What happened, Eric?

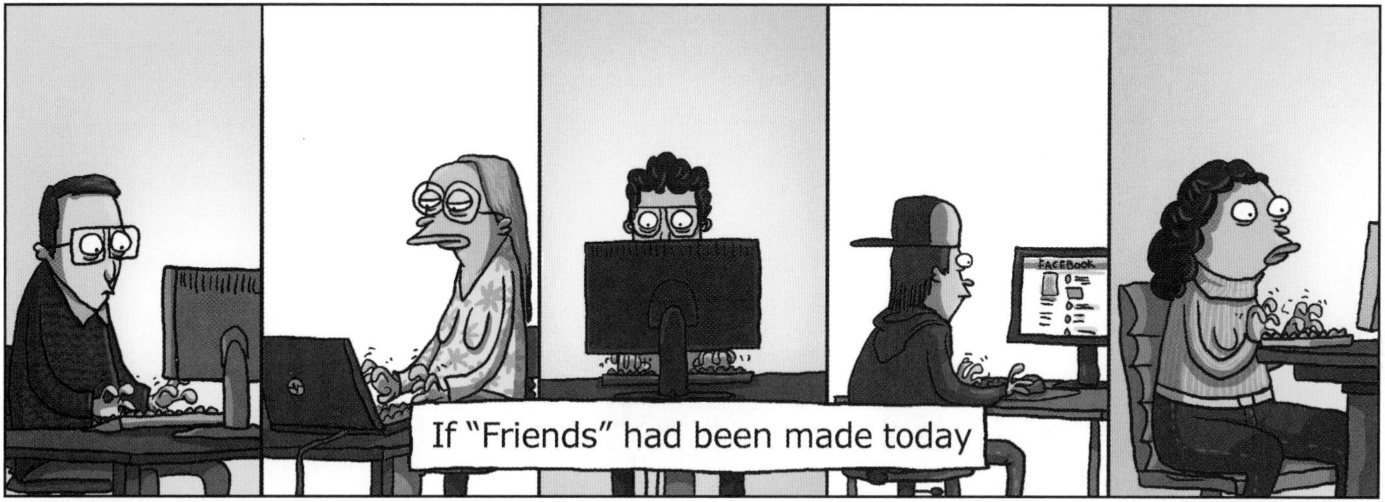

FACEBOOK
If "Friends" had been made today

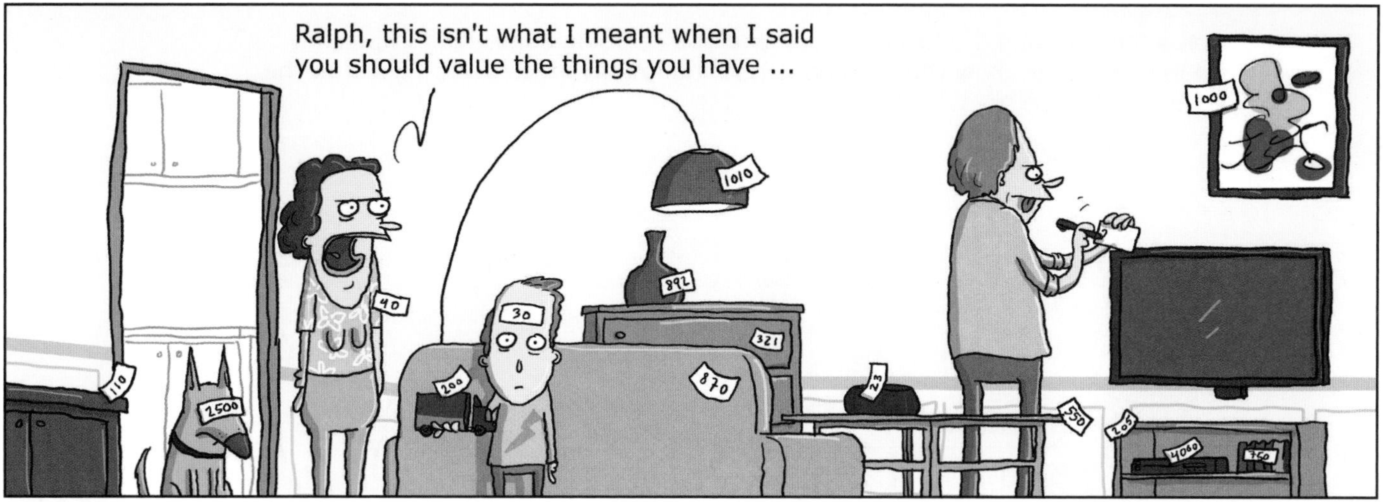

Ralph, this isn't what I meant when I said you should value the things you have ...
1000
1010
892
40
30
321
870
200
110
2500
23
550
205
4060
750

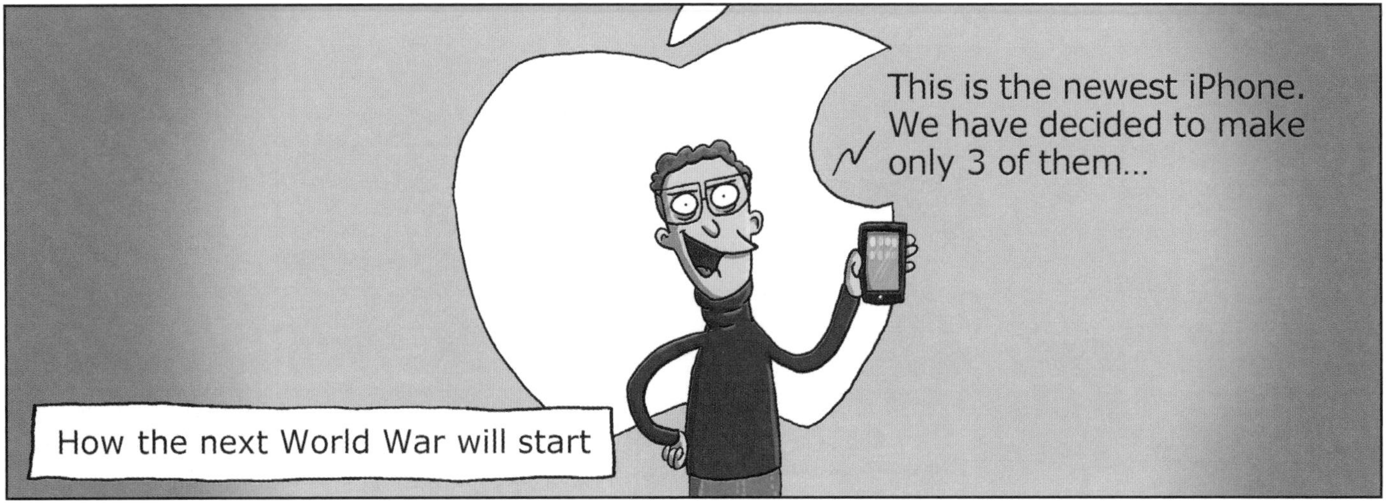
How the next World War will start
This is the newest iPhone. We have decided to make only 3 of them...

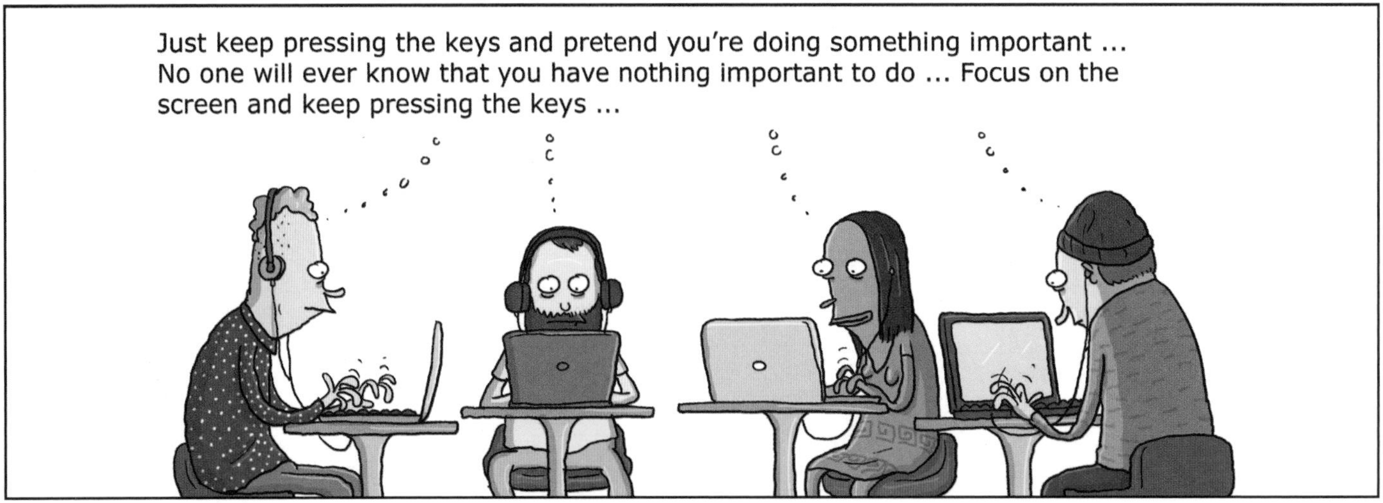
Just keep pressing the keys and pretend you're doing something important ... No one will ever know that you have nothing important to do ... Focus on the screen and keep pressing the keys ...

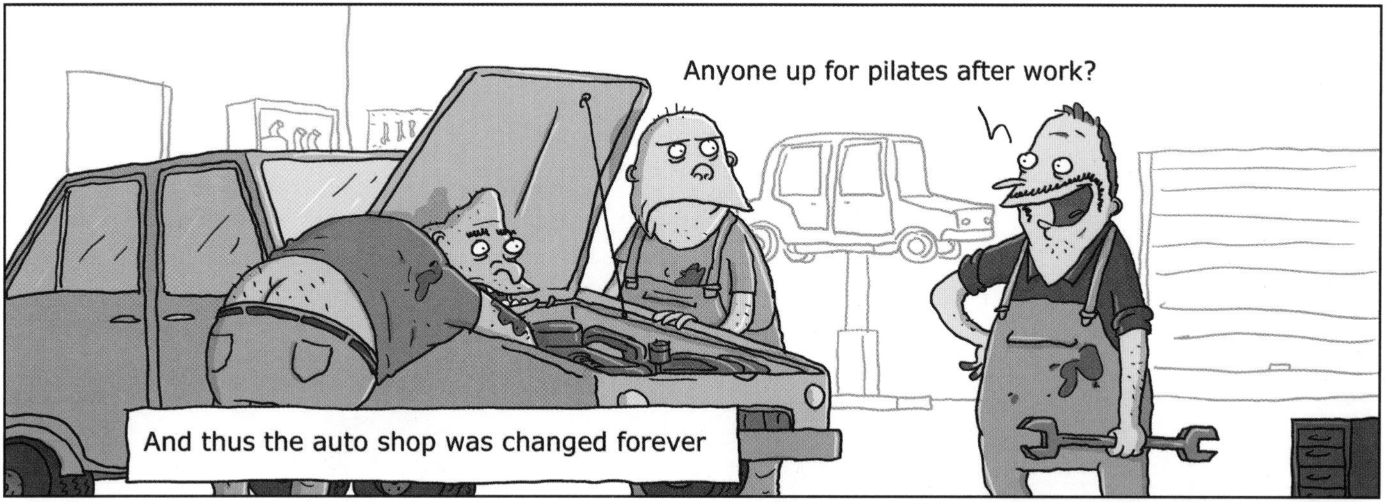
Anyone up for pilates after work?
And thus the auto shop was changed forever

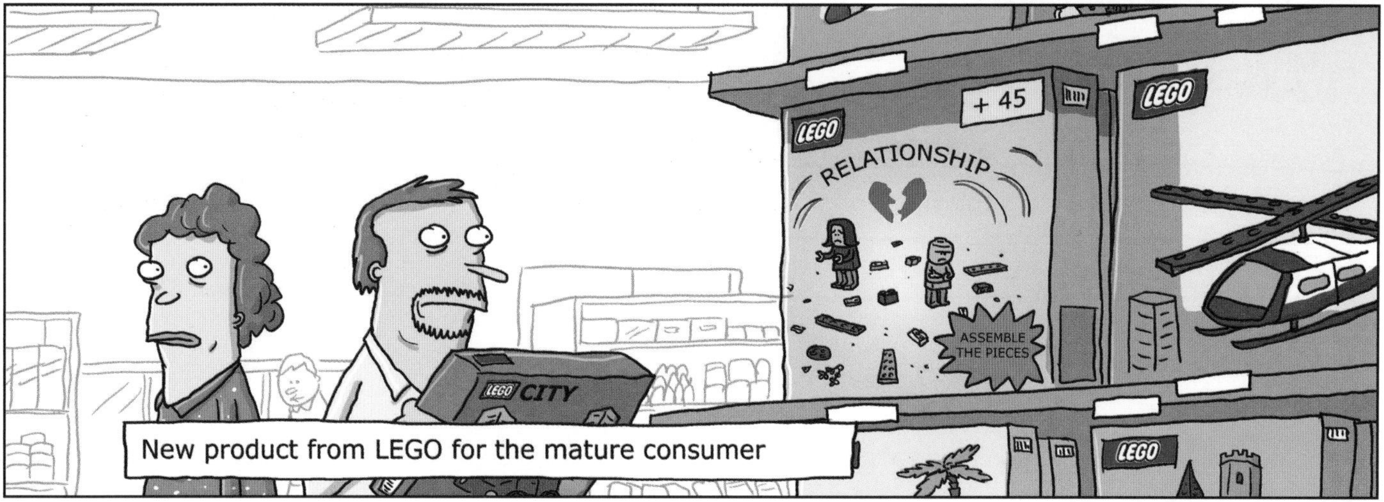
LEGO
+ 45
RELATIONSHIP
ASSEMBLE THE PIECES
LEGO
LEGO CITY
LEGO
New product from LEGO for the mature consumer

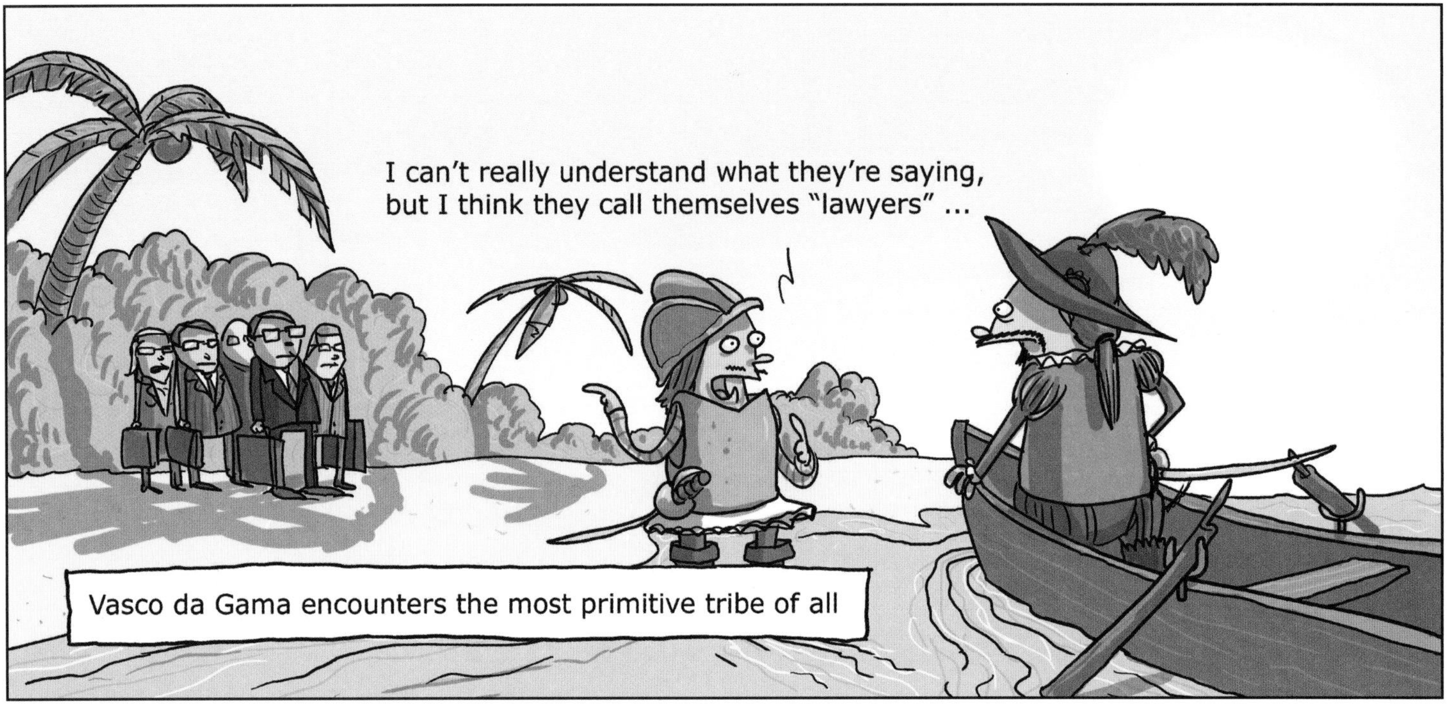
I can't really understand what they're saying, but I think they call themselves "lawyers" ...
Vasco da Gama encounters the most primitive tribe of all

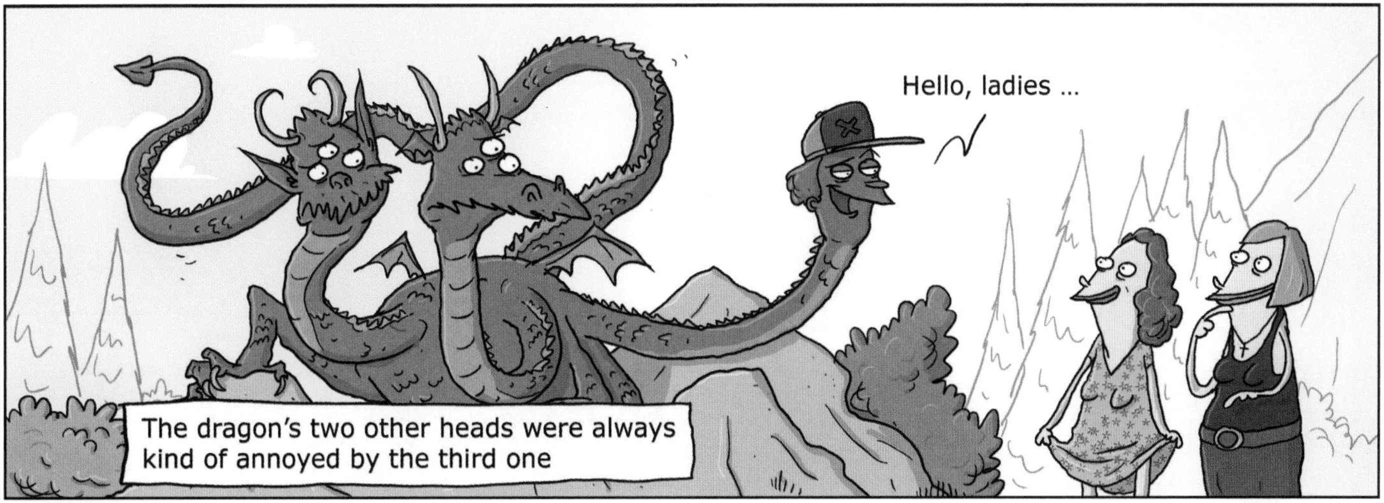
Hello, ladies ...
The dragon's two other heads were always kind of annoyed by the third one

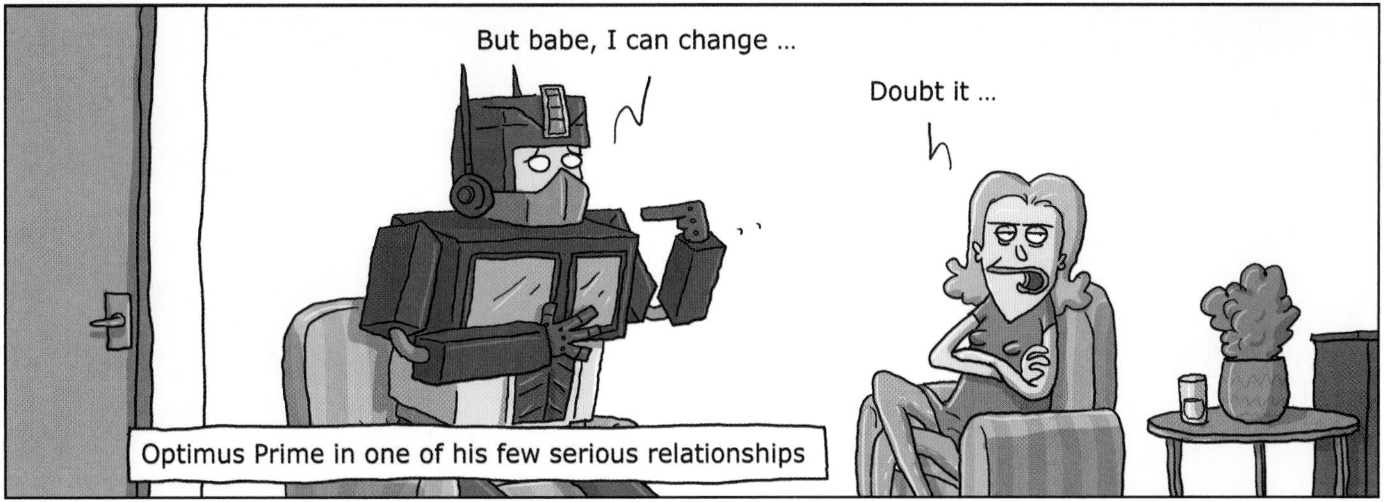
But babe, I can change ...
Doubt it ...
Optimus Prime in one of his few serious relationships

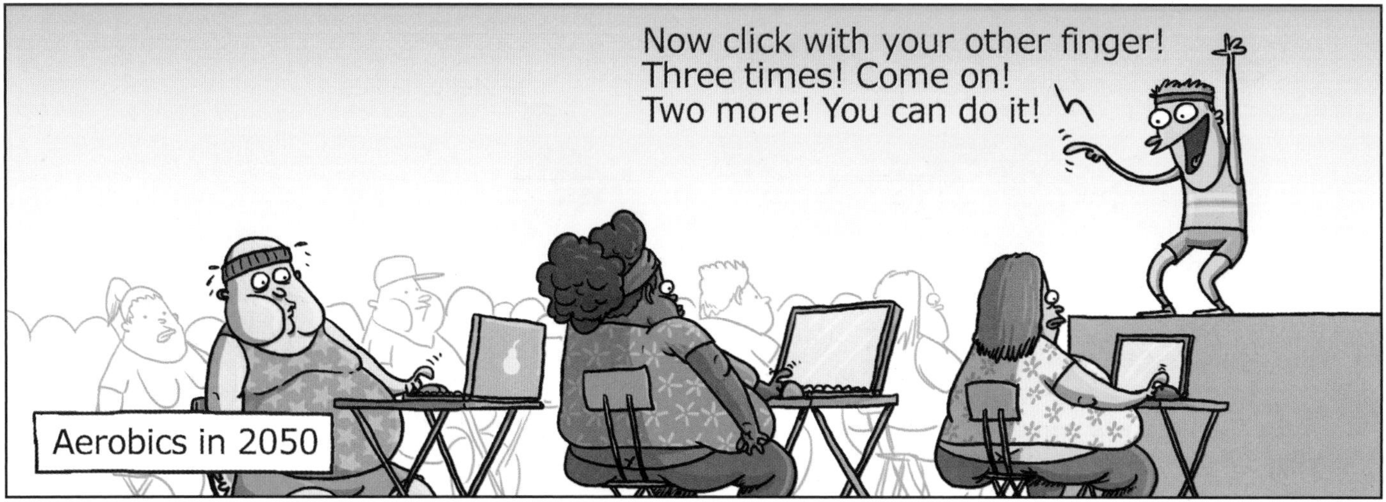
Now click with your other finger! Three times! Come on! Two more! You can do it!
Aerobics in 2050

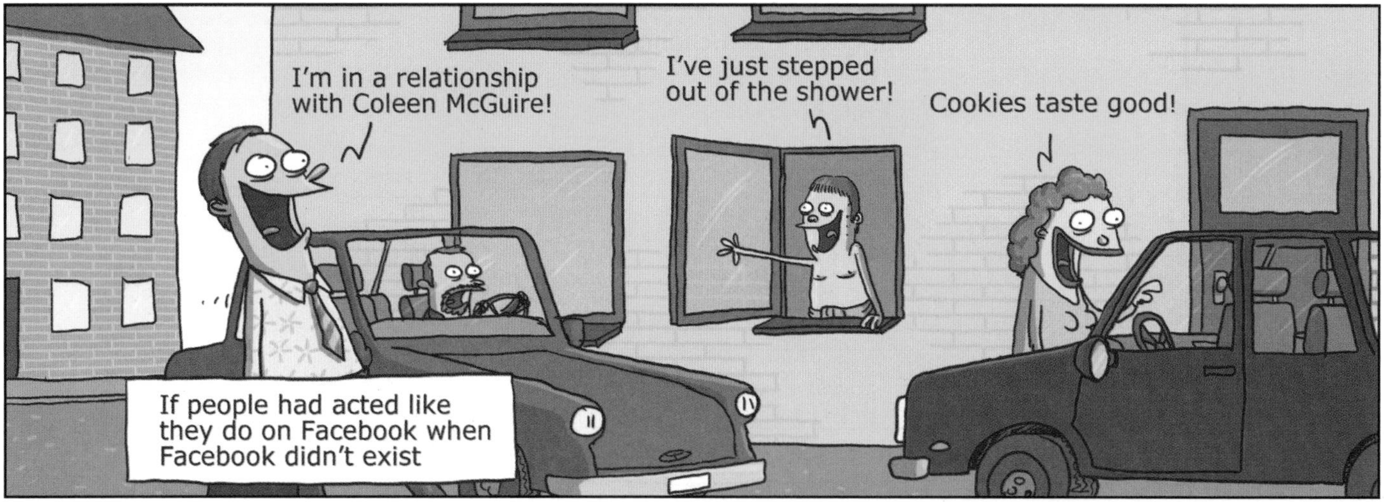
I'm in a relationship with Coleen McGuire!
I've just stepped out of the shower!
Cookies taste good!
If people had acted like they do on Facebook when Facebook didn't exist

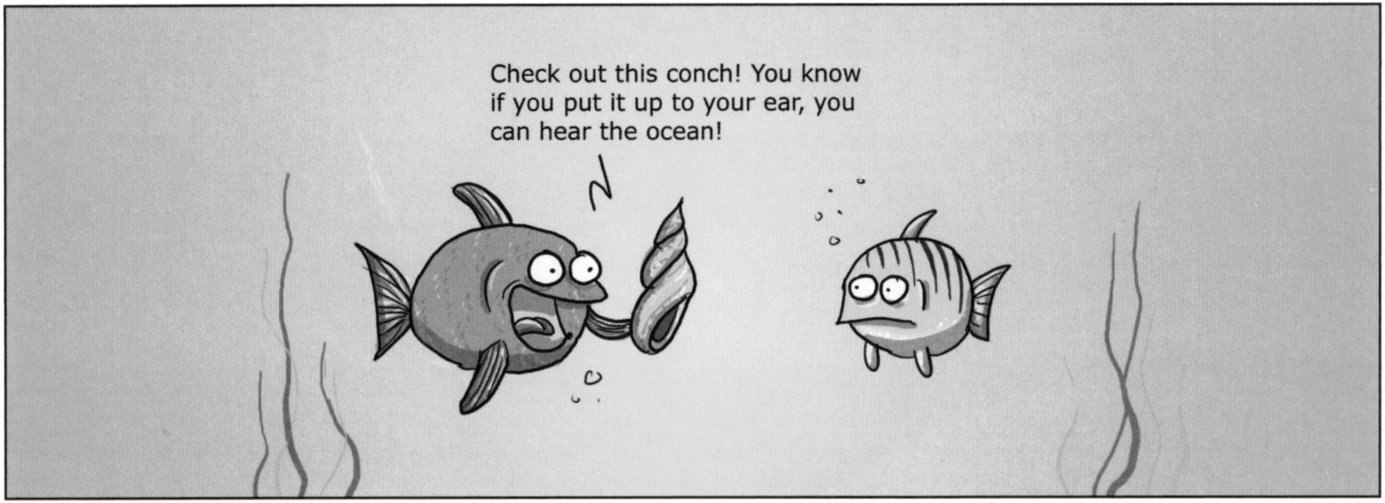
Check out this conch! You know if you put it up to your ear, you can hear the ocean!

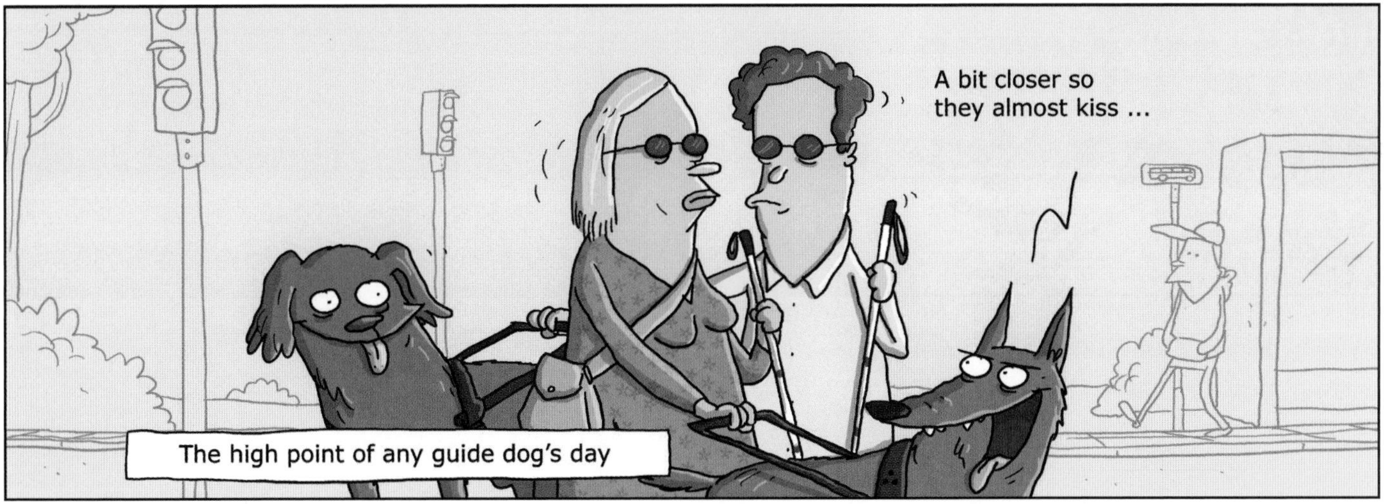
A bit closer so they almost kiss ...
The high point of any guide dog's day

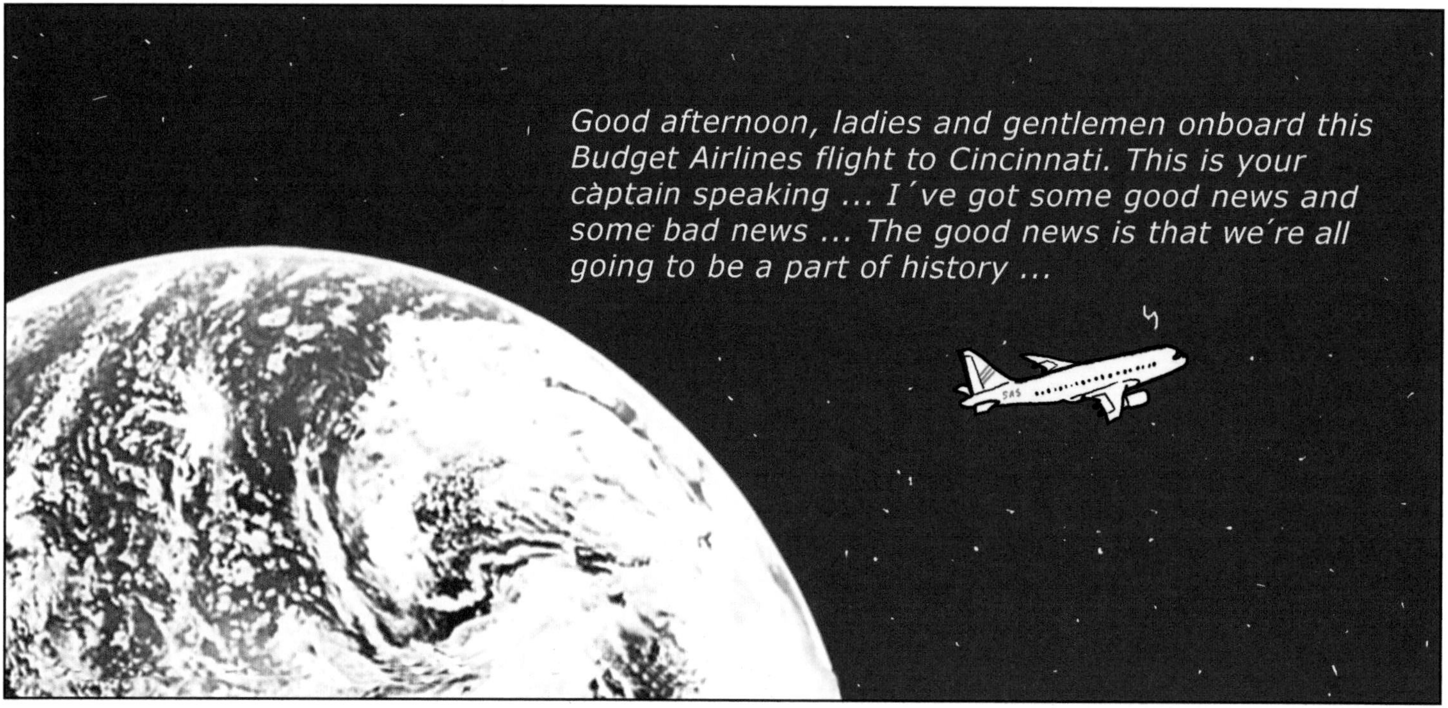
Good afternoon, ladies and gentlemen onboard this Budget Airlines flight to Cincinnati. This is your càptain speaking ... I´ve got some good news and some bad news ... The good news is that we're all going to be a part of history ...
SAS

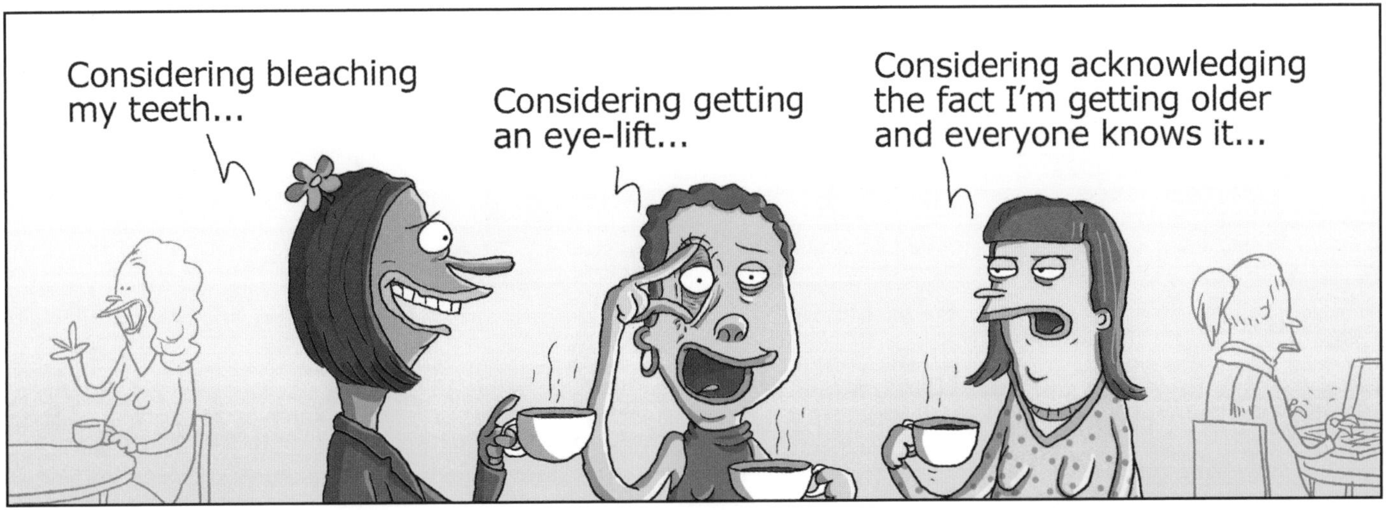
Considering bleaching my teeth...
Considering getting an eye-lift...
Considering acknowledging the fact I'm getting older and everyone knows it...

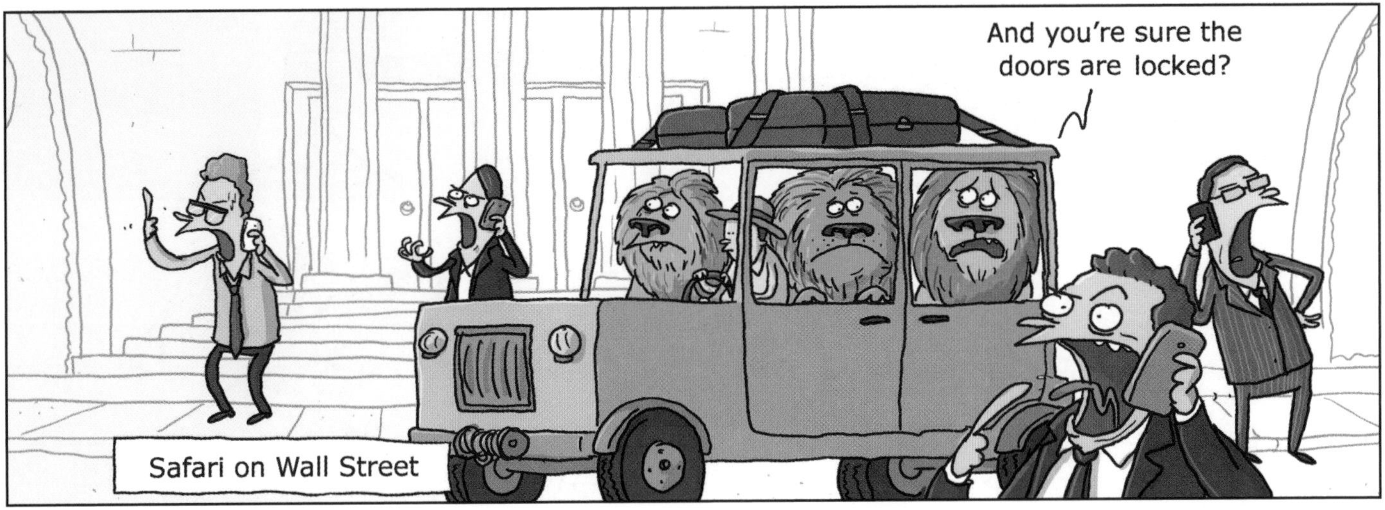
And you're sure the doors are locked?
Safari on Wall Street

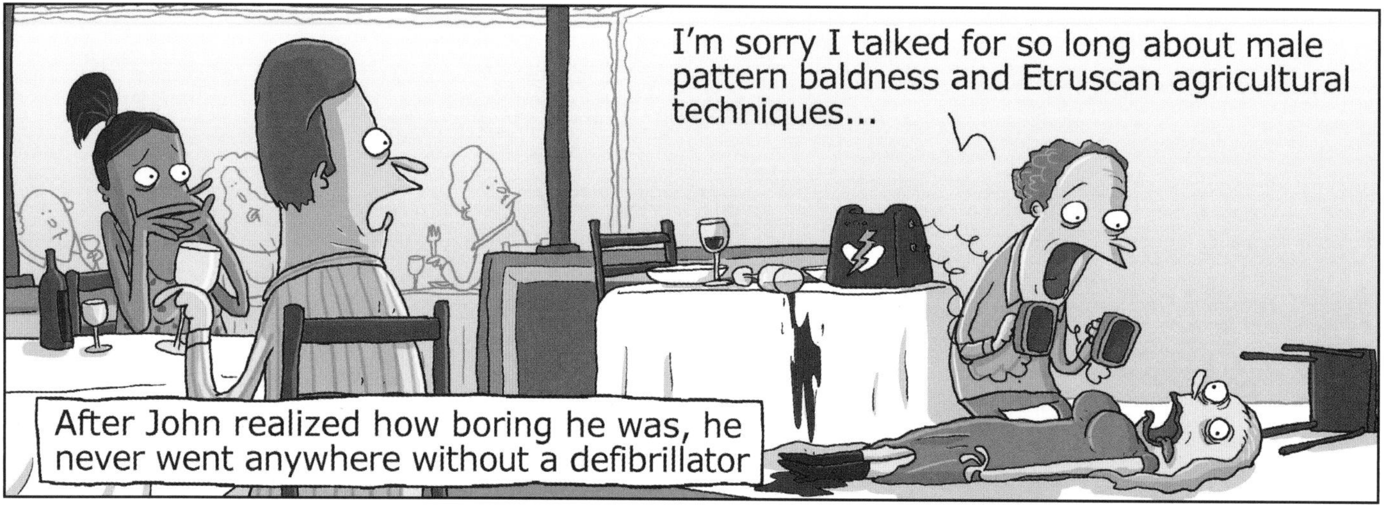
I'm sorry I talked for so long about male pattern baldness and Etruscan agricultural techniques...
After John realized how boring he was, he never went anywhere without a defibrillator

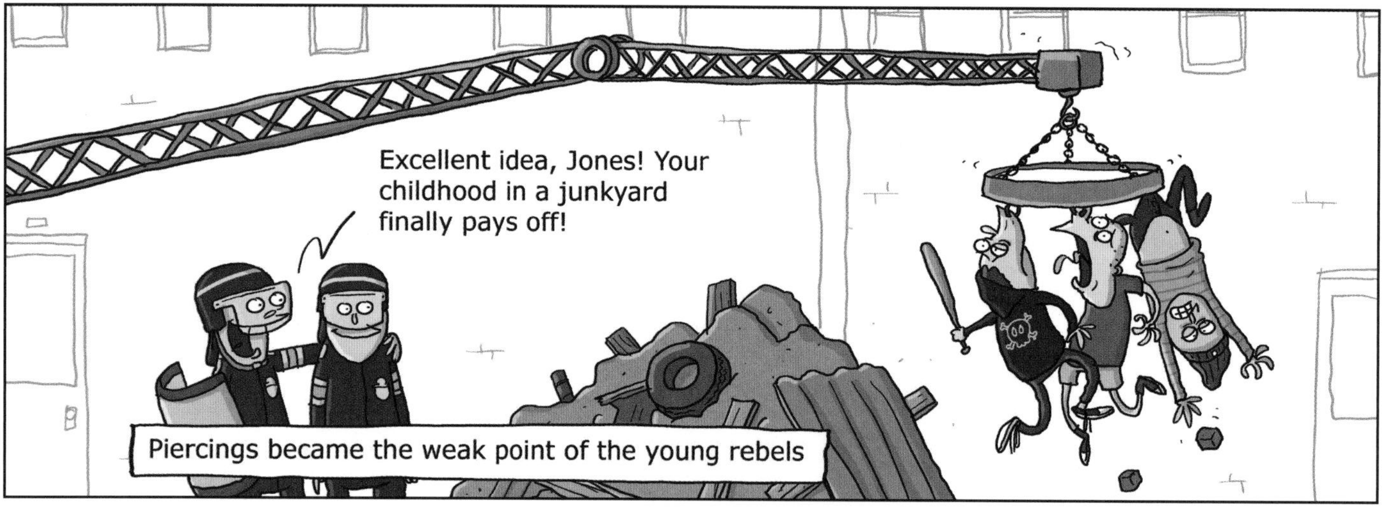
Excellent idea, Jones! Your childhood in a junkyard finally pays off!
Piercings became the weak point of the young rebels

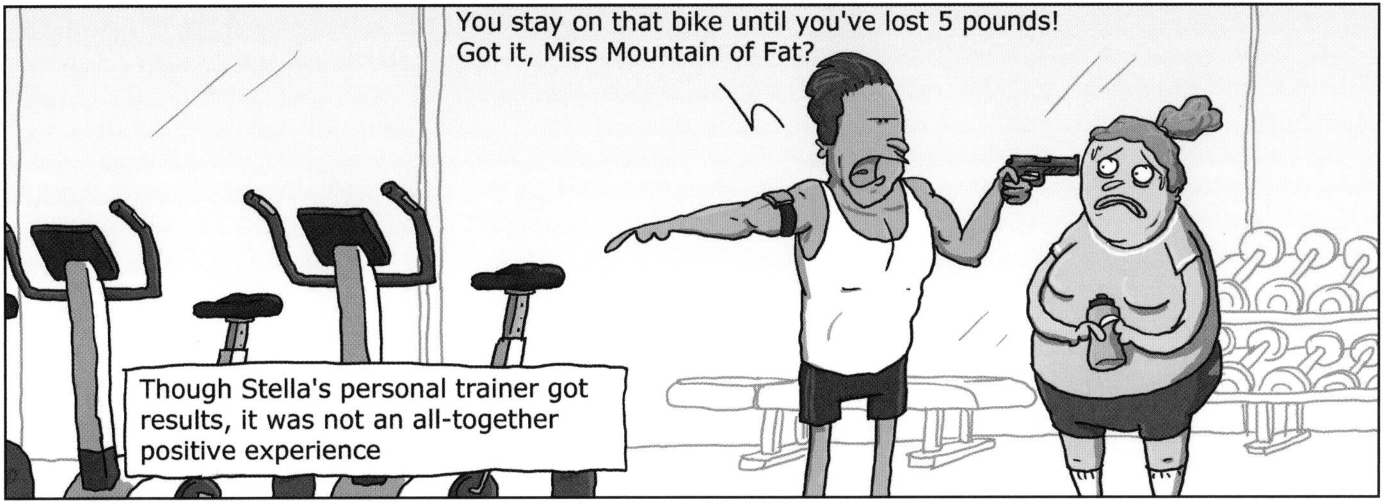
You stay on that bike until you've lost 5 pounds!
Got it, Miss Mountain of Fat?
Though Stella's personal trainer got results, it was not an all-together positive experience

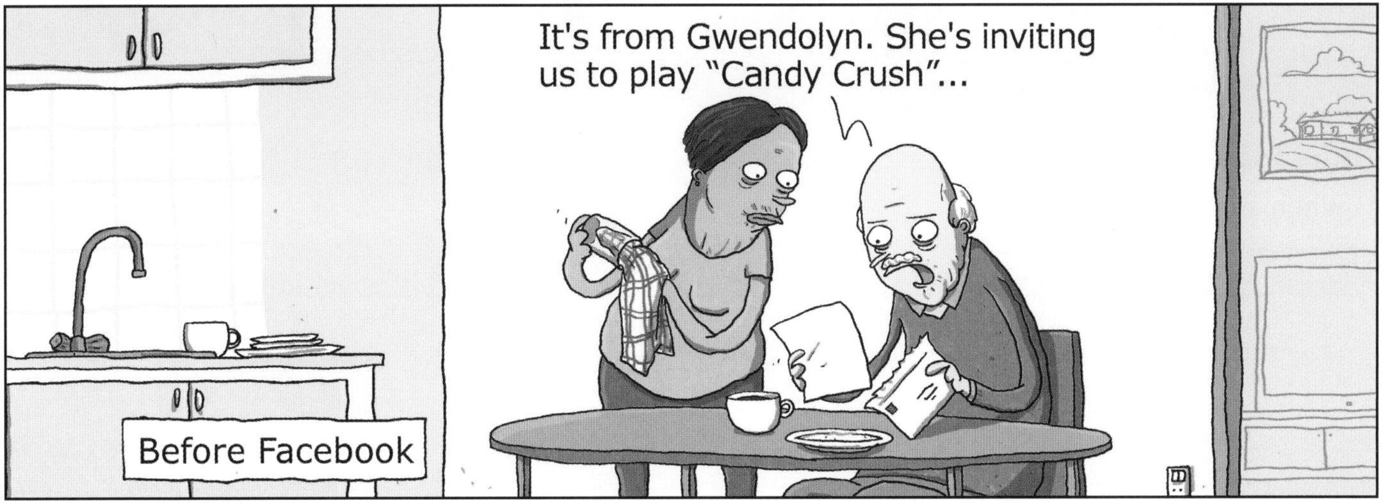
Before Facebook
It's from Gwendolyn. She's inviting us to play “Candy Crush”...

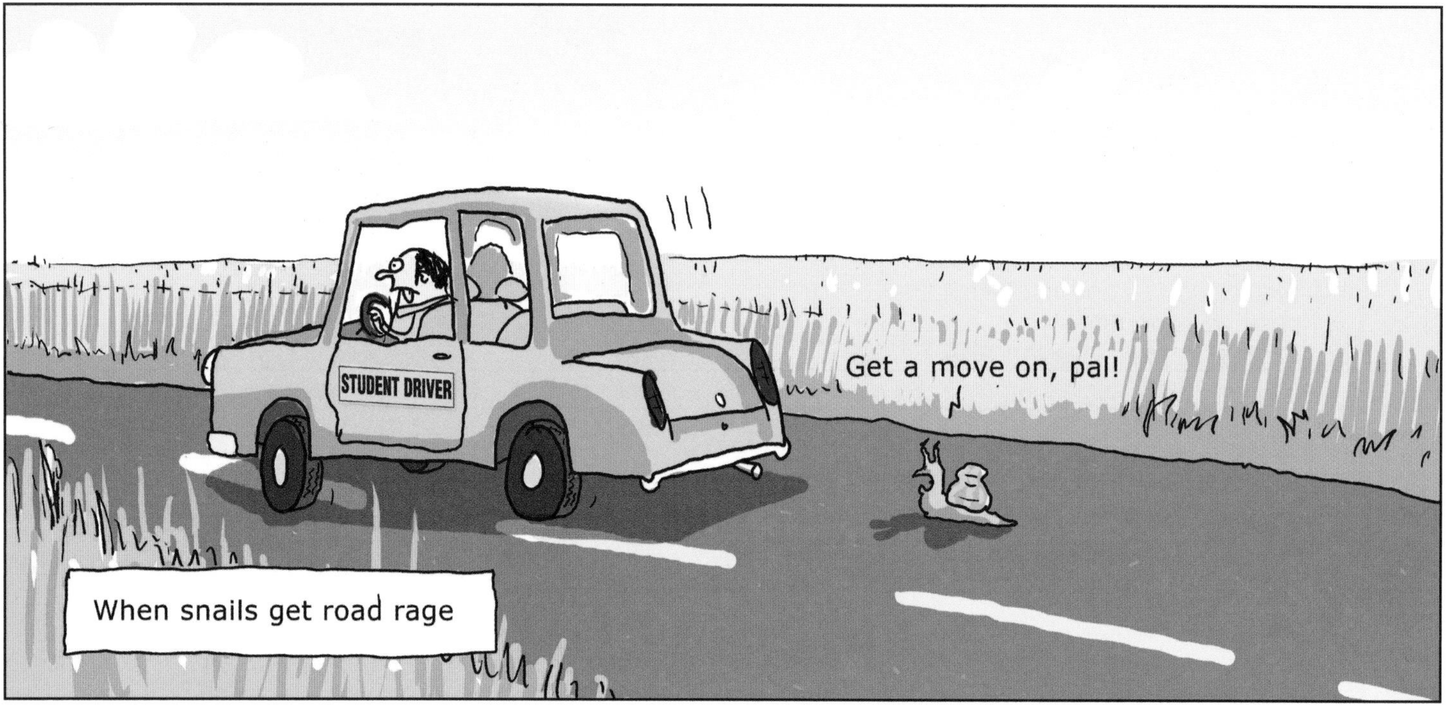
STUDENT DRIVER
Get a move on, pal!
When snails get road rage

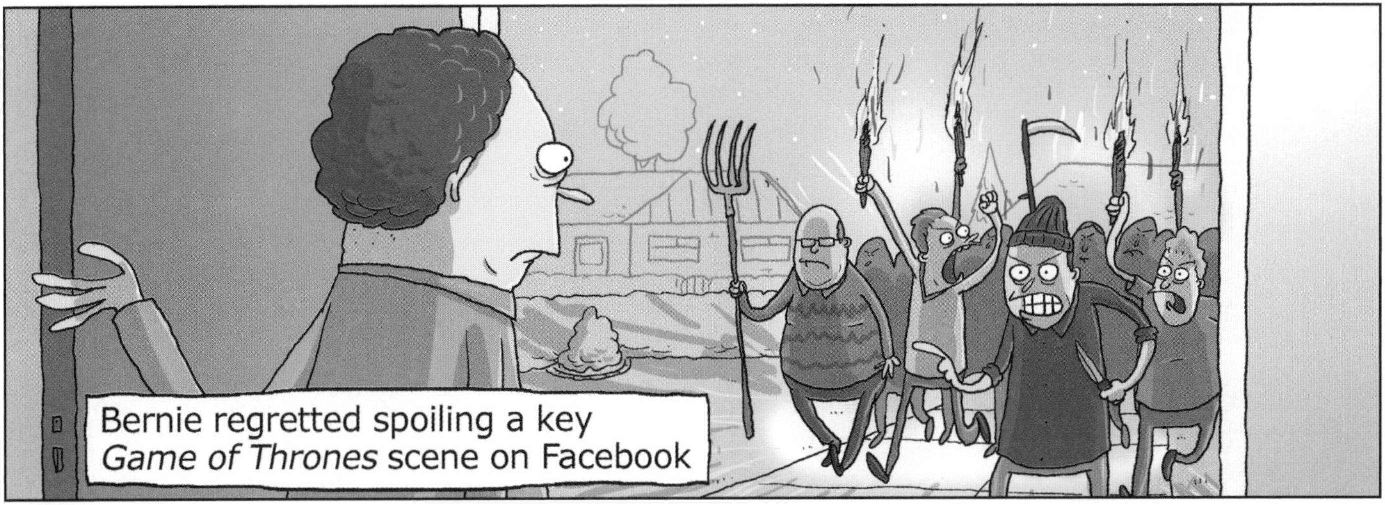
Bernie regretted spoiling a key *Game of Thrones* scene on Facebook

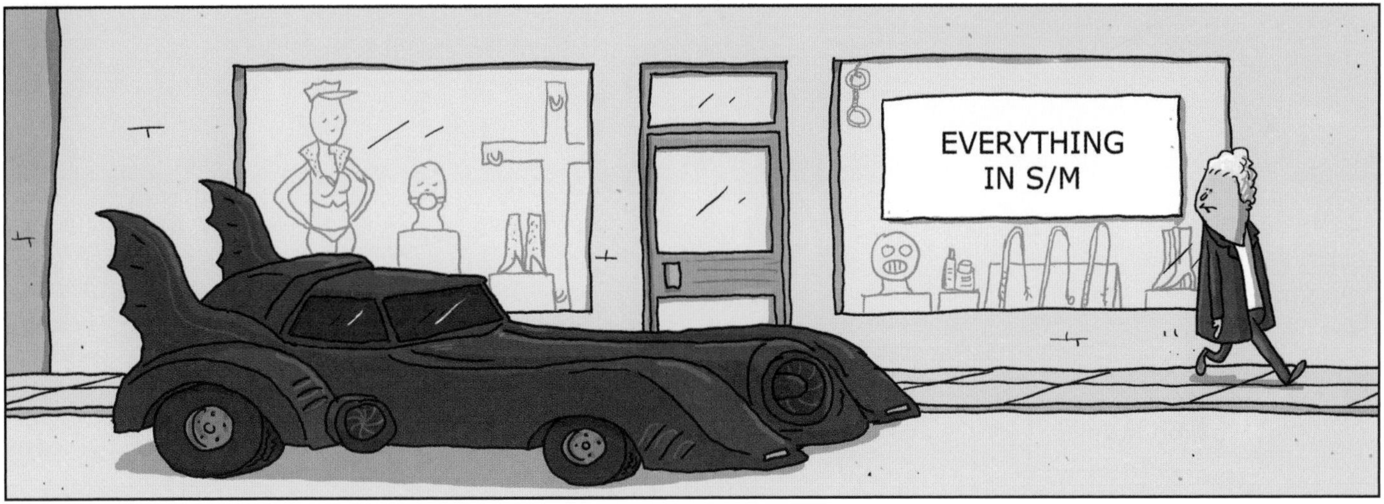
EVERYTHING IN S/M

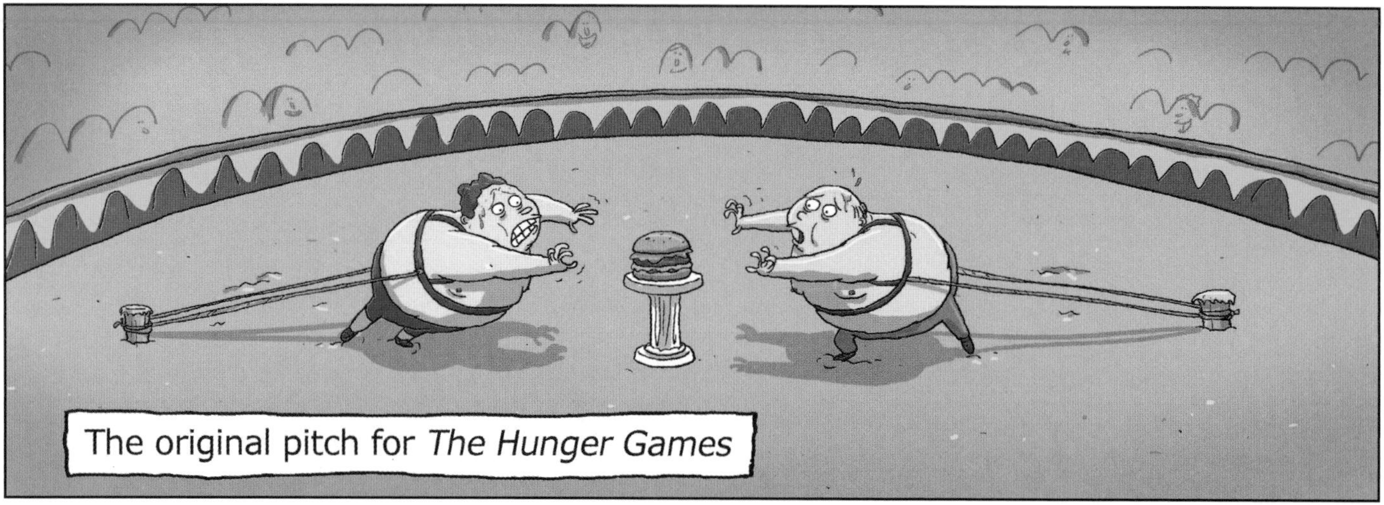
The original pitch for *The Hunger Games*

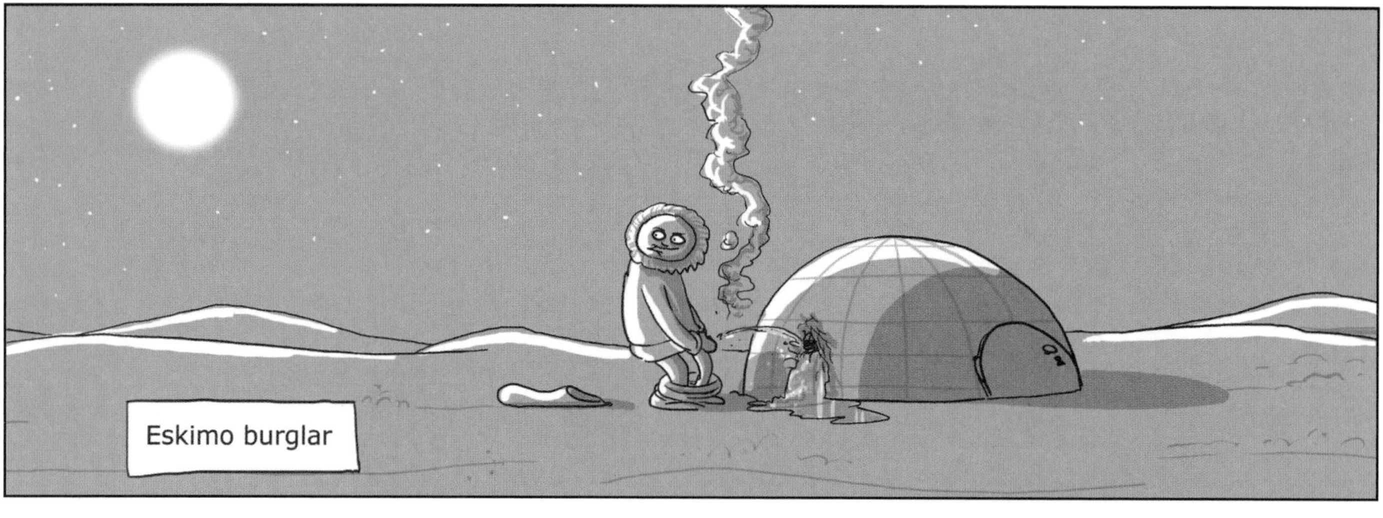
Eskimo burglar

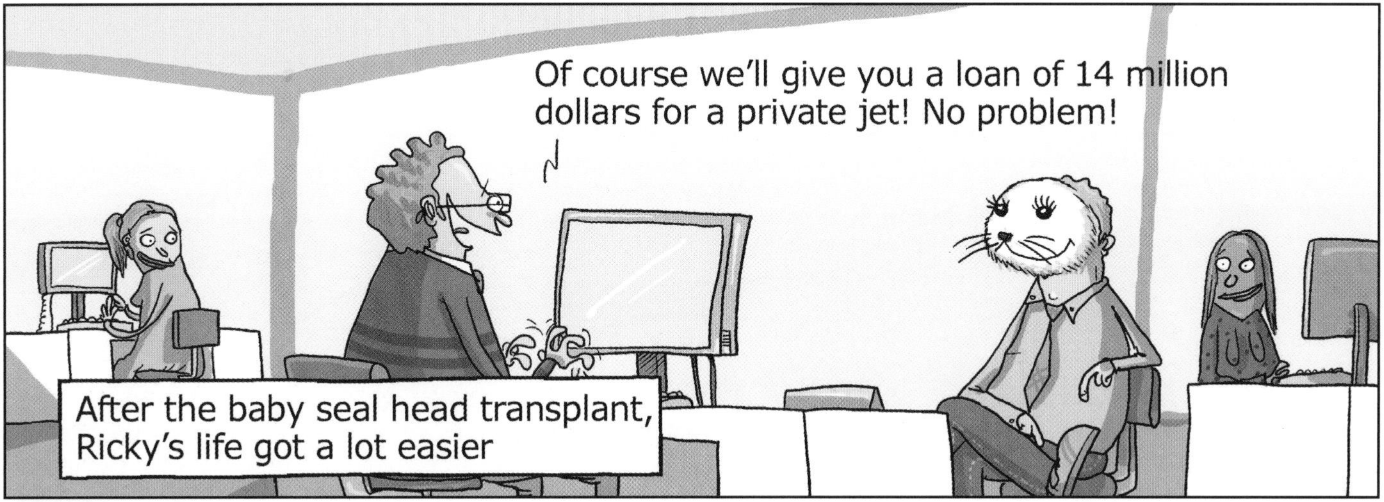
Of course we'll give you a loan of 14 million dollars for a private jet! No problem!
After the baby seal head transplant, Ricky's life got a lot easier

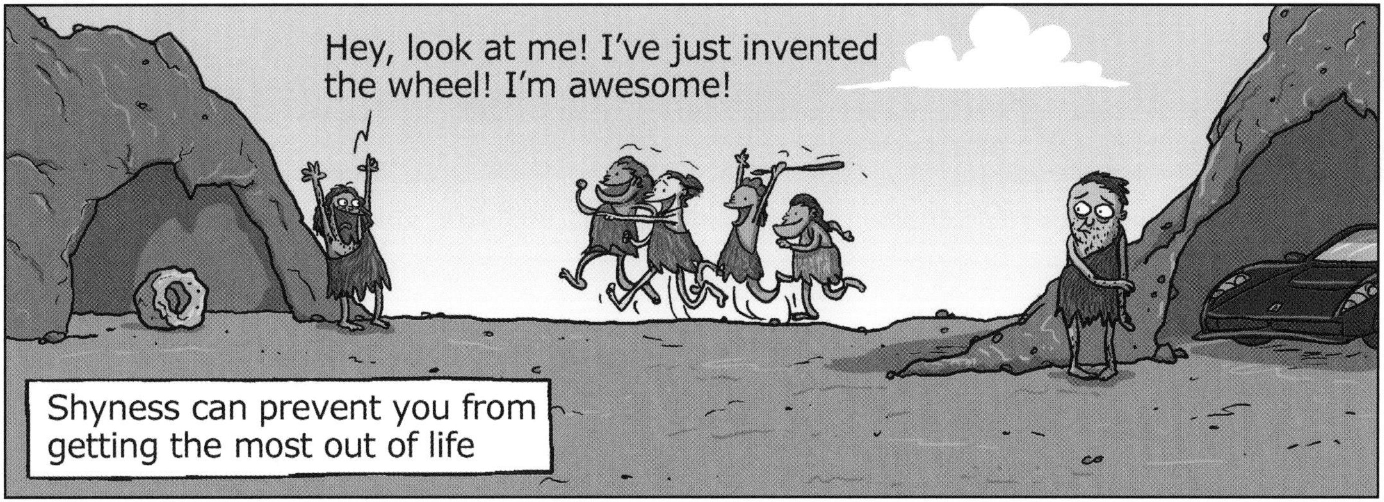
Hey, look at me! I've just invented the wheel! I'm awesome!
Shyness can prevent you from getting the most out of life

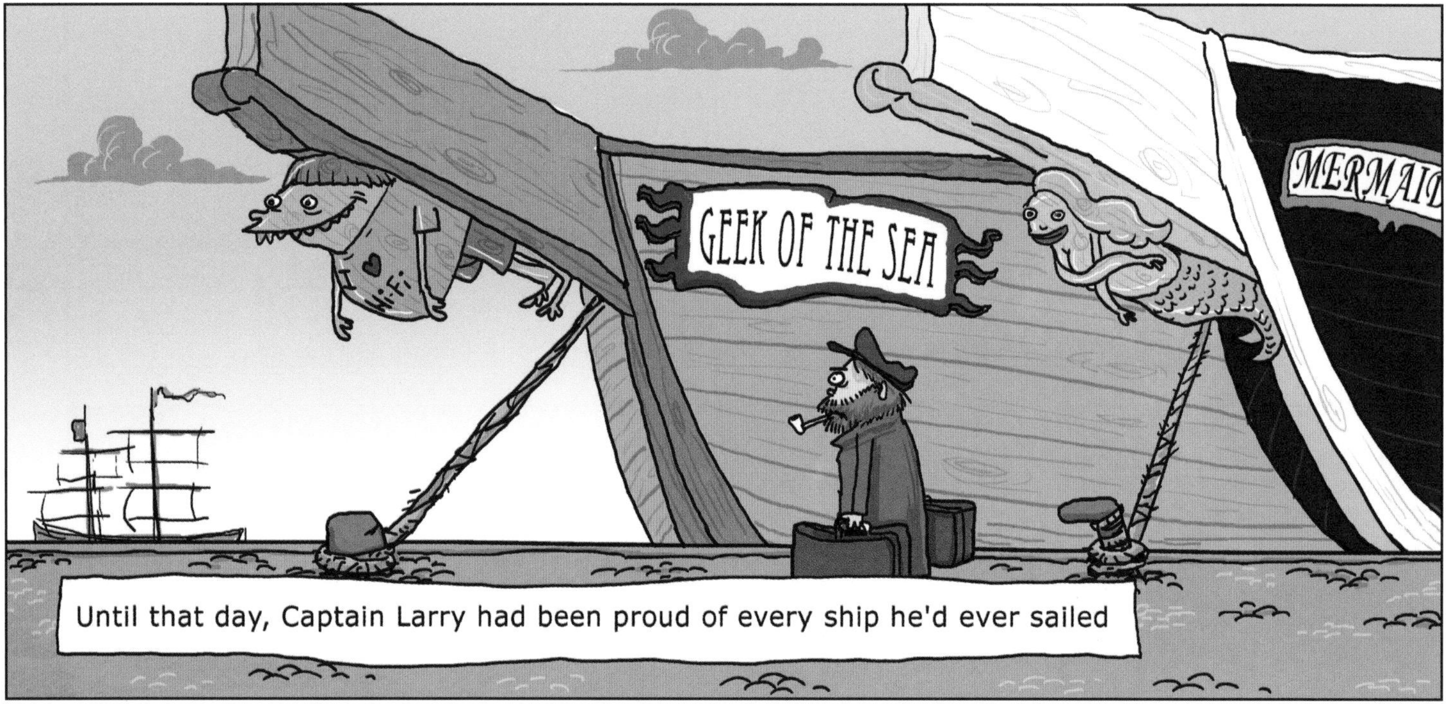
GEEK OF THE SEA
MERMAID
Until that day, Captain Larry had been proud of every ship he'd ever sailed

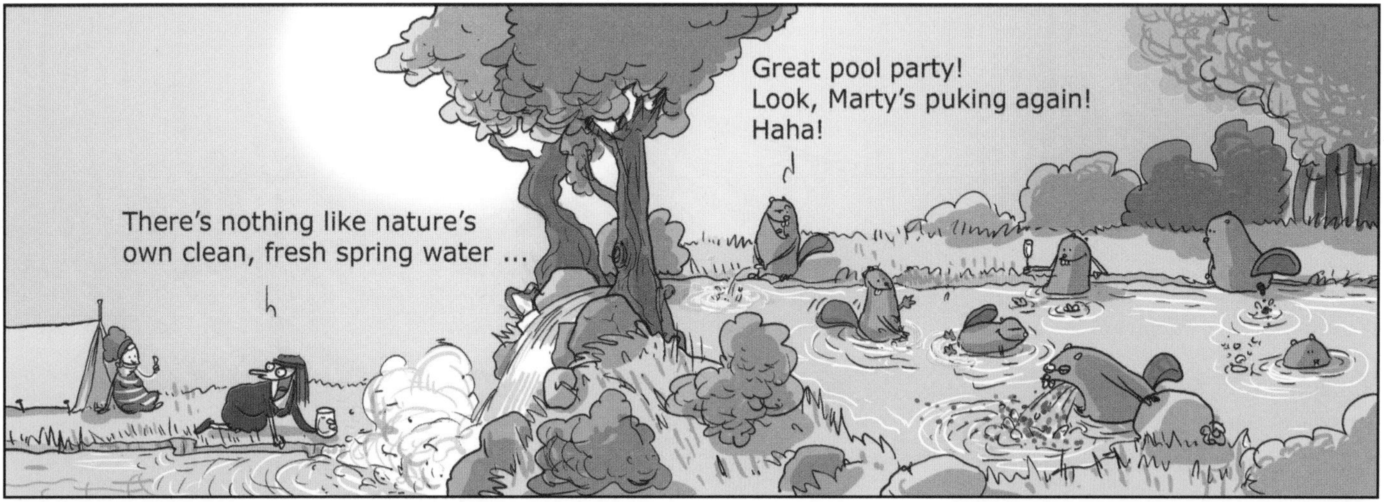
Great pool party!
Look, Marty's puking again!
Haha!
There's nothing like nature's
own clean, fresh spring water ...

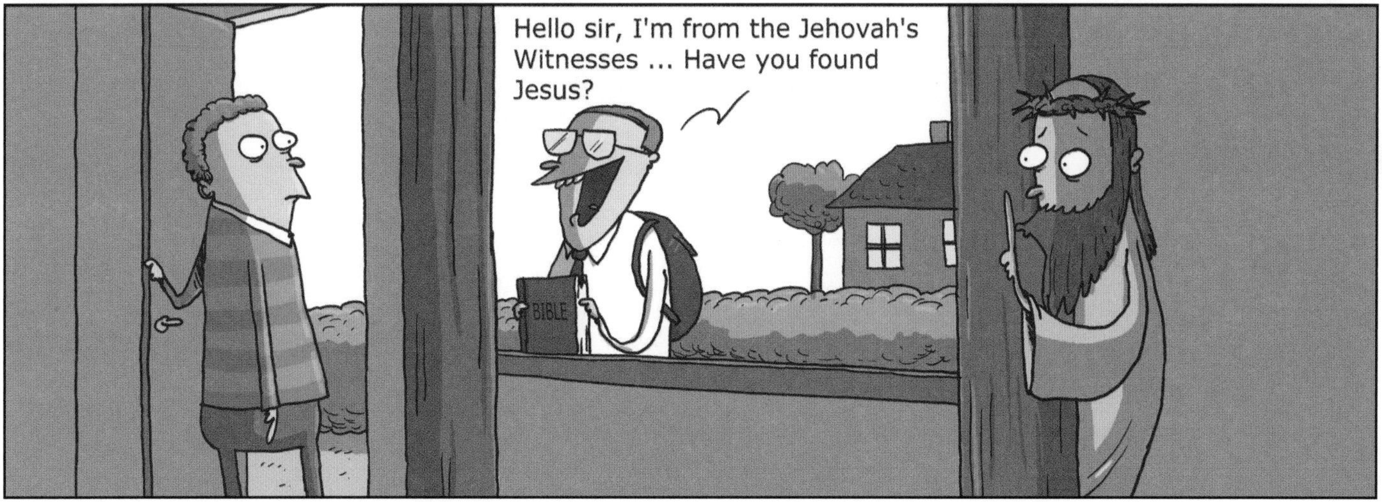
Hello sir, I'm from the Jehovah's
Witnesses ... Have you found
Jesus?
BIBLE

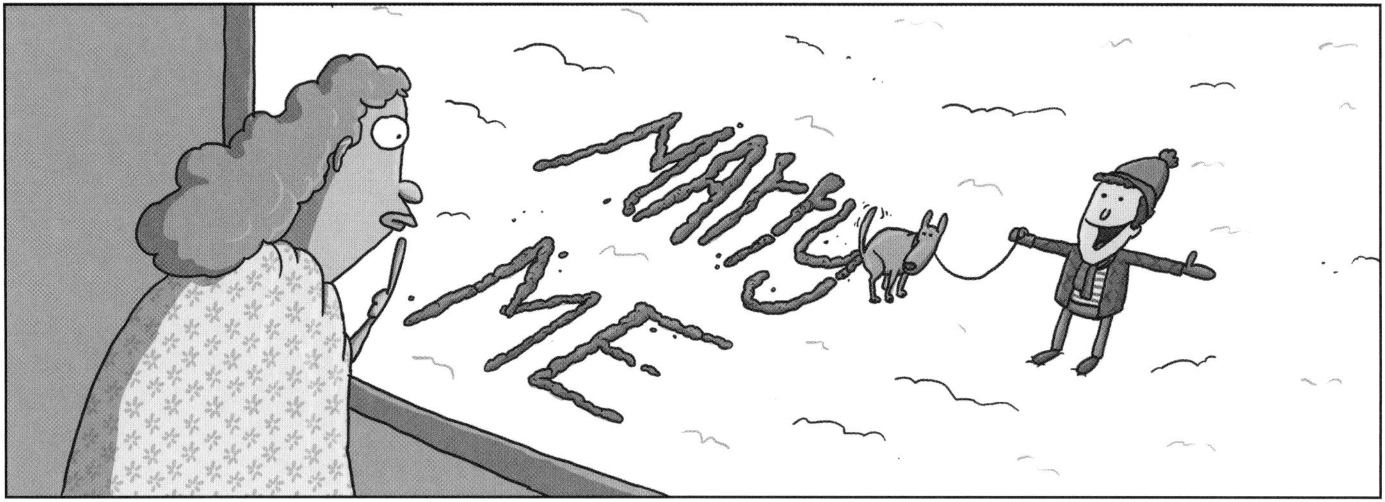
MARRY ME

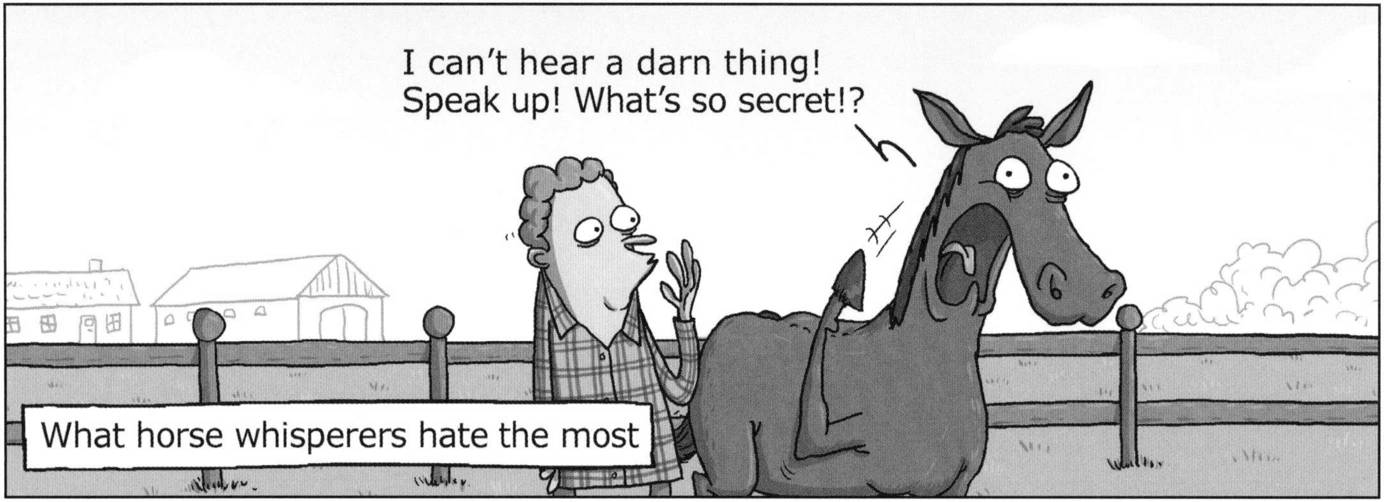
I can't hear a darn thing!
Speak up! What's so secret!?
What horse whisperers hate the most

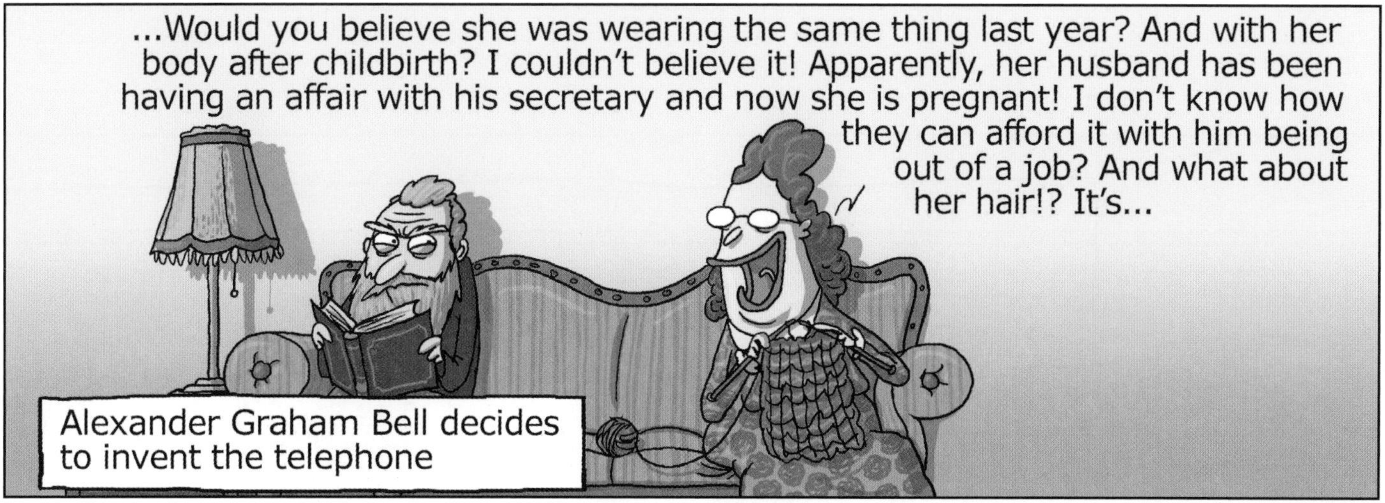
...Would you believe she was wearing the same thing last year? And with her body after childbirth? I couldn't believe it! Apparently, her husband has been having an affair with his secretary and now she is pregnant! I don't know how they can afford it with him being out of a job? And what about her hair!? It's...
Alexander Graham Bell decides to invent the telephone

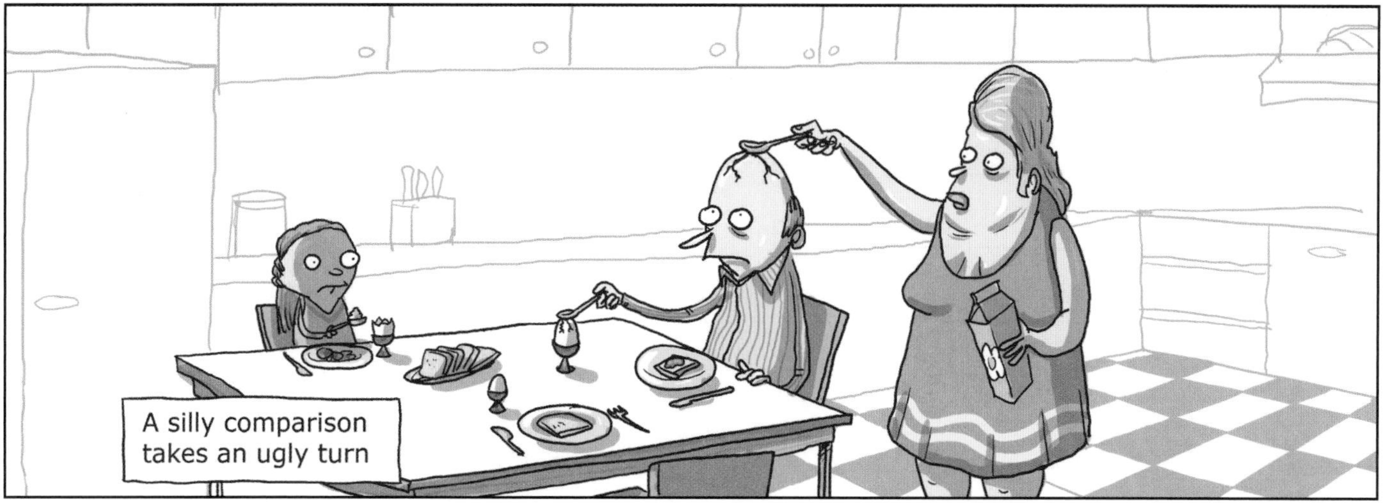
A silly comparison takes an ugly turn

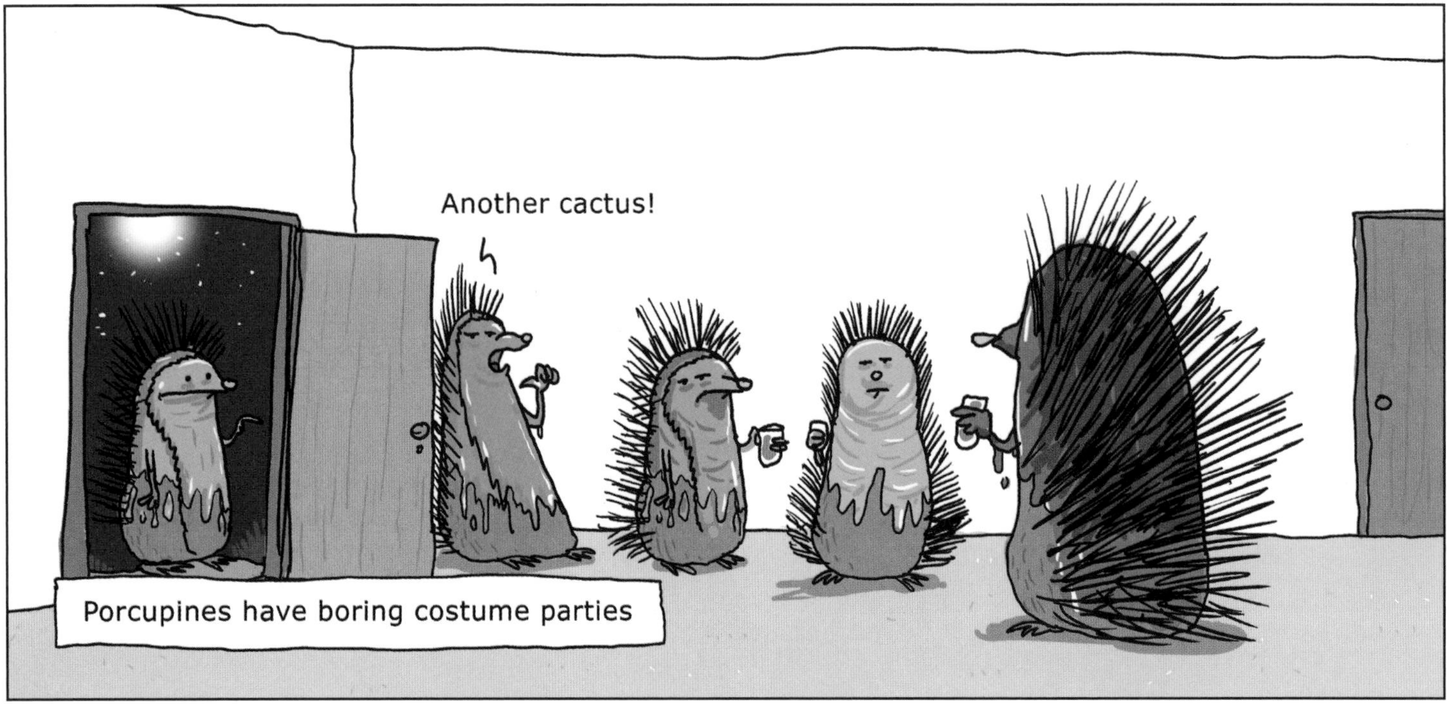
Another cactus!
Porcupines have boring costume parties

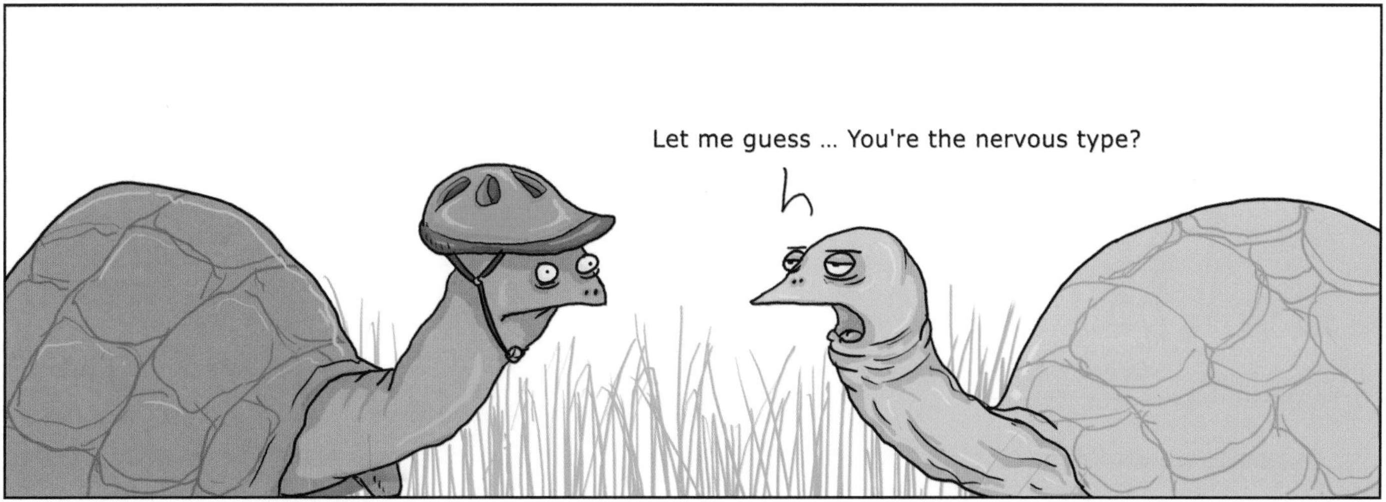
Let me guess ... You're the nervous type?

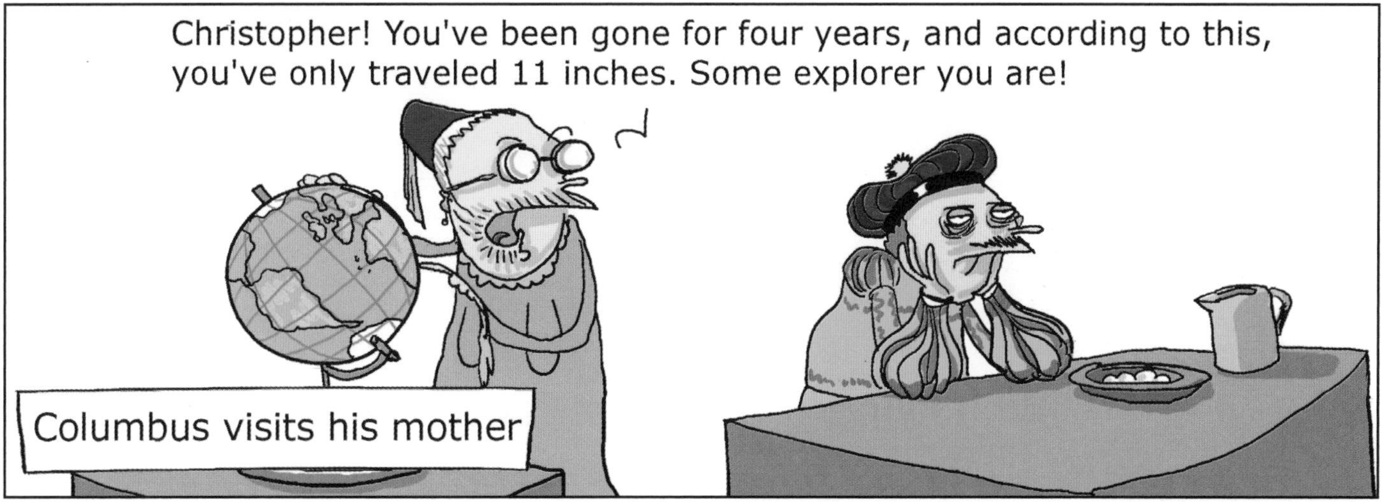
Christopher! You've been gone for four years, and according to this, you've only traveled 11 inches. Some explorer you are!
Columbus visits his mother

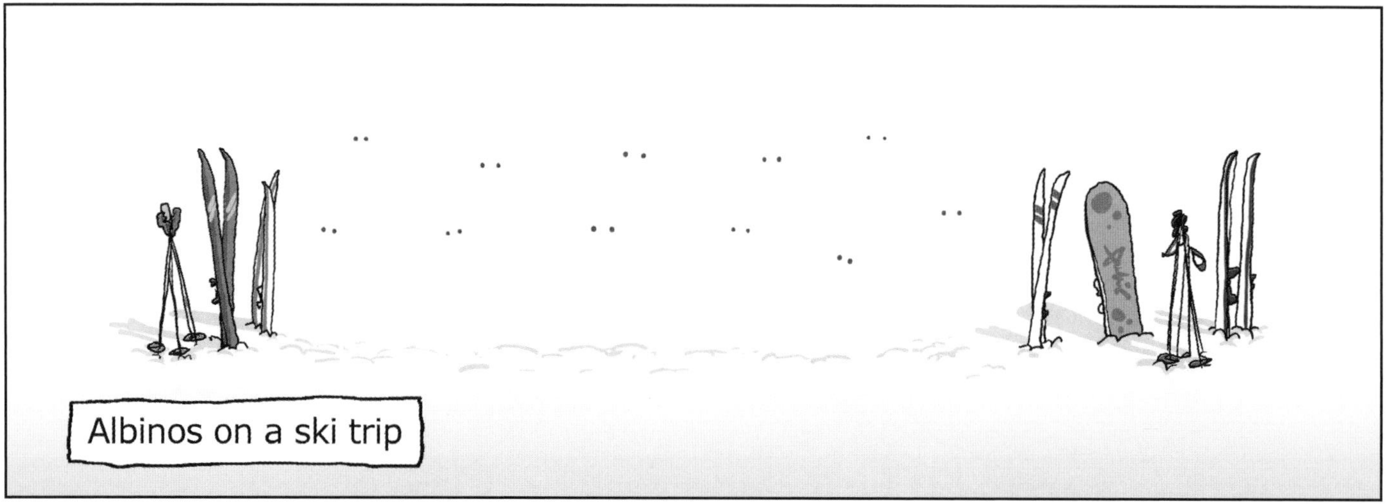
Albinos on a ski trip

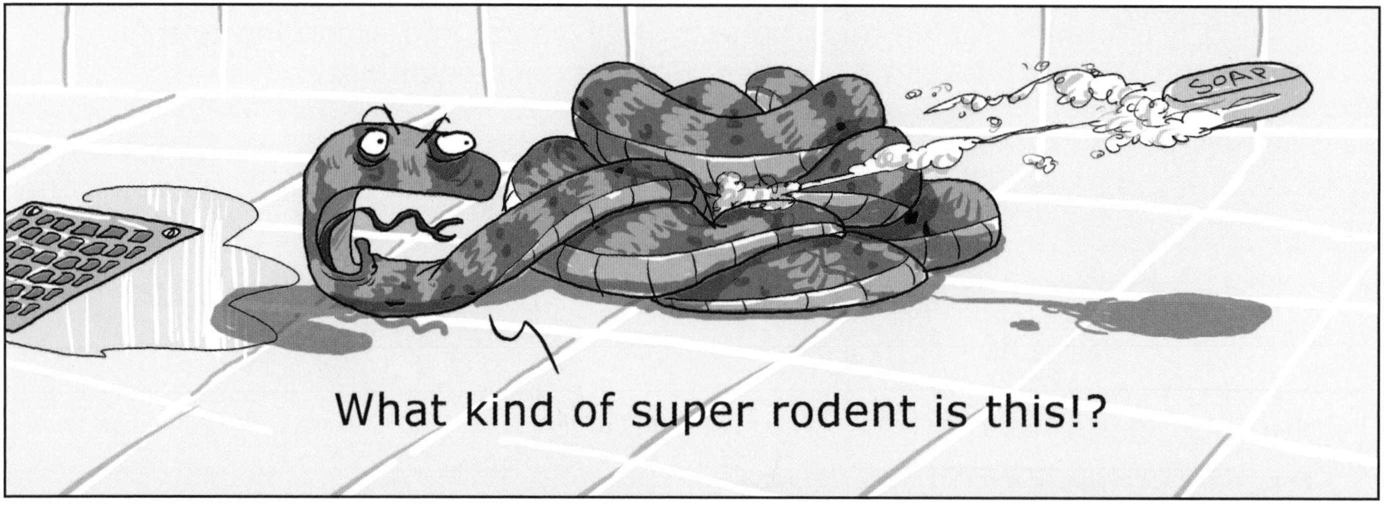
SOAP
What kind of super rodent is this!?

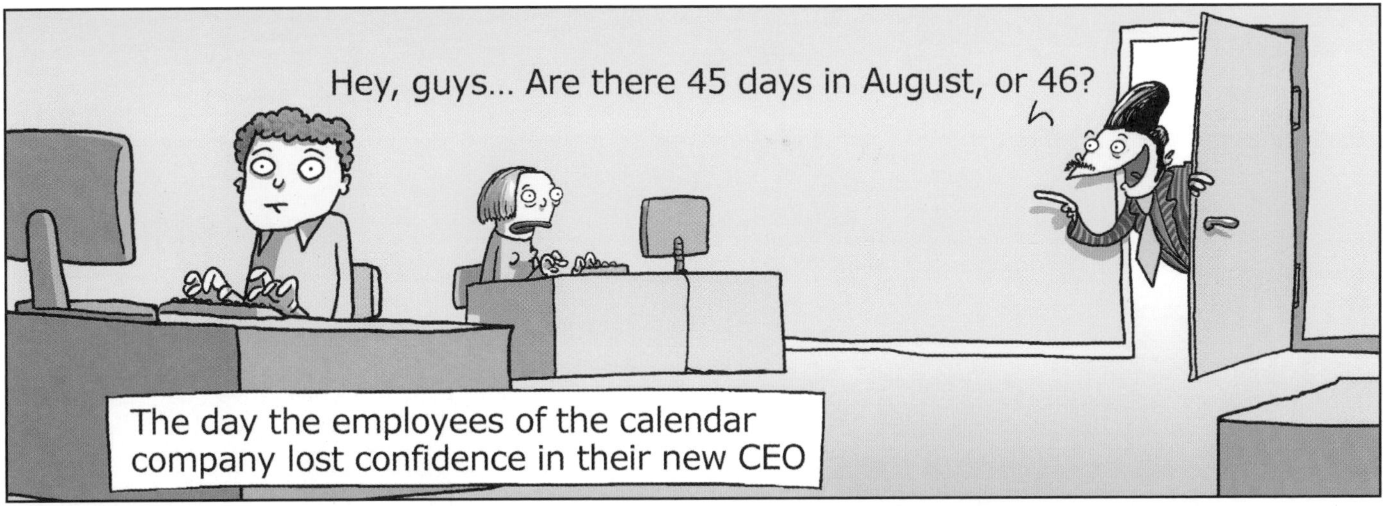
Hey, guys... Are there 45 days in August, or 46?
The day the employees of the calendar company lost confidence in their new CEO

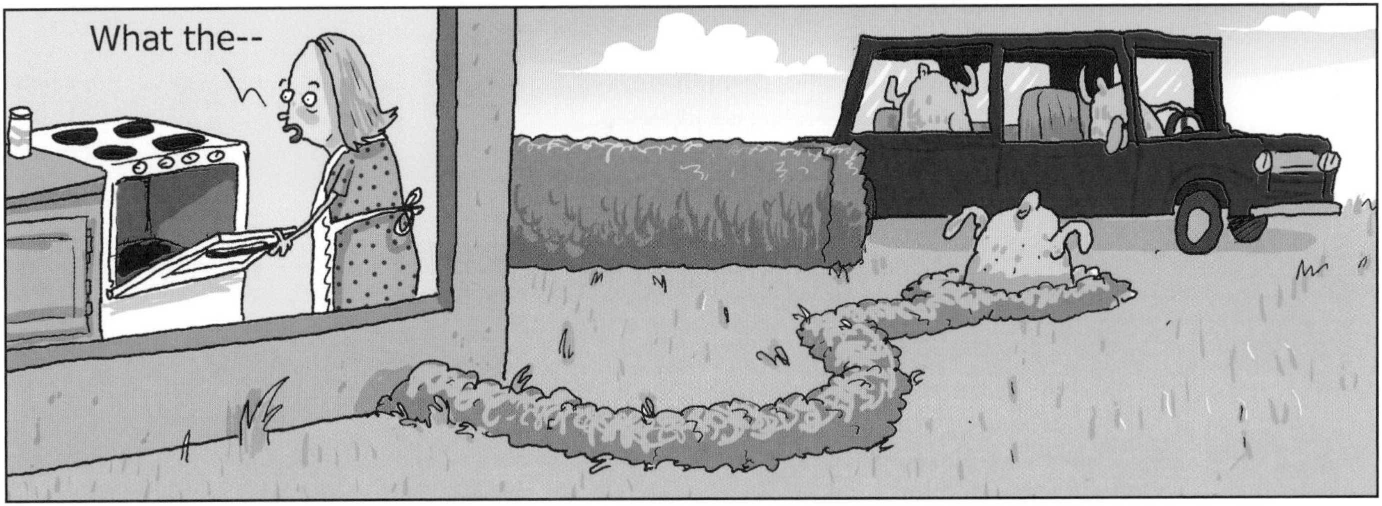
What the--

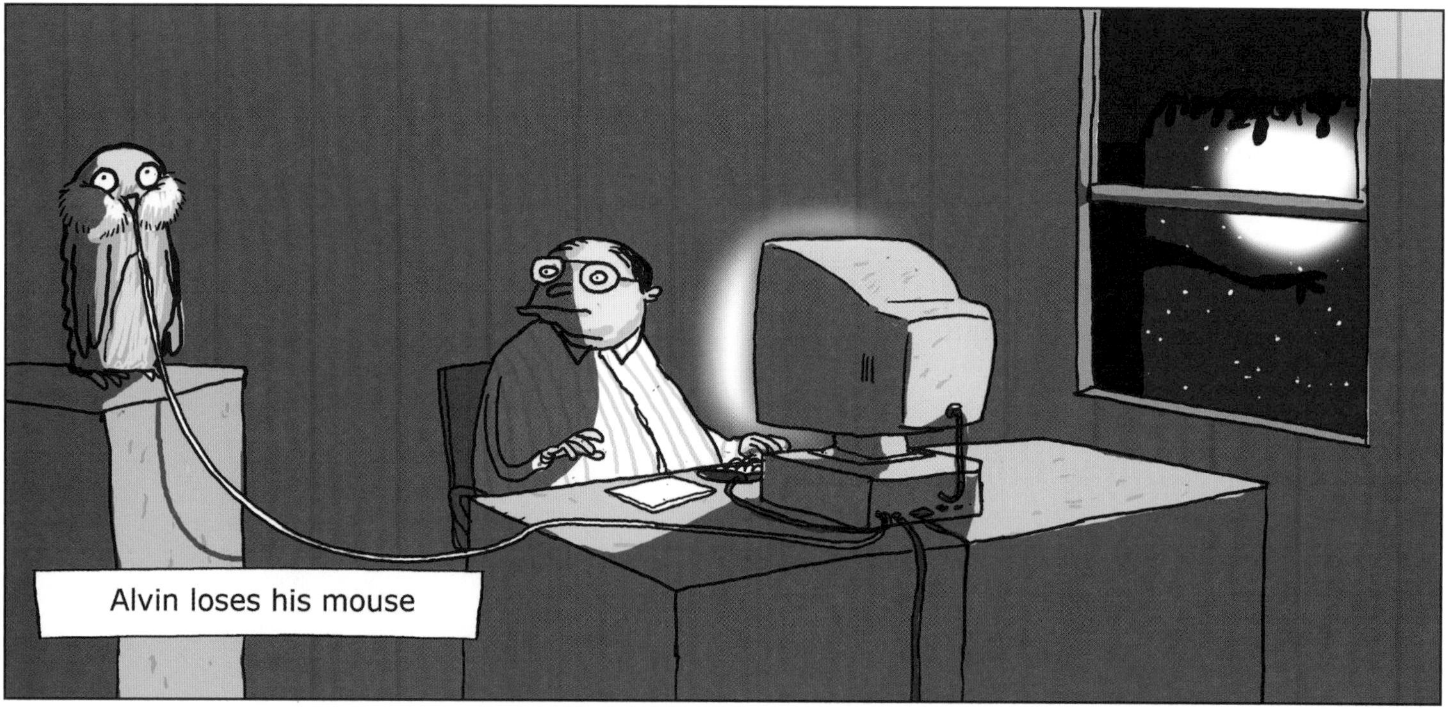
Alvin loses his mouse

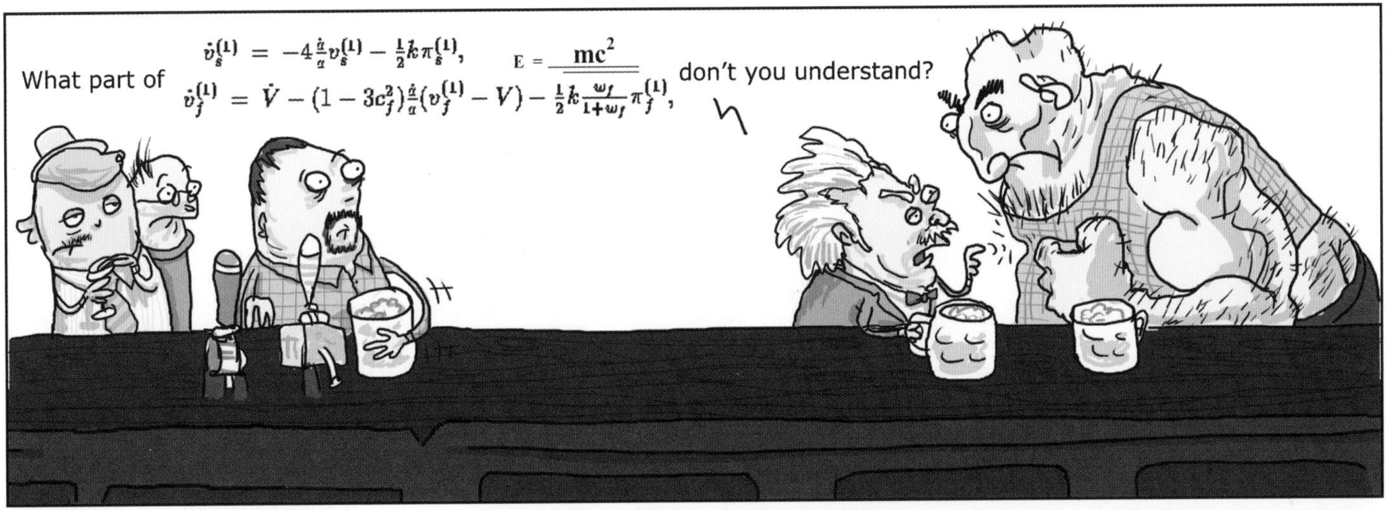
What part of
$\dot{v}_s^{(1)} = -4\frac{\dot{a}}{a}v_s^{(1)} - \frac{1}{2}k\pi_s^{(1)},$
$\dot{v}_f^{(1)} = \dot{V} - (1 - 3c_f^2)\frac{\dot{a}}{a}(v_f^{(1)} - V) - \frac{1}{2}k\frac{w_f}{1+w_f}\pi_f^{(1)},$
$E = \frac{mc^2}{}$
don't you understand?

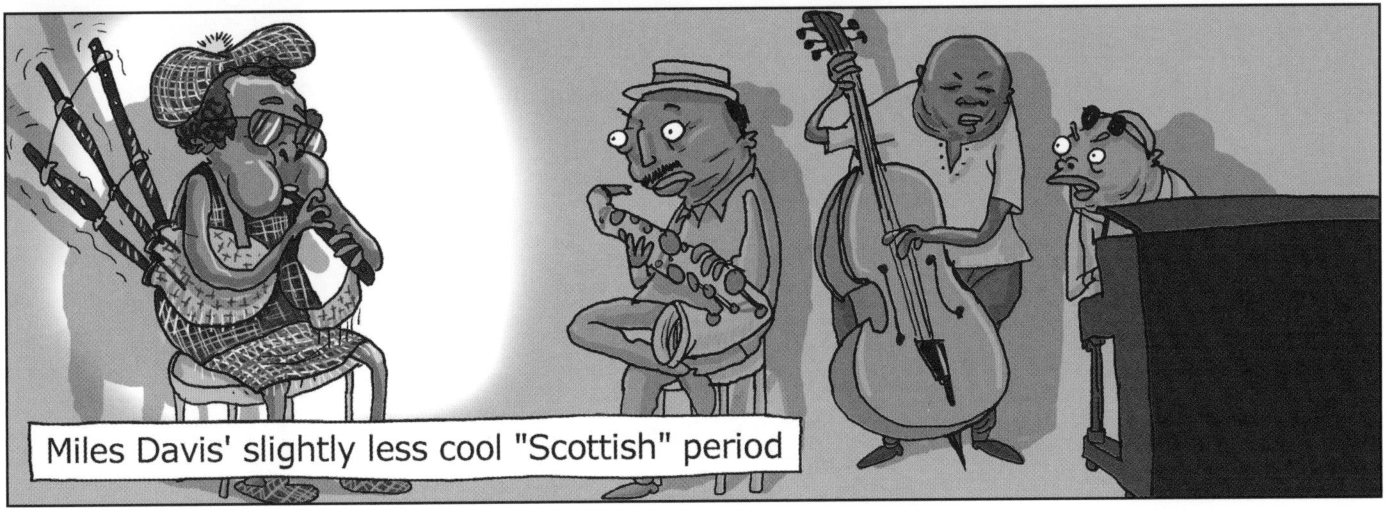
Miles Davis' slightly less cool "Scottish" period

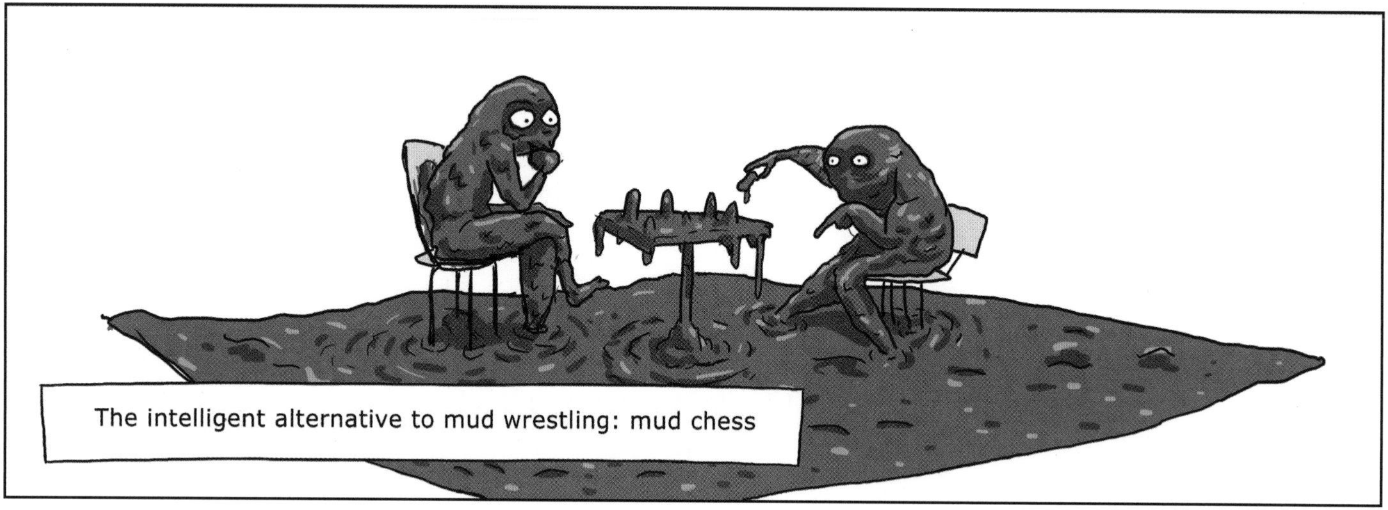
The intelligent alternative to mud wrestling: mud chess

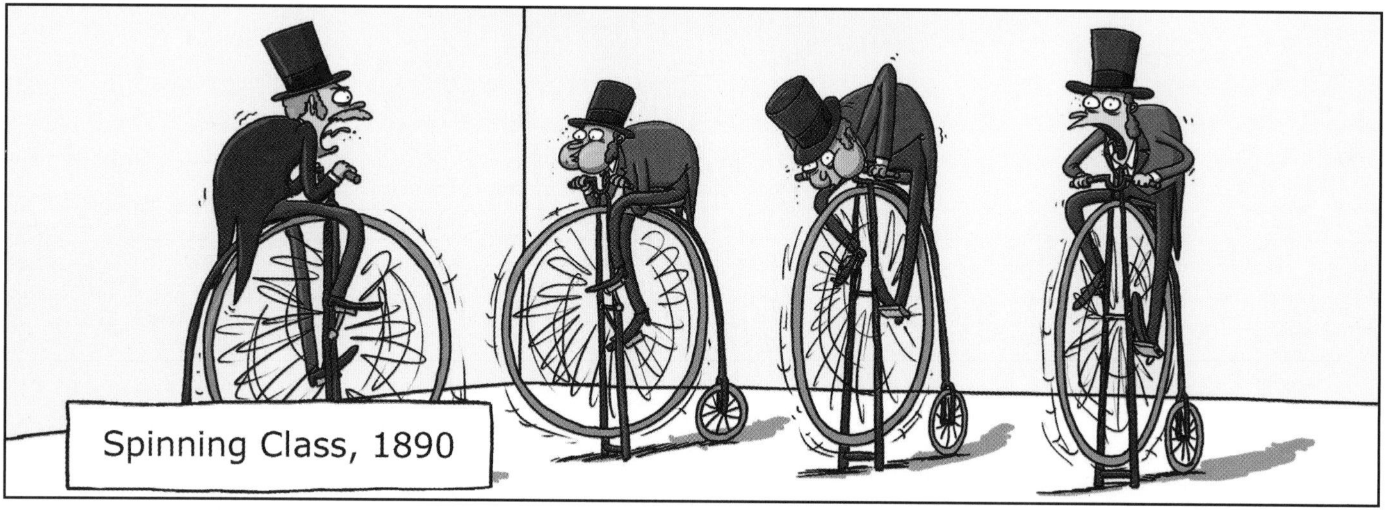
Spinning Class, 1890

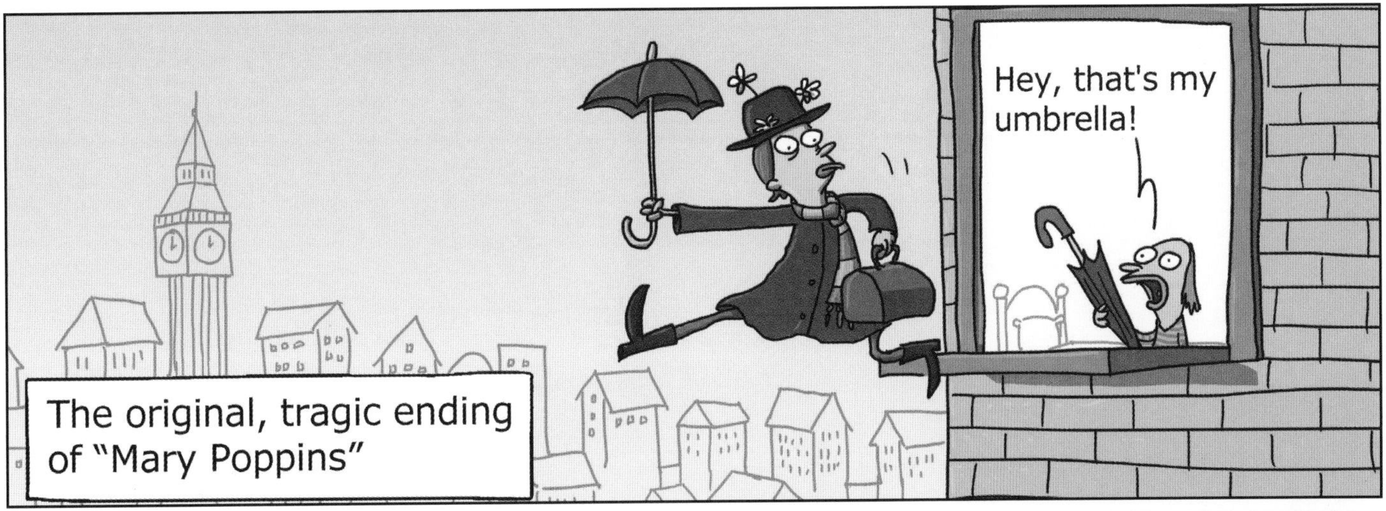
The original, tragic ending of "Mary Poppins"
Hey, that's my umbrella!

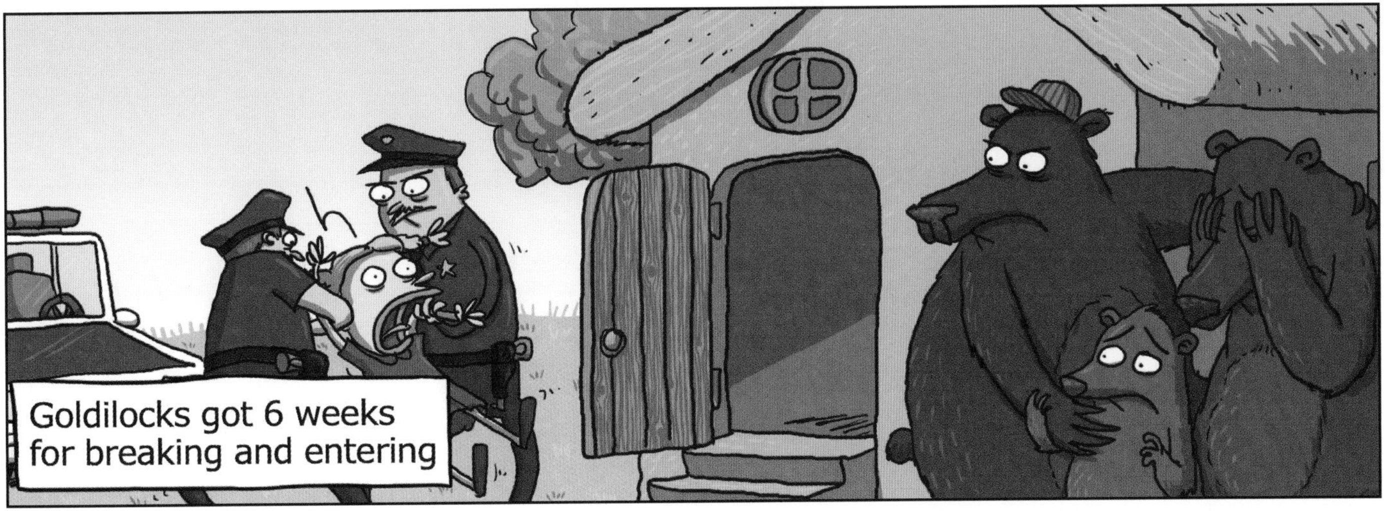
Goldilocks got 6 weeks for breaking and entering

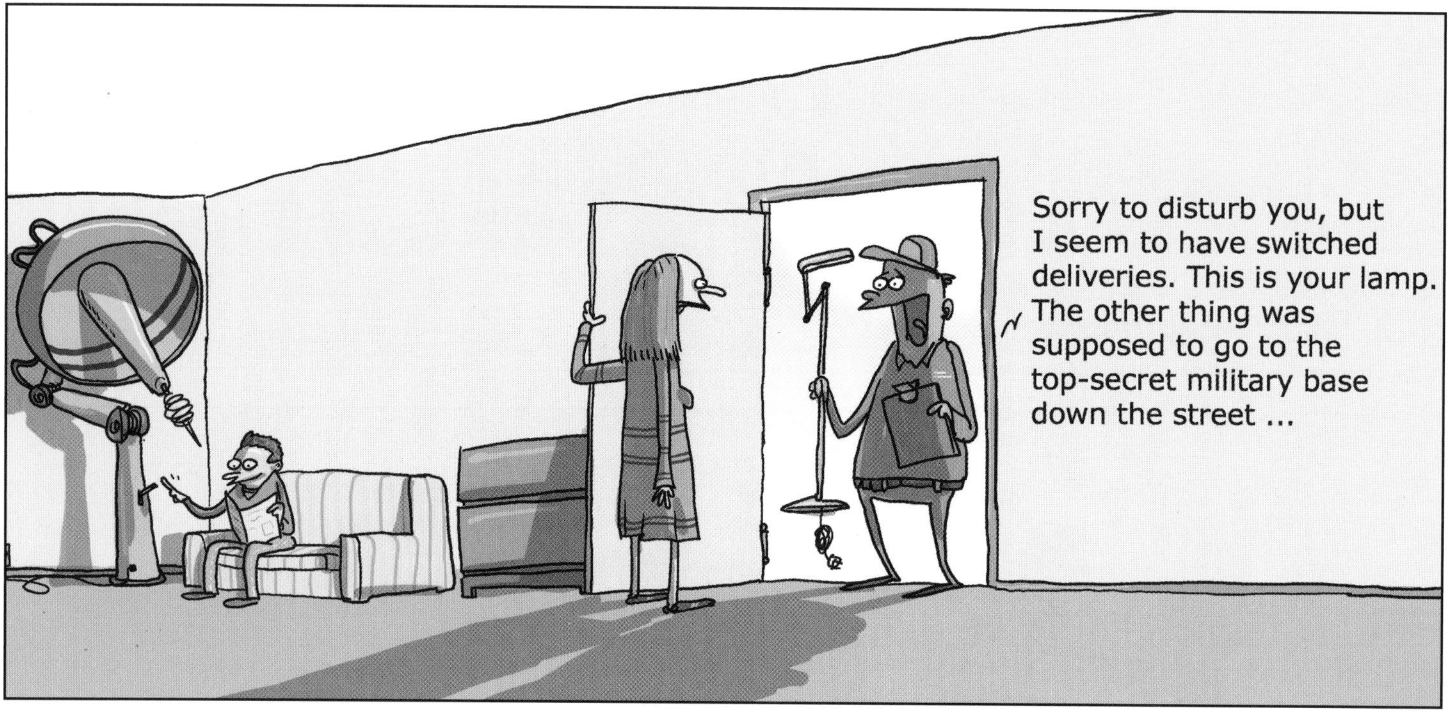
Sorry to disturb you, but I seem to have switched deliveries. This is your lamp. The other thing was supposed to go to the top-secret military base down the street ...

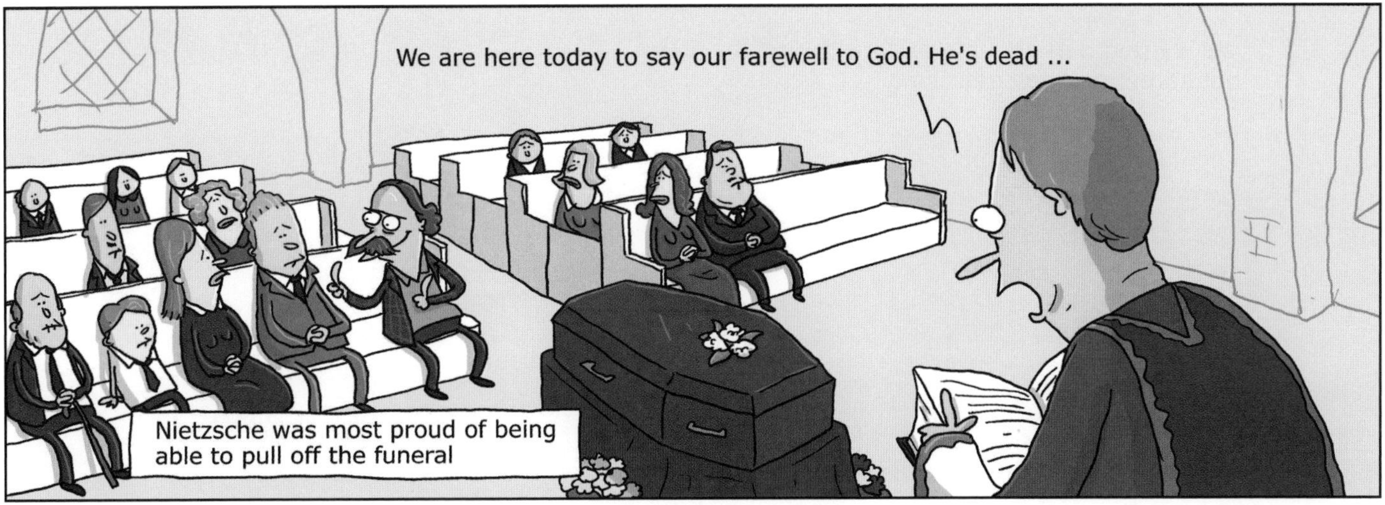
We are here today to say our farewell to God. He's dead ...
Nietzsche was most proud of being able to pull off the funeral

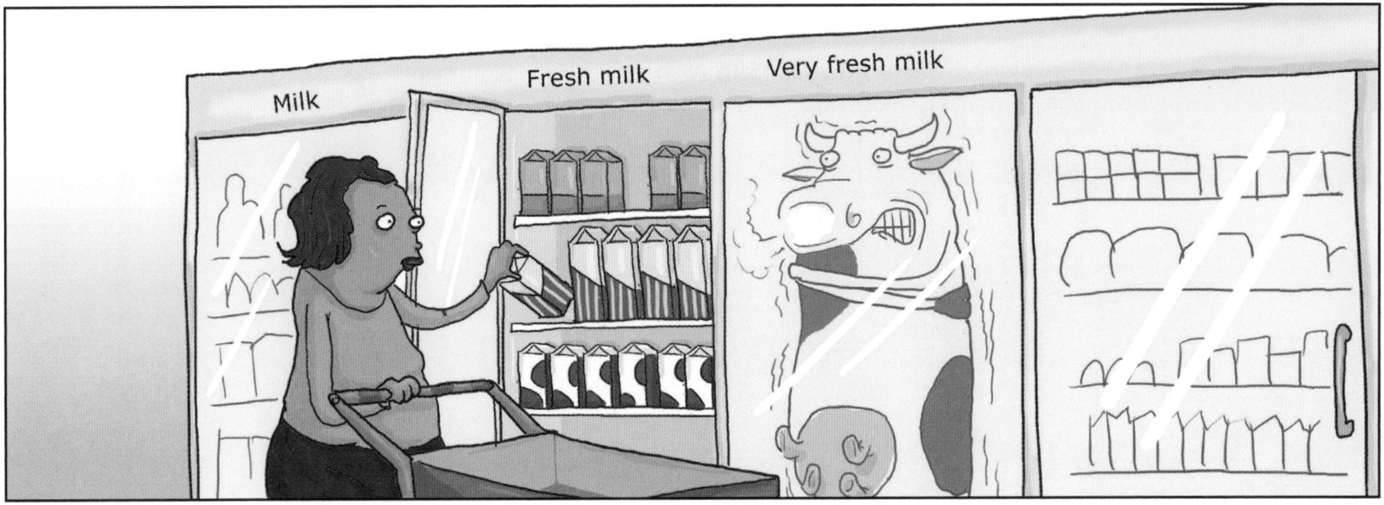
Milk
Fresh milk
Very fresh milk

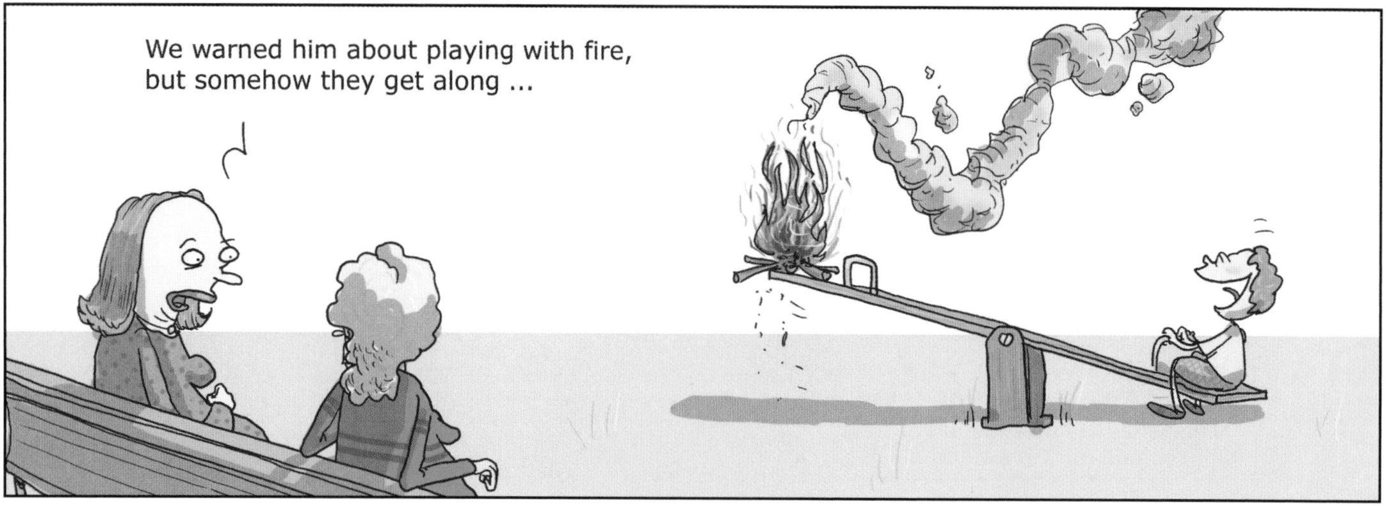
We warned him about playing with fire, but somehow they get along ...

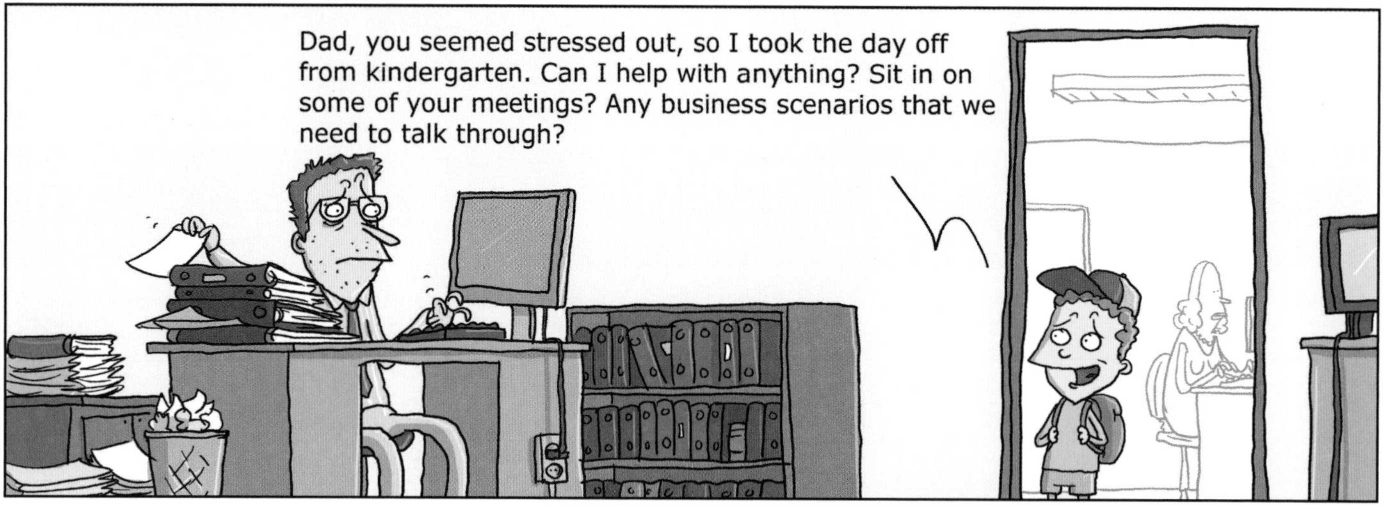
Dad, you seemed stressed out, so I took the day off from kindergarten. Can I help with anything? Sit in on some of your meetings? Any business scenarios that we need to talk through?

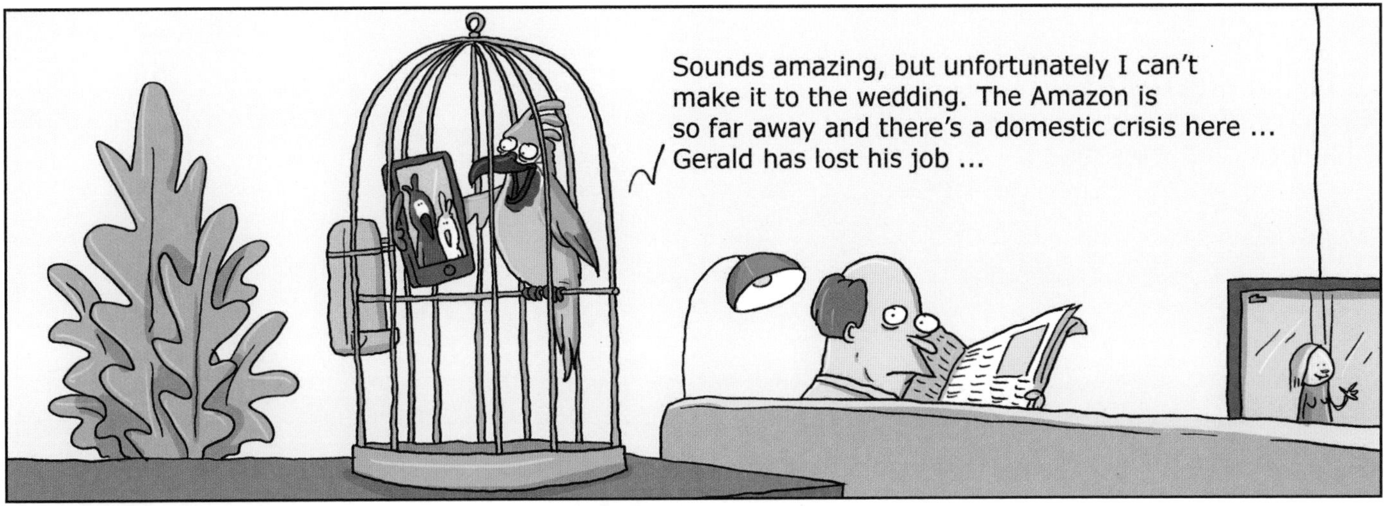
Sounds amazing, but unfortunately I can't make it to the wedding. The Amazon is so far away and there's a domestic crisis here ... Gerald has lost his job ...

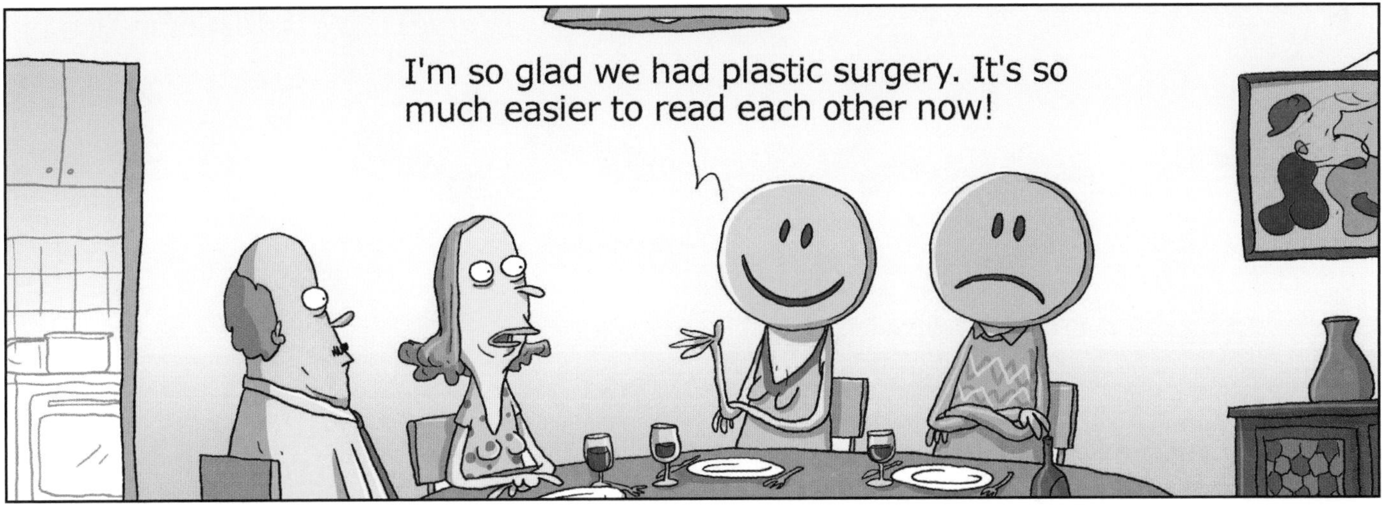
I'm so glad we had plastic surgery. It's so much easier to read each other now!

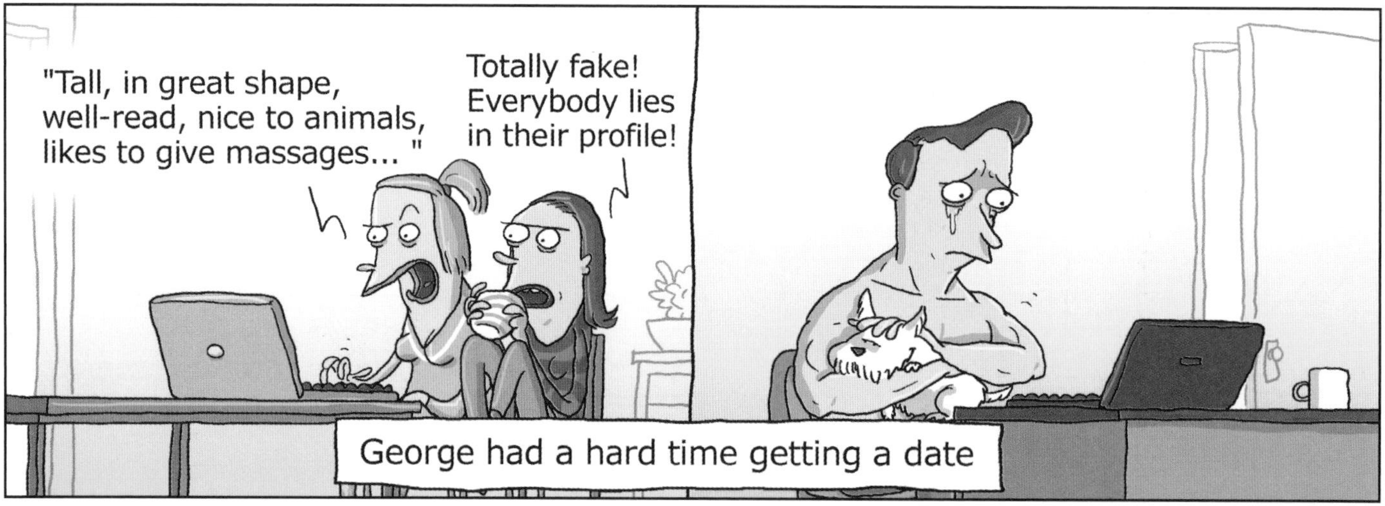

"Tall, in great shape, well-read, nice to animals, likes to give massages... "
Totally fake! Everybody lies in their profile!
George had a hard time getting a date

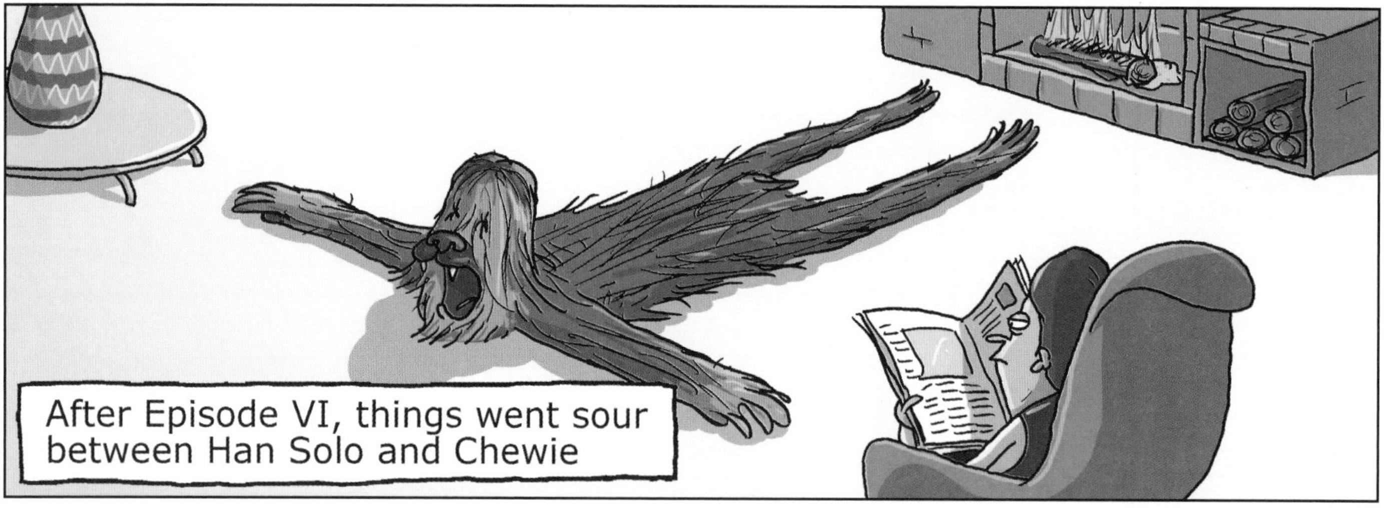

After Episode VI, things went sour between Han Solo and Chewie

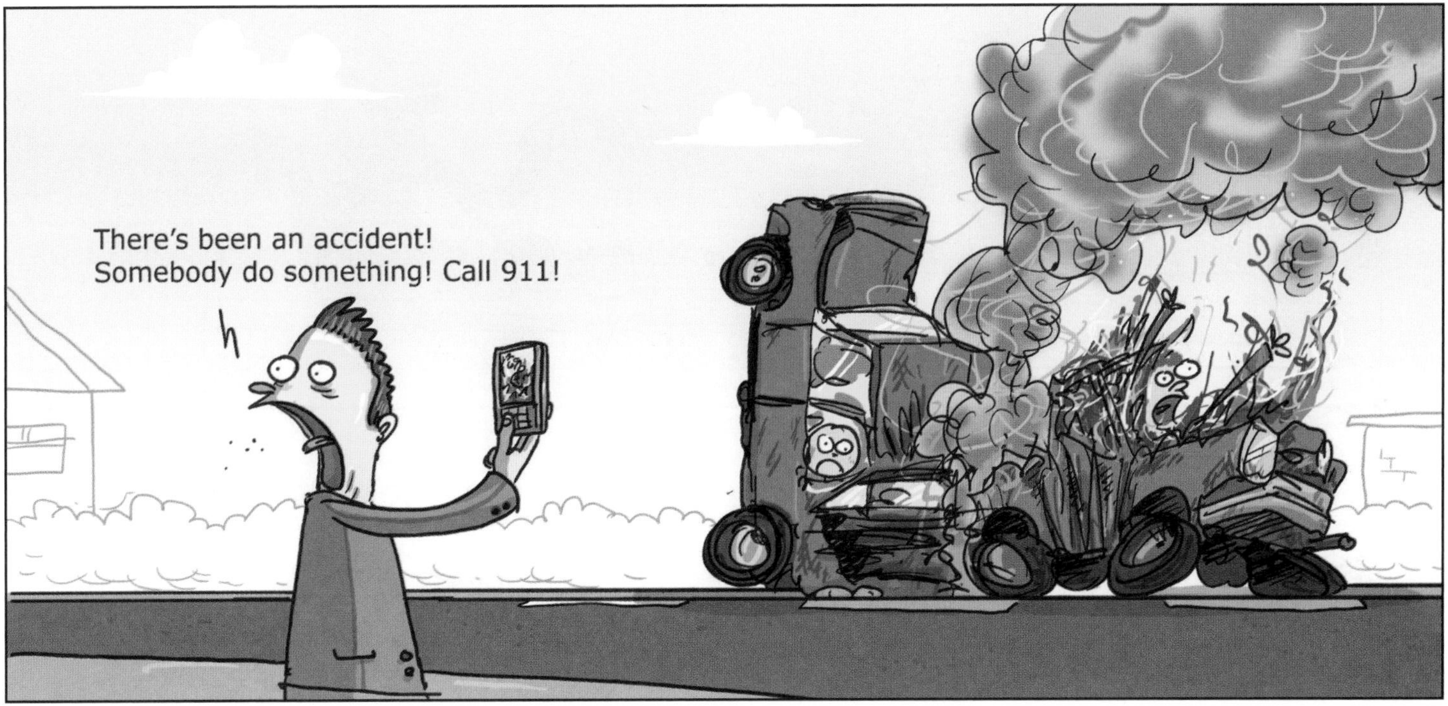
There's been an accident!
Somebody do something! Call 911!

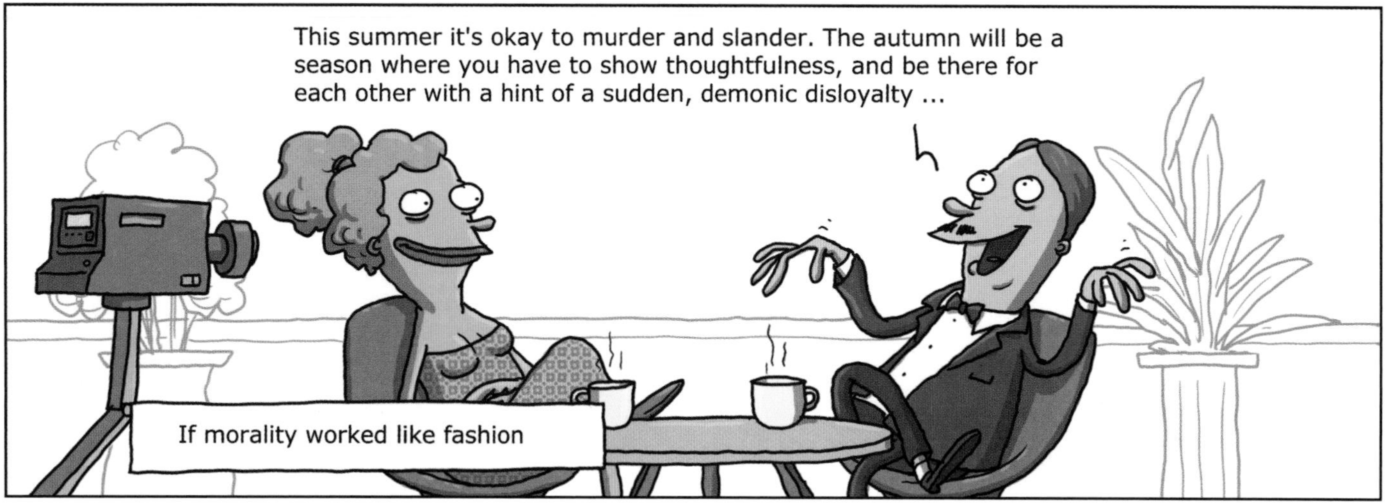
This summer it's okay to murder and slander. The autumn will be a season where you have to show thoughtfulness, and be there for each other with a hint of a sudden, demonic disloyalty ...
If morality worked like fashion

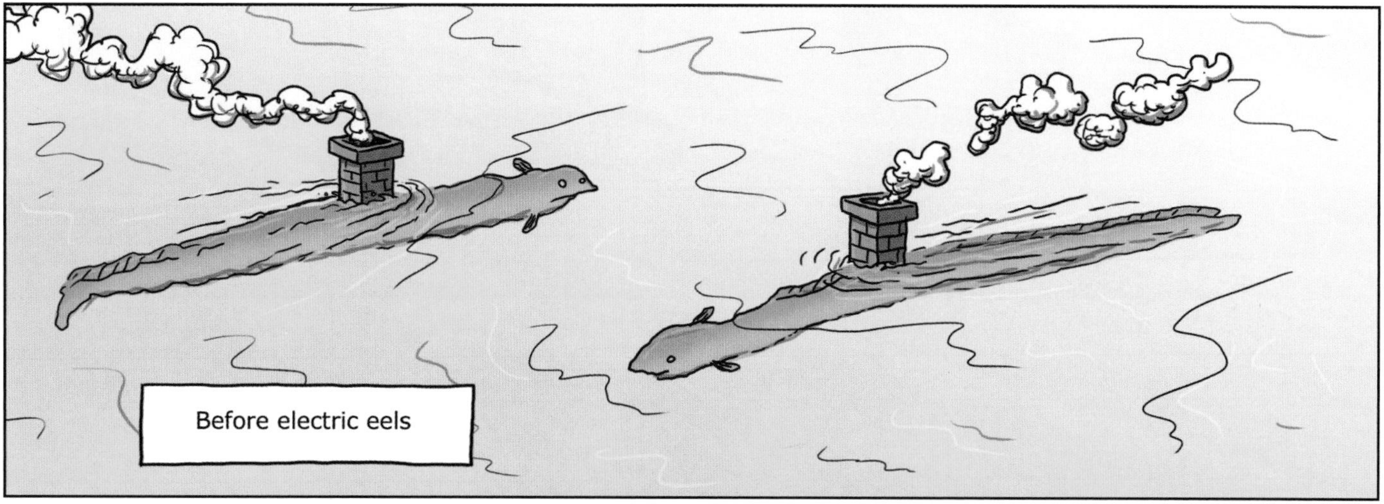
Before electric eels

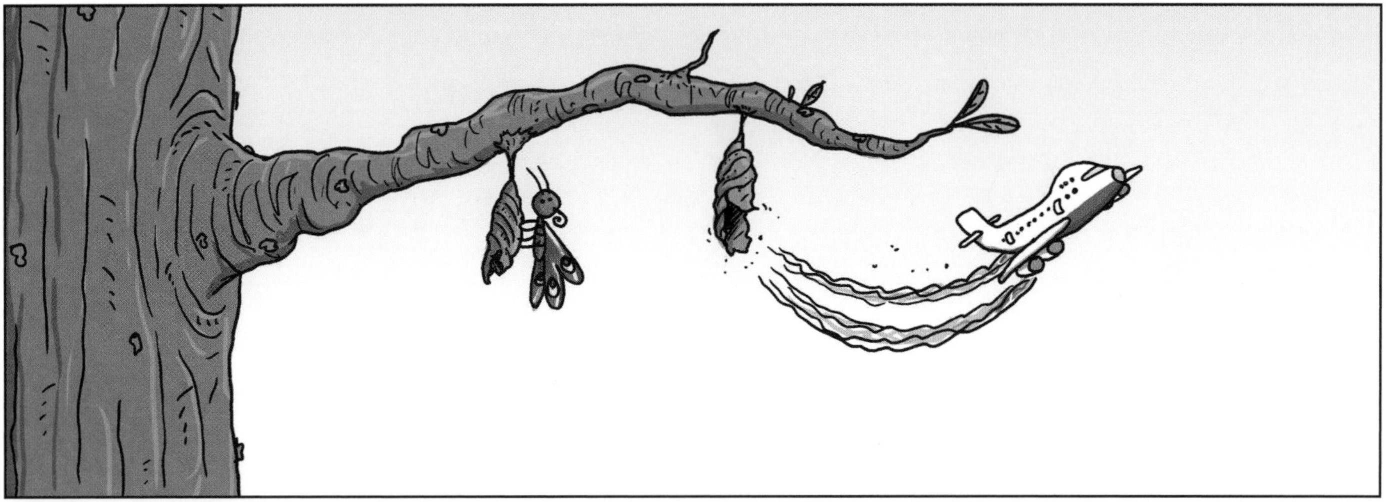

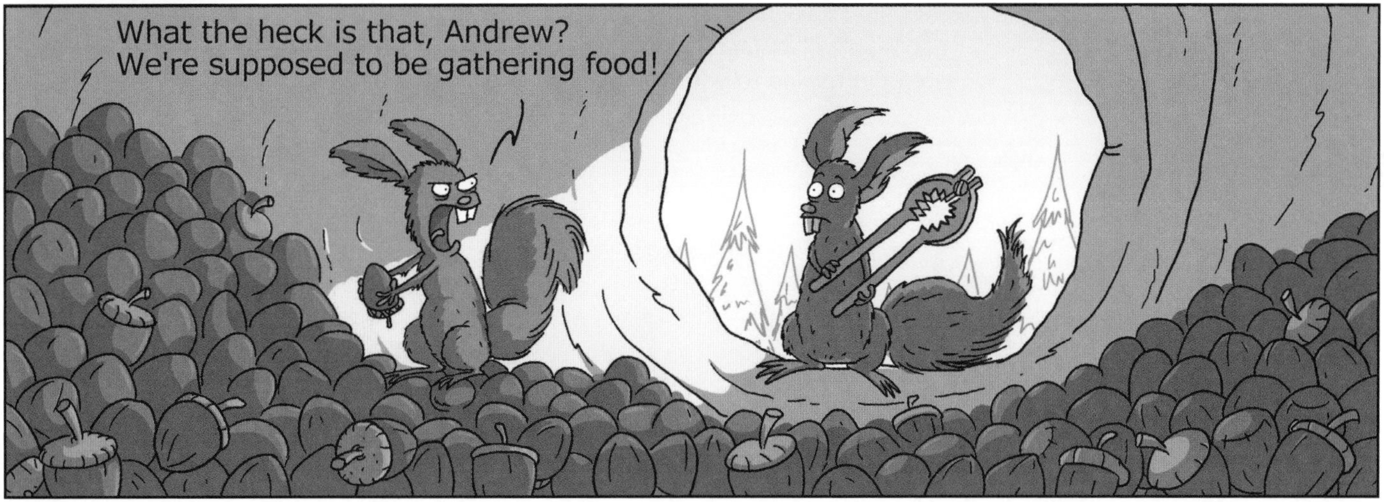
What the heck is that, Andrew?
We're supposed to be gathering food!

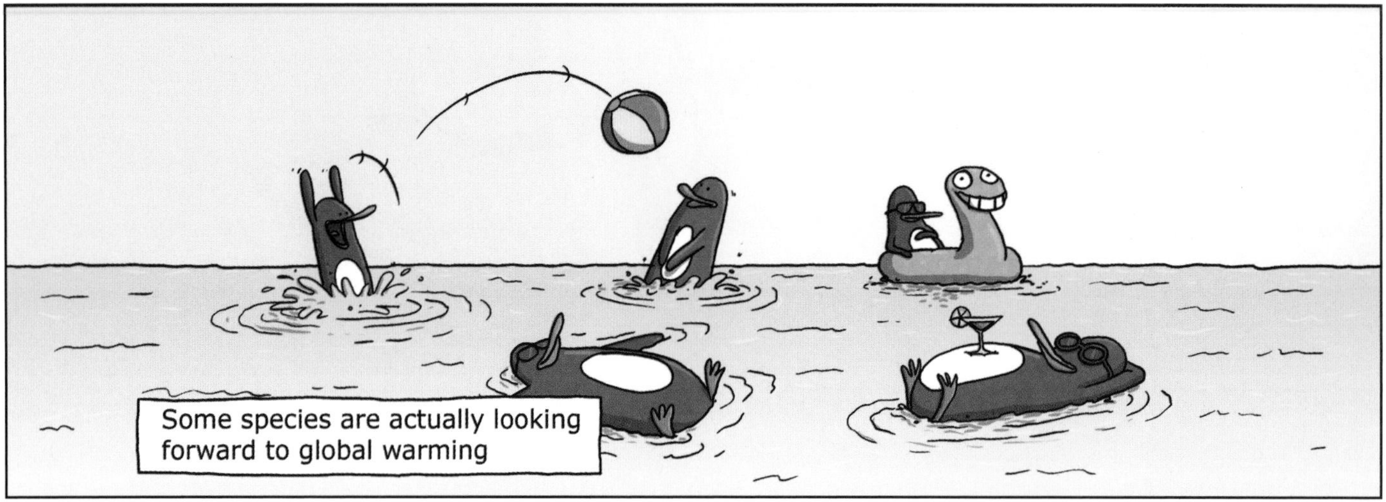
Some species are actually looking forward to global warming

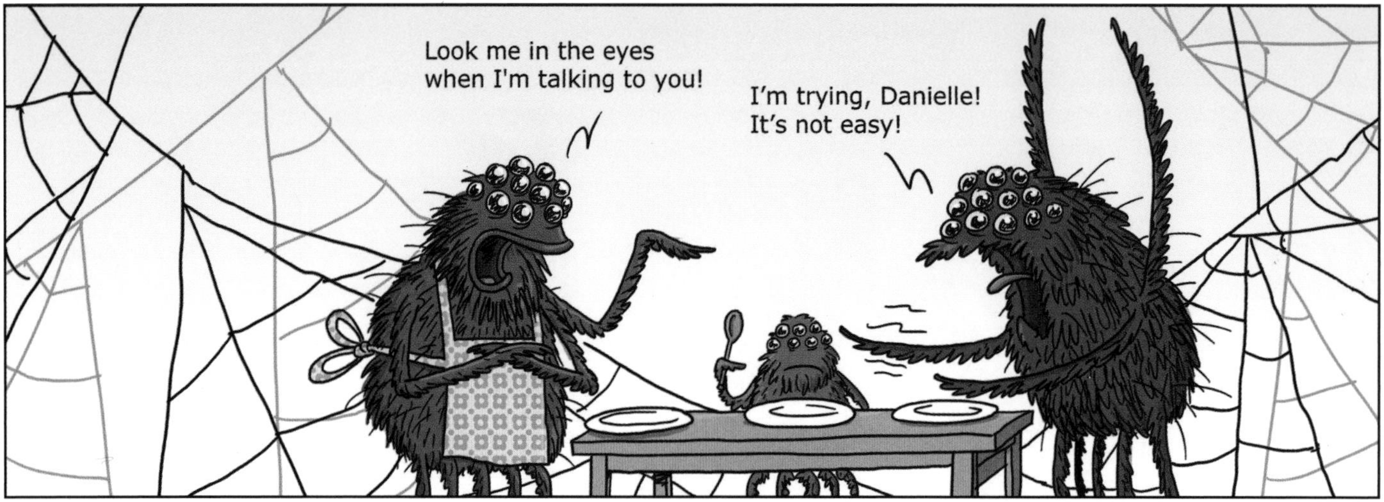
Look me in the eyes when I'm talking to you!
I'm trying, Danielle! It's not easy!

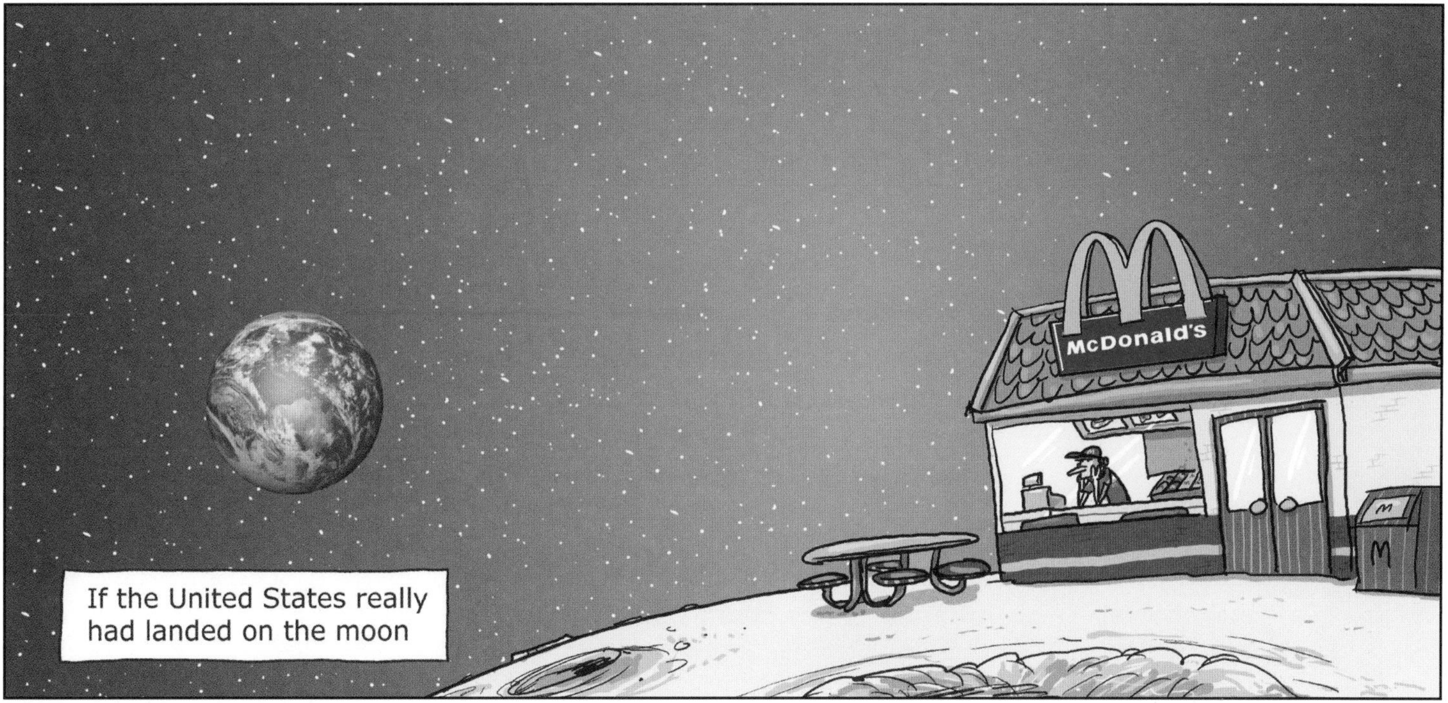
If the United States really had landed on the moon
McDonald's
M
M

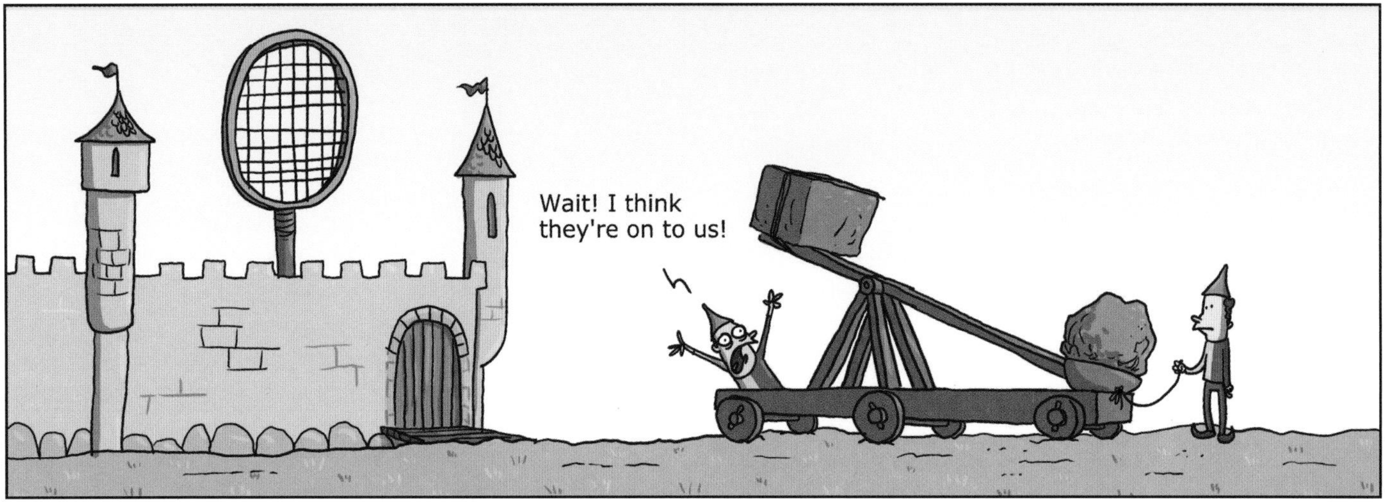
Wait! I think
they're on to us!

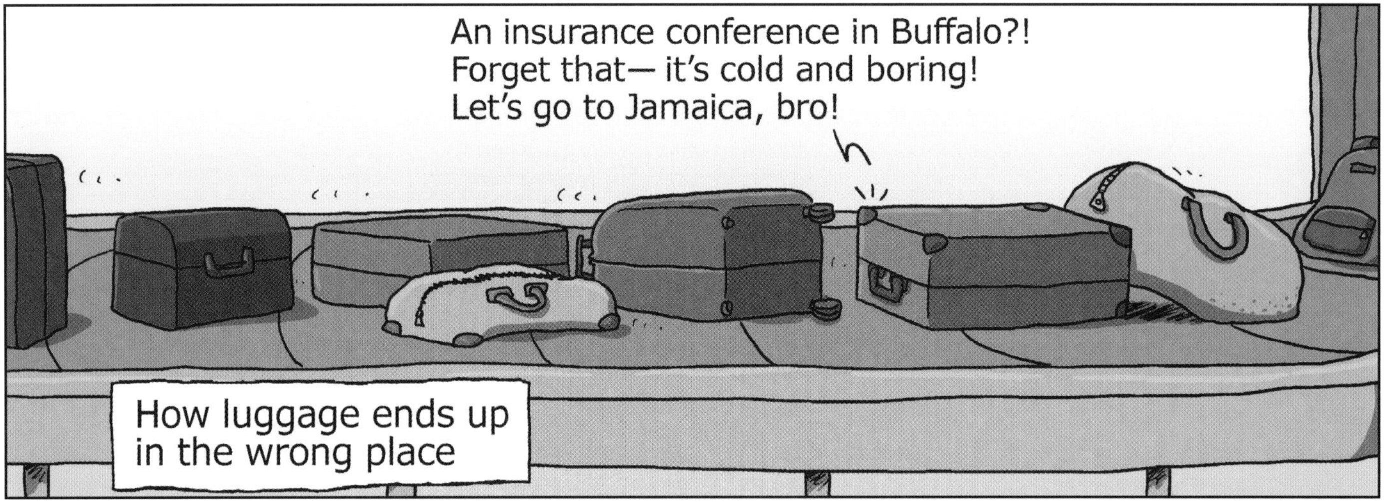
An insurance conference in Buffalo?!
Forget that— it's cold and boring!
Let's go to Jamaica, bro!
How luggage ends up
in the wrong place

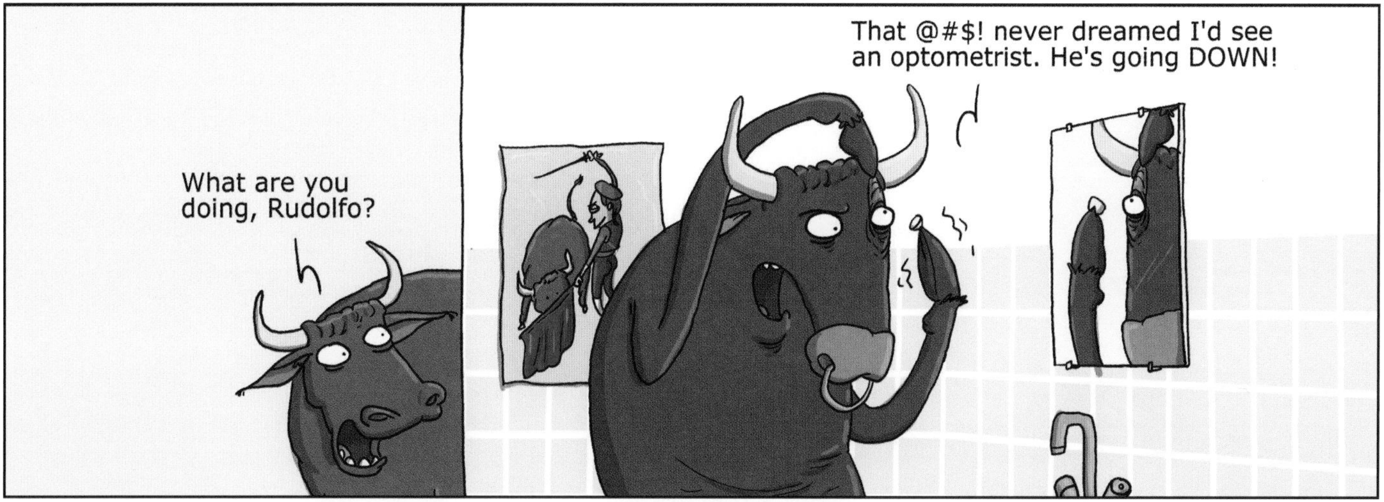
What are you doing, Rudolfo?
That @#$! never dreamed I'd see an optometrist. He's going DOWN!

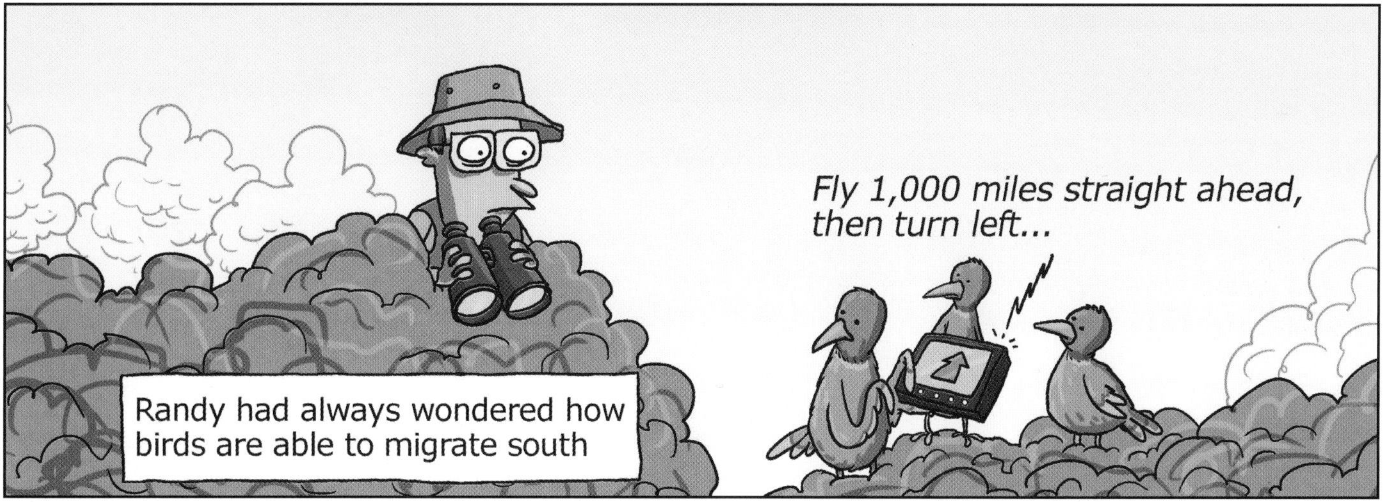
Randy had always wondered how birds are able to migrate south
Fly 1,000 miles straight ahead, then turn left...

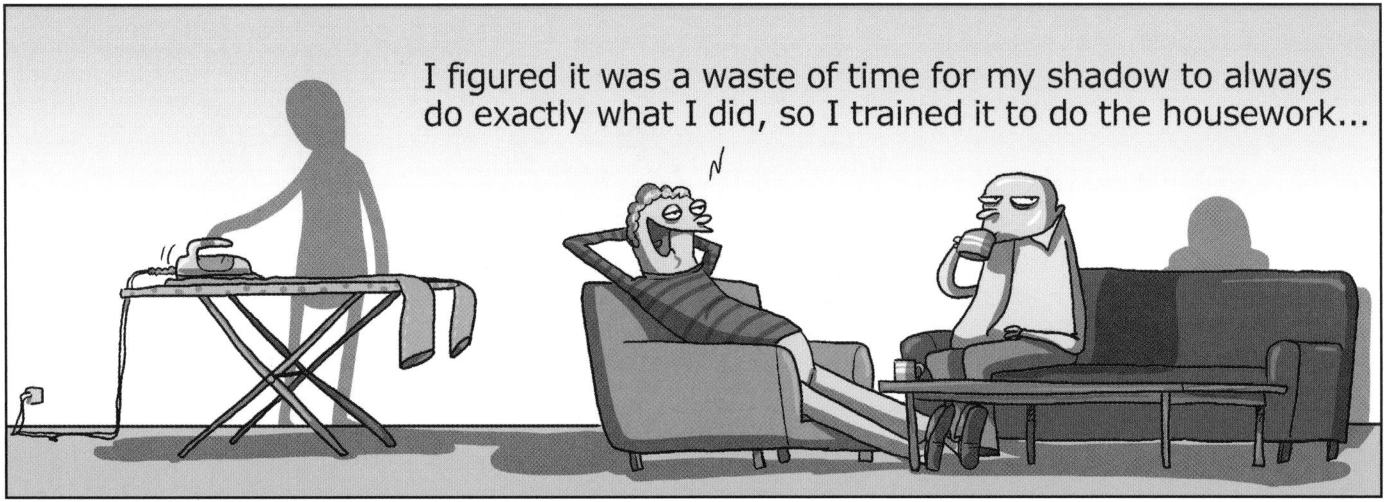
I figured it was a waste of time for my shadow to always do exactly what I did, so I trained it to do the housework...

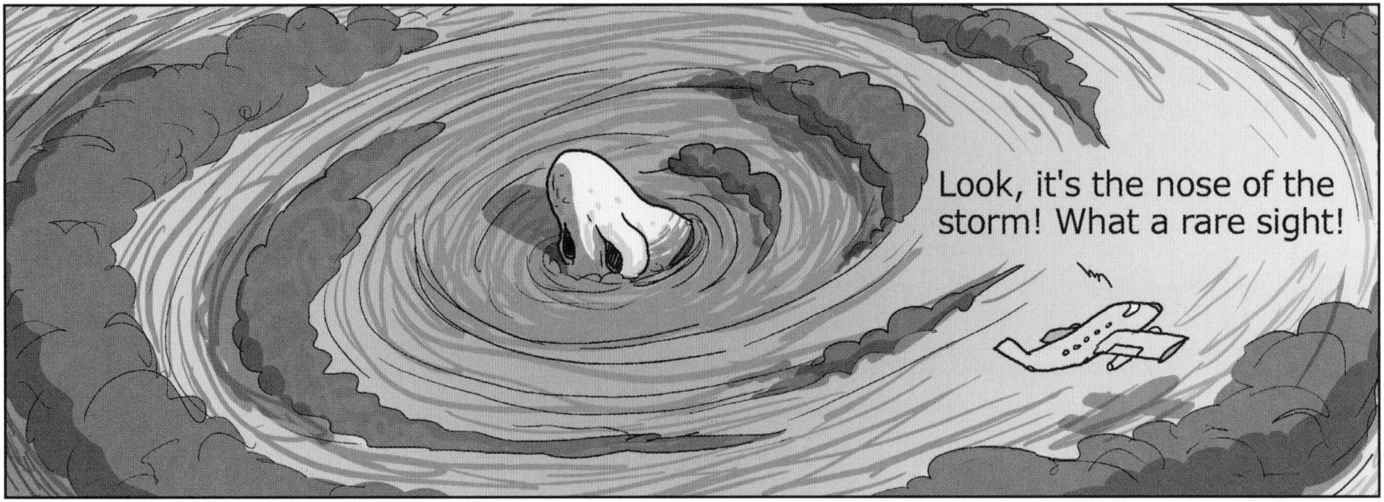
Look, it's the nose of the storm! What a rare sight!

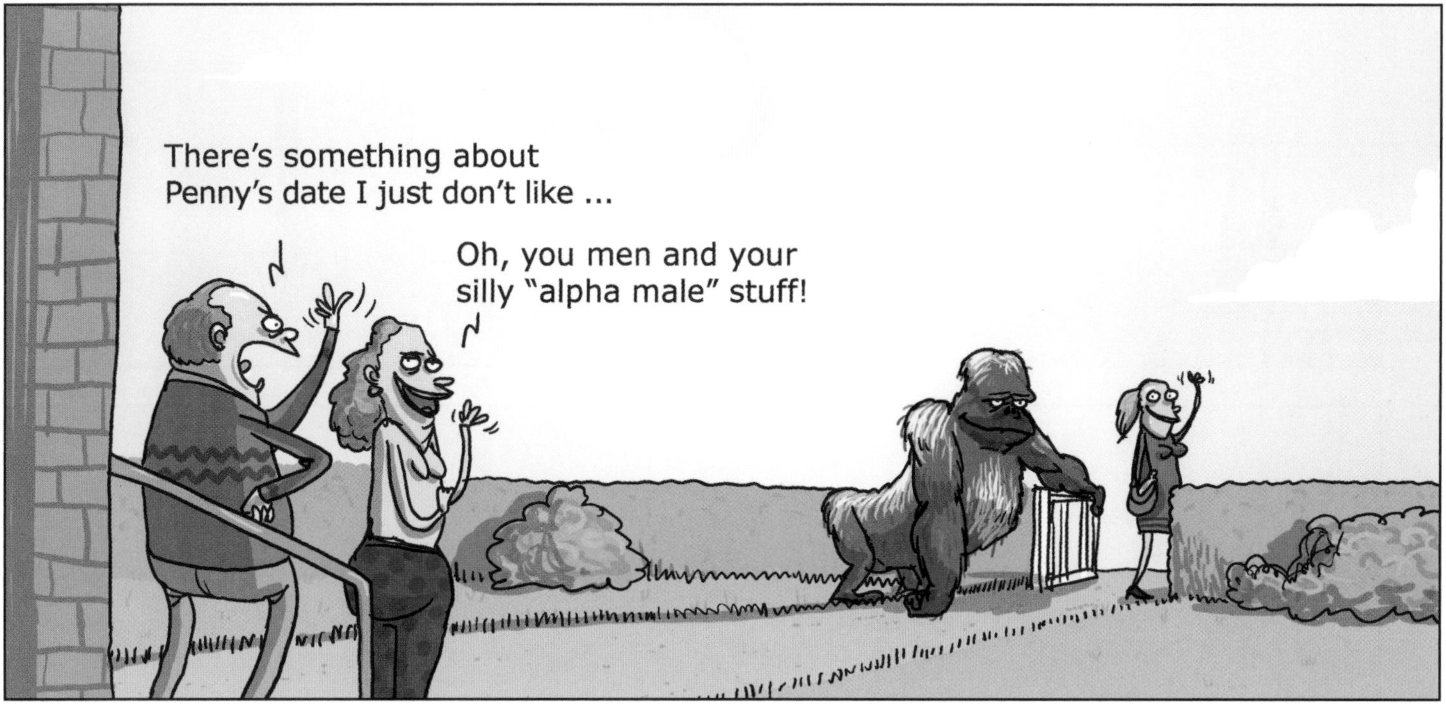
There's something about
Penny's date I just don't like ...
Oh, you men and your
silly "alpha male" stuff!

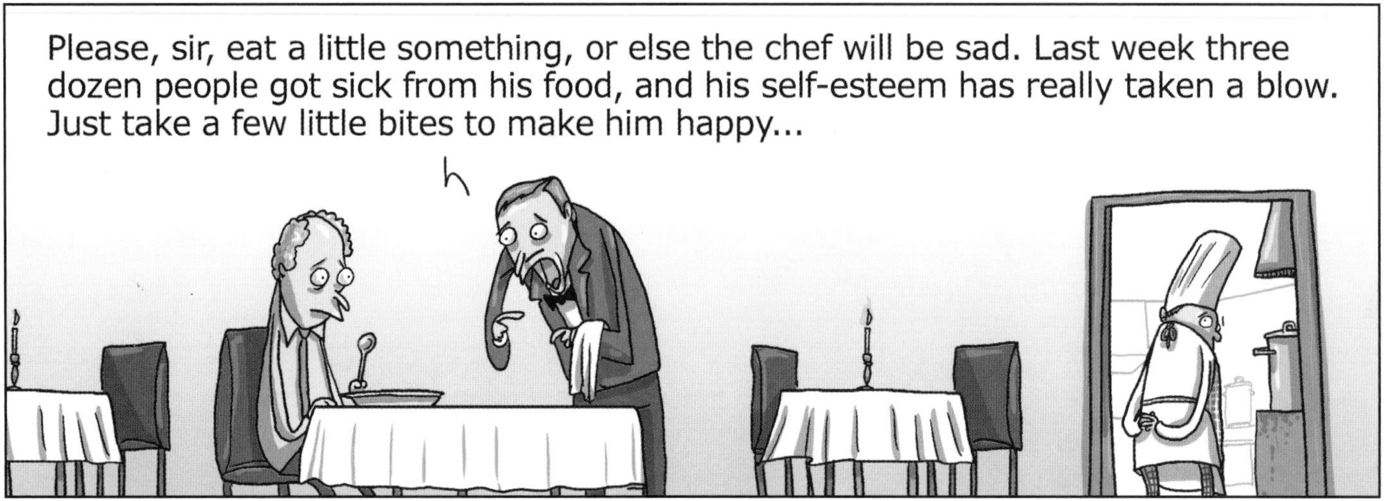
Please, sir, eat a little something, or else the chef will be sad. Last week three dozen people got sick from his food, and his self-esteem has really taken a blow. Just take a few little bites to make him happy...
h

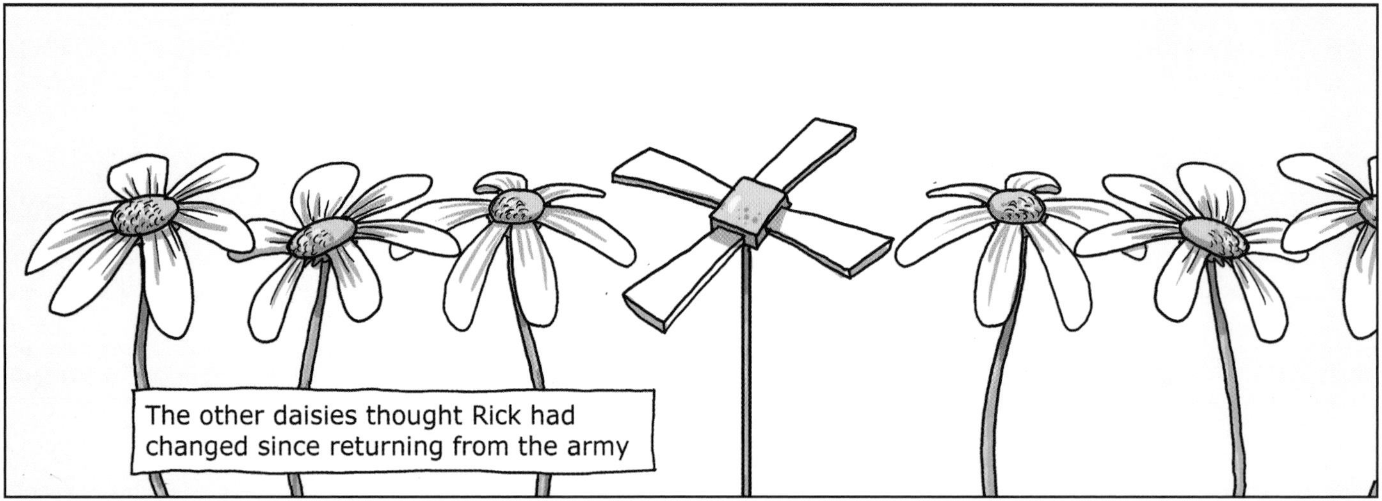
The other daisies thought Rick had changed since returning from the army

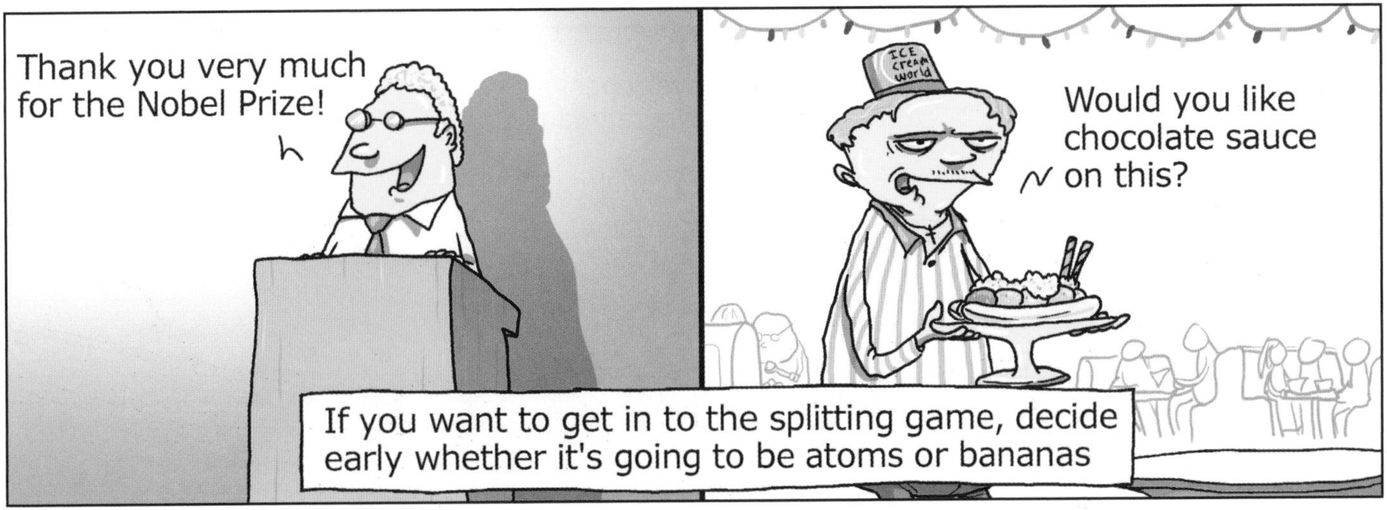
Thank you very much for the Nobel Prize!
ICE cream world
Would you like chocolate sauce on this?
If you want to get in to the splitting game, decide early whether it's going to be atoms or bananas

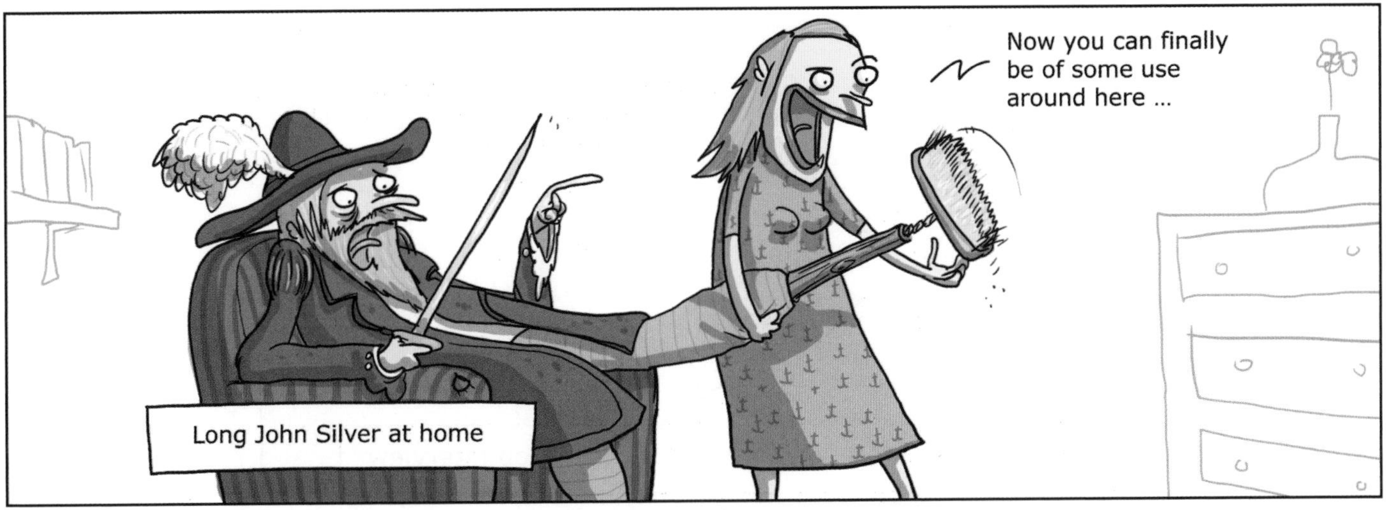
Now you can finally be of some use around here ...
Long John Silver at home

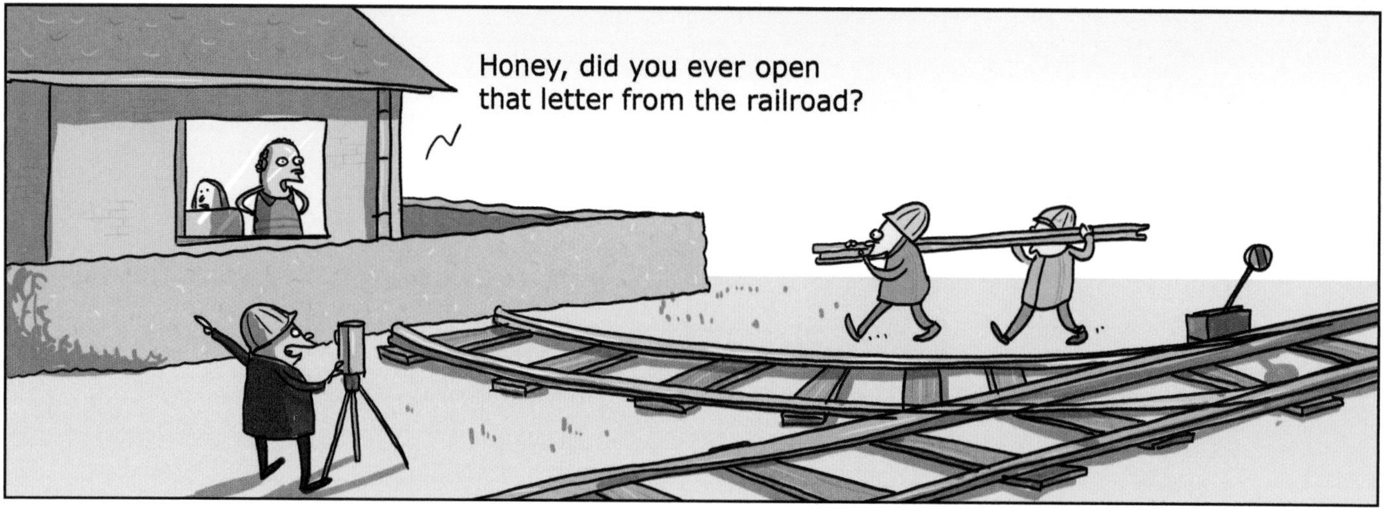
Honey, did you ever open
that letter from the railroad?

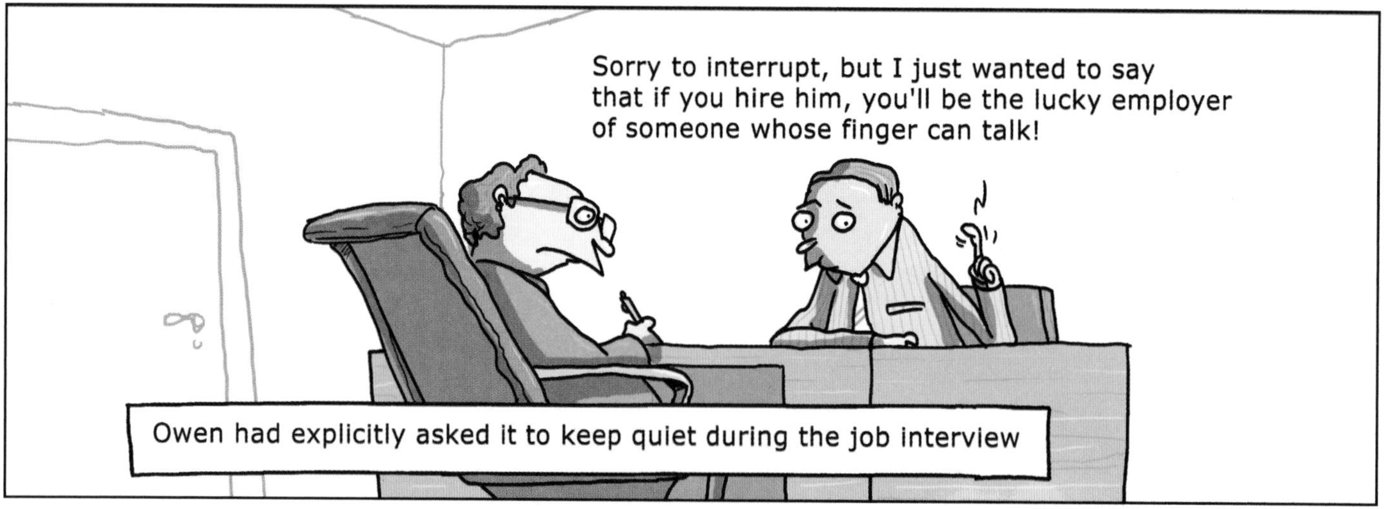
Sorry to interrupt, but I just wanted to say
that if you hire him, you'll be the lucky employer
of someone whose finger can talk!
Owen had explicitly asked it to keep quiet during the job interview

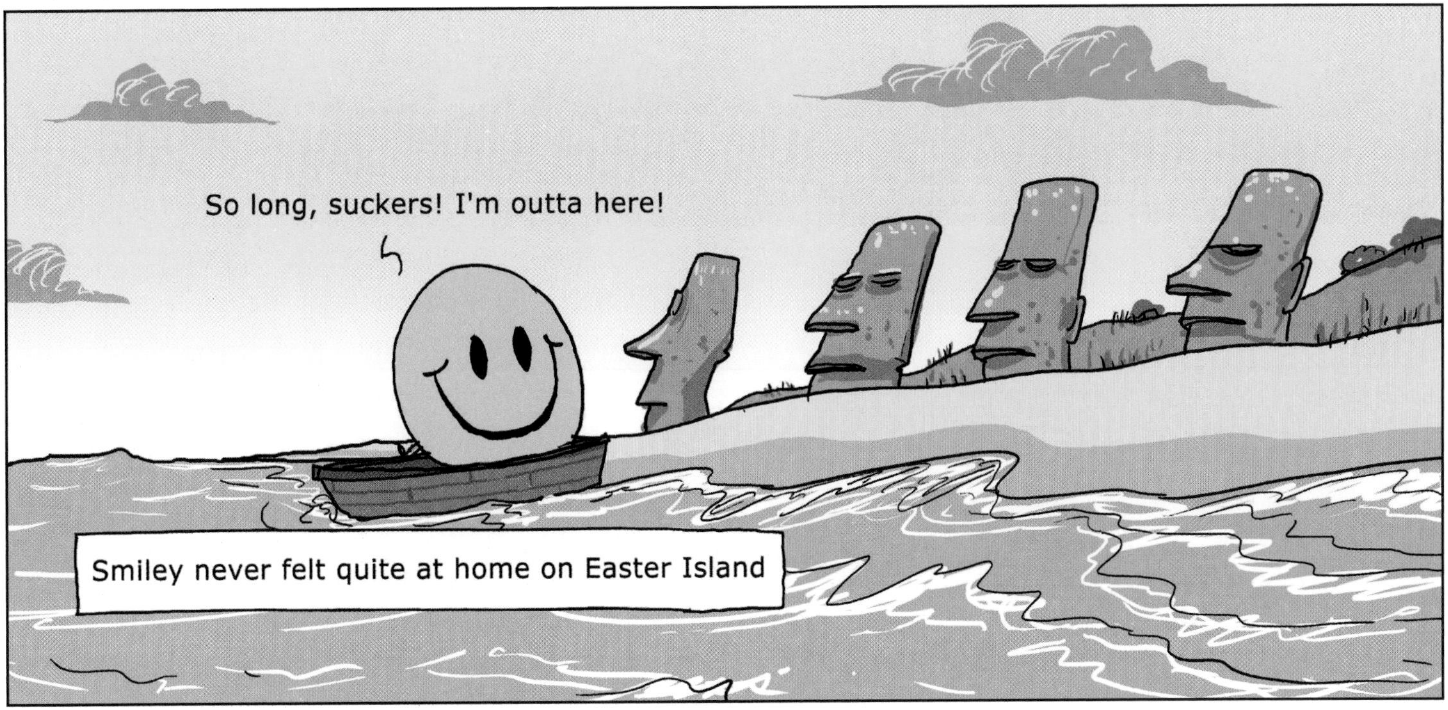
So long, suckers! I'm outta here!
Smiley never felt quite at home on Easter Island

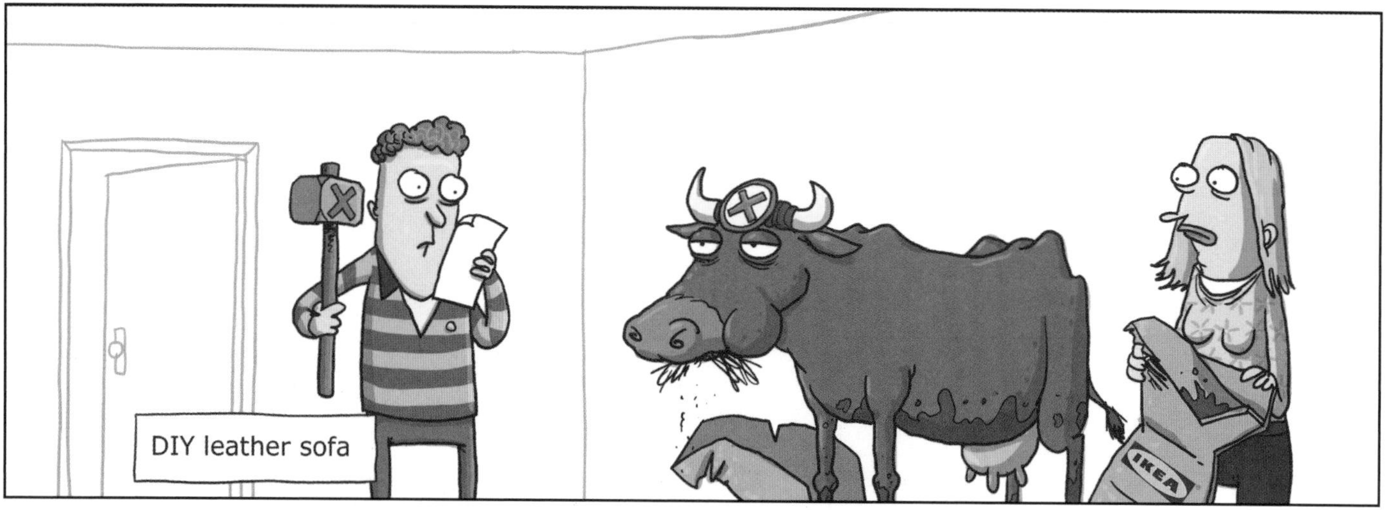
DIY leather sofa
IKEA

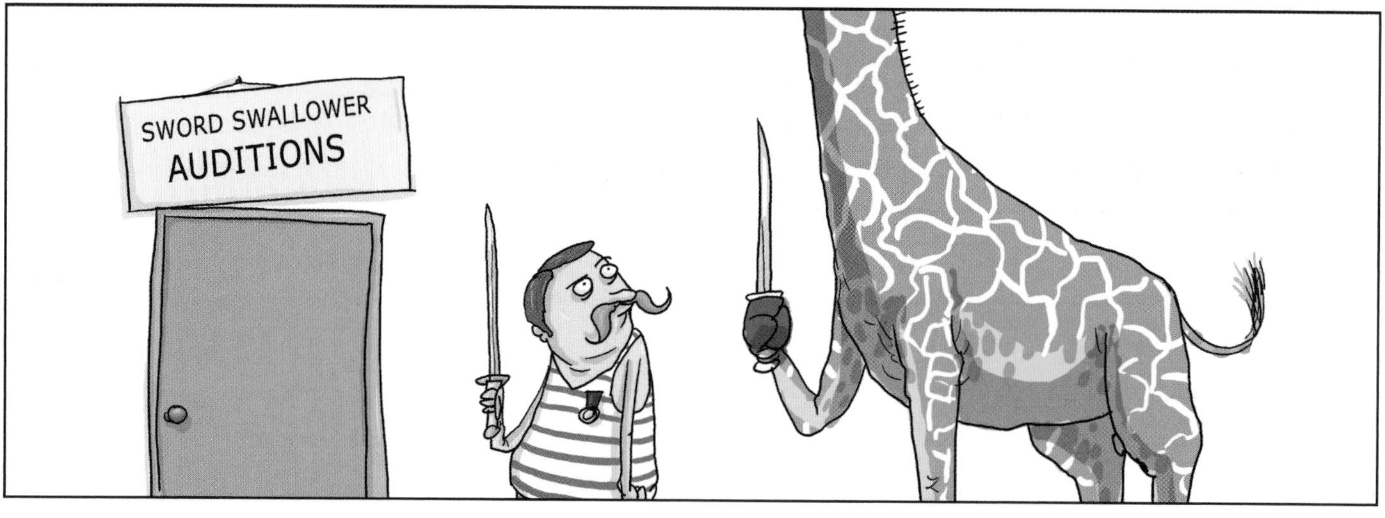
SWORD SWALLOWER
AUDITIONS

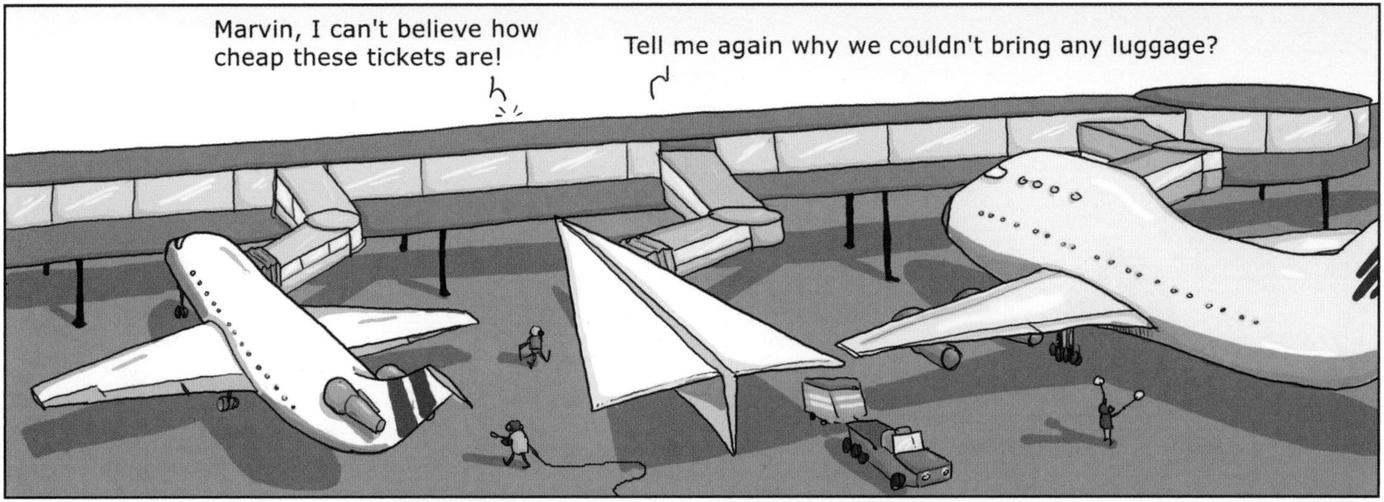
Marvin, I can't believe how cheap these tickets are!
Tell me again why we couldn't bring any luggage?

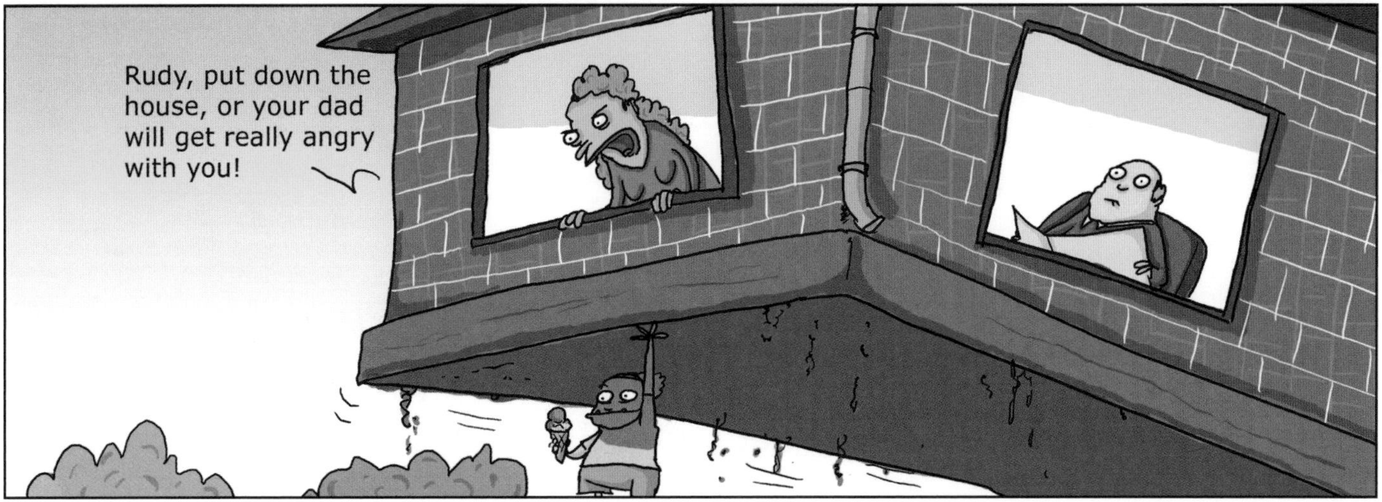
Rudy, put down the house, or your dad will get really angry with you!

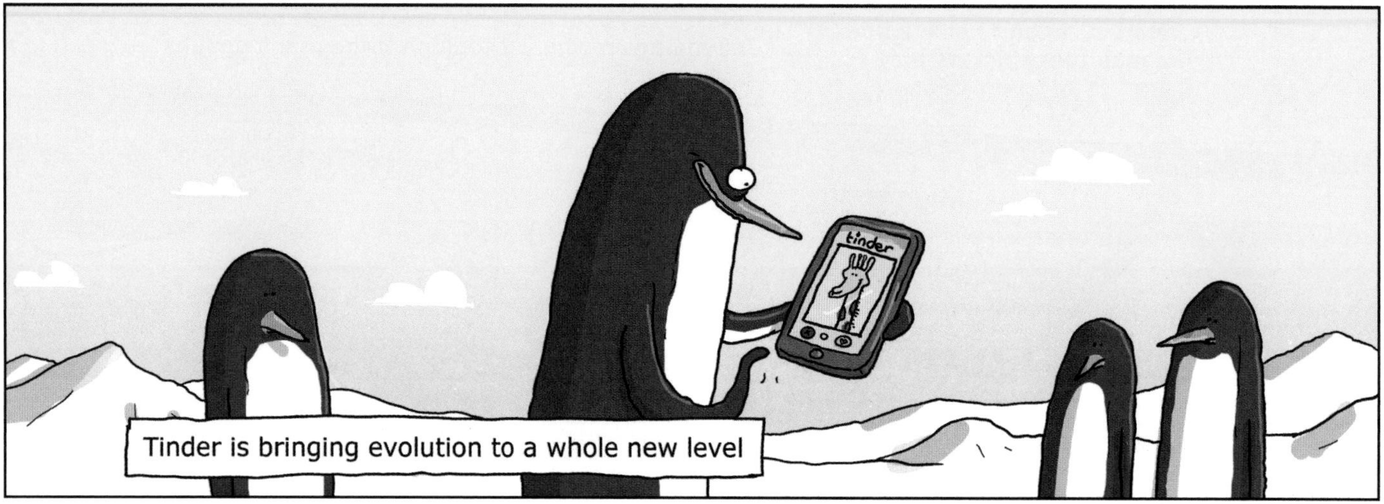
Tinder is bringing evolution to a whole new level
tinder

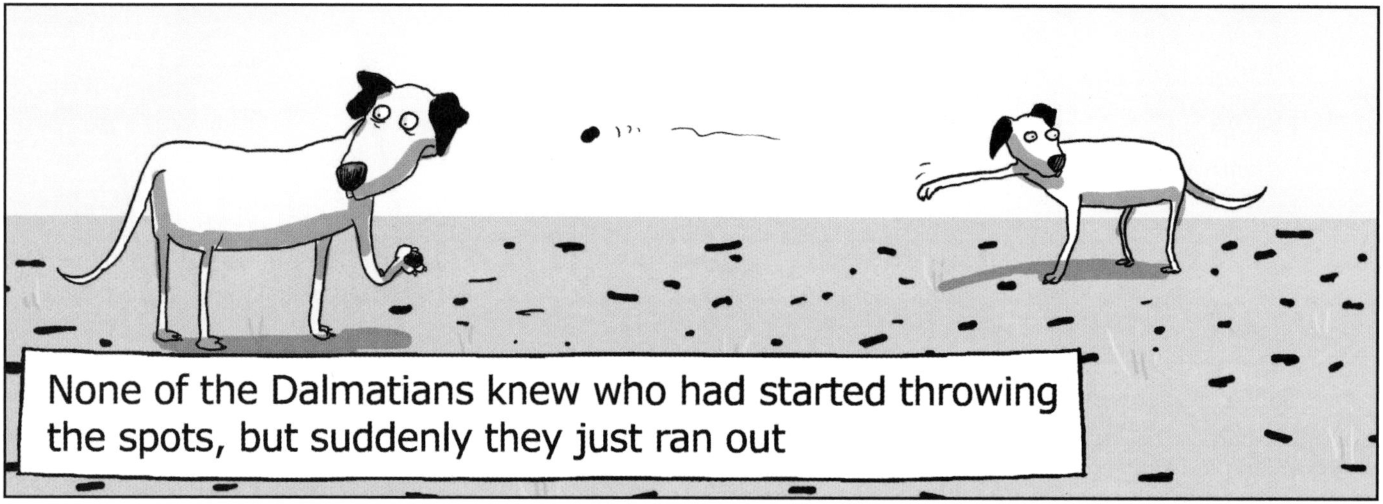
None of the Dalmatians knew who had started throwing the spots, but suddenly they just ran out

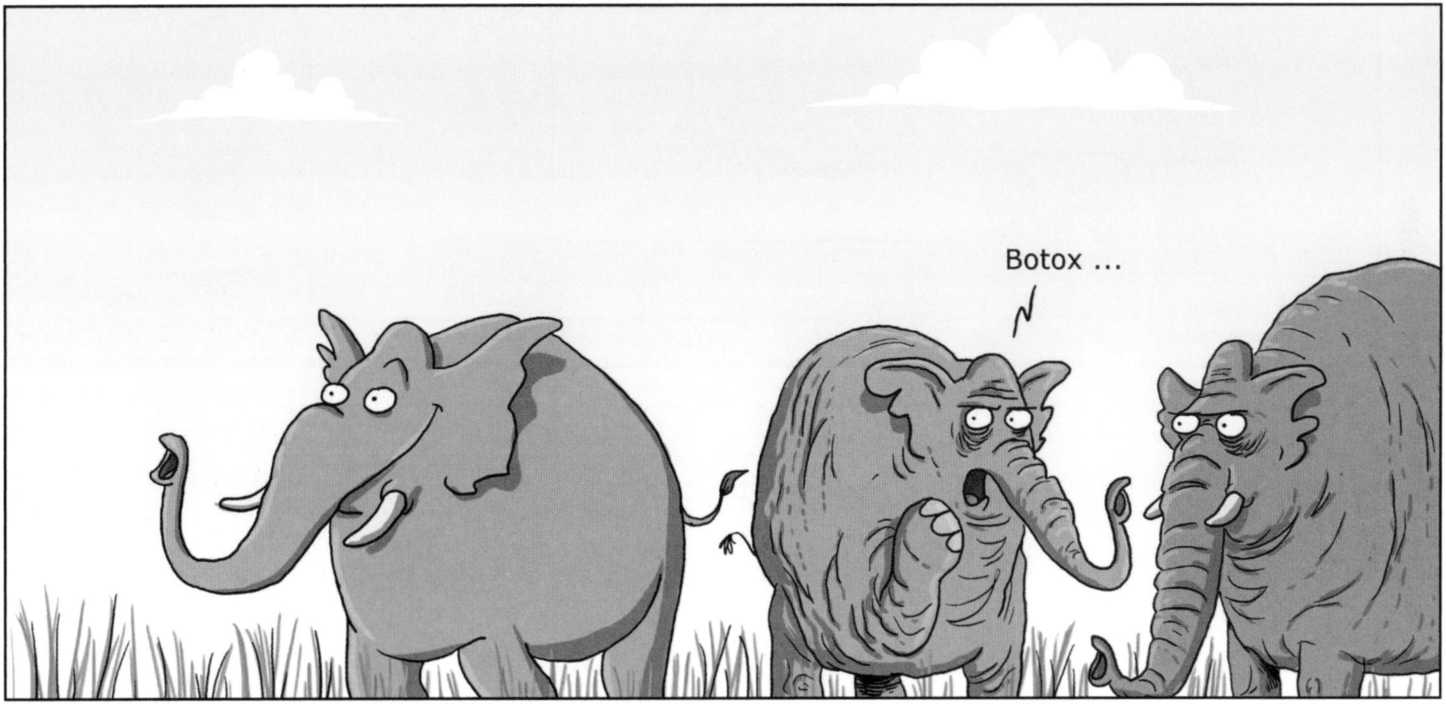
Botox ...

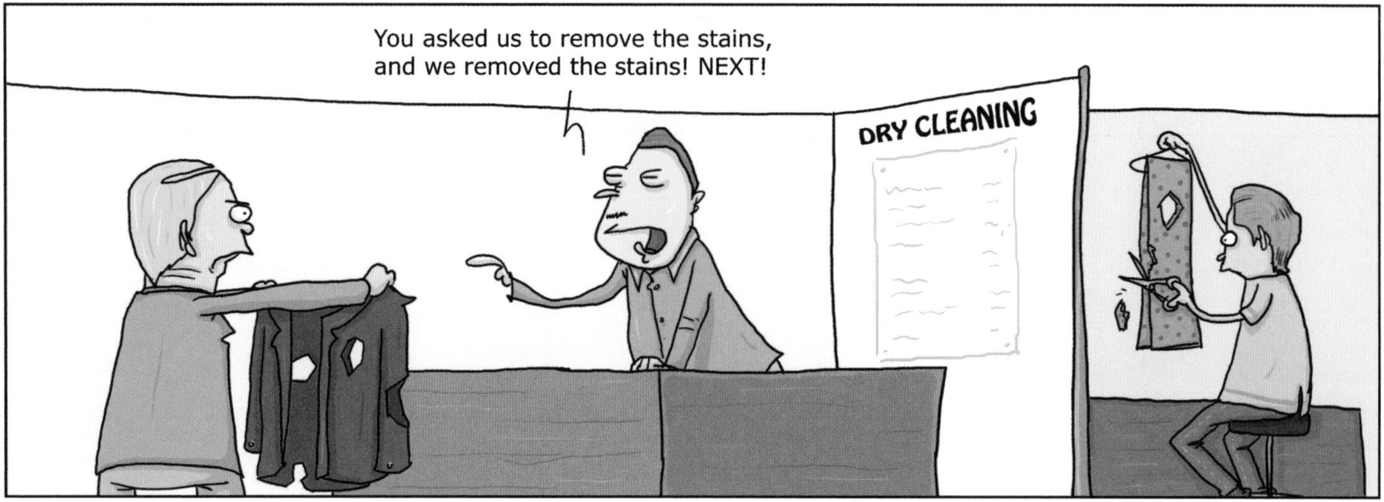
You asked us to remove the stains, and we removed the stains! NEXT!
DRY CLEANING

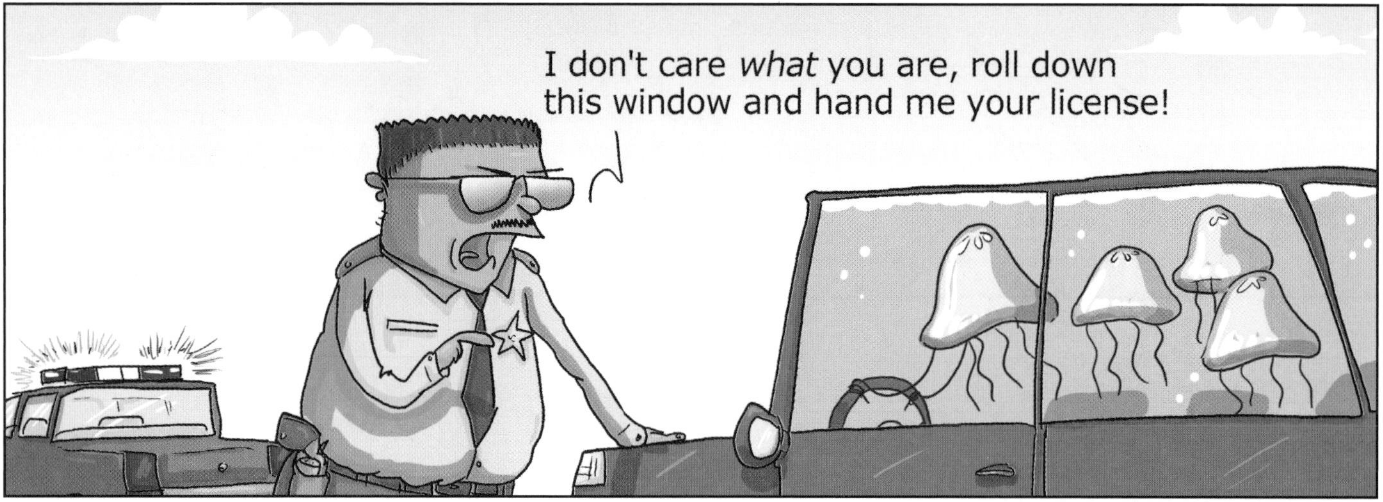
I don't care *what* you are, roll down this window and hand me your license!

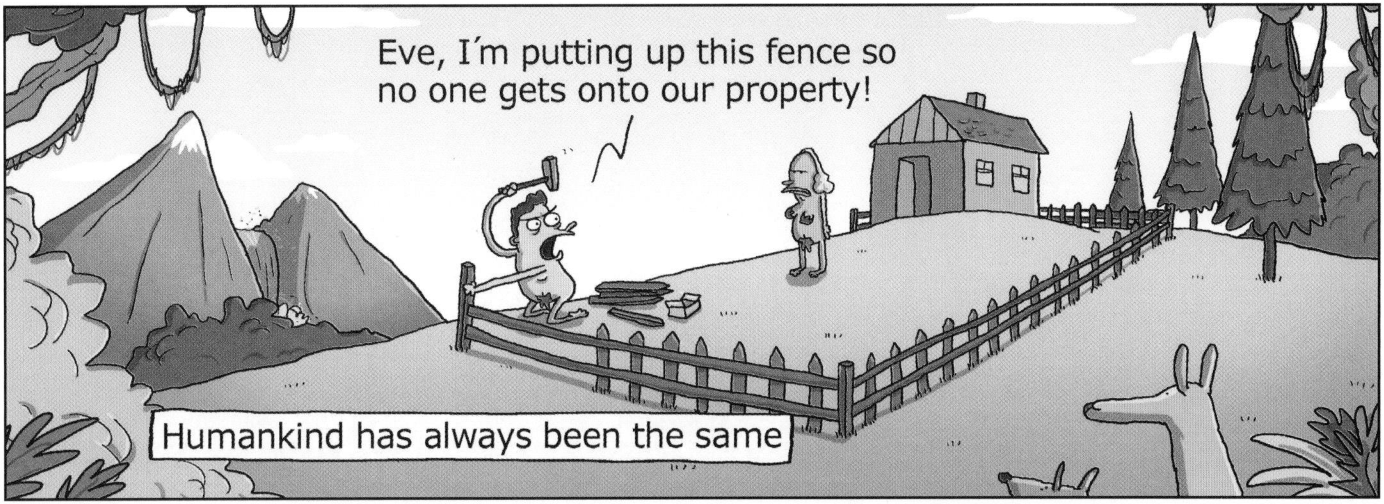
Eve, I´m putting up this fence so
no one gets onto our property!
Humankind has always been the same

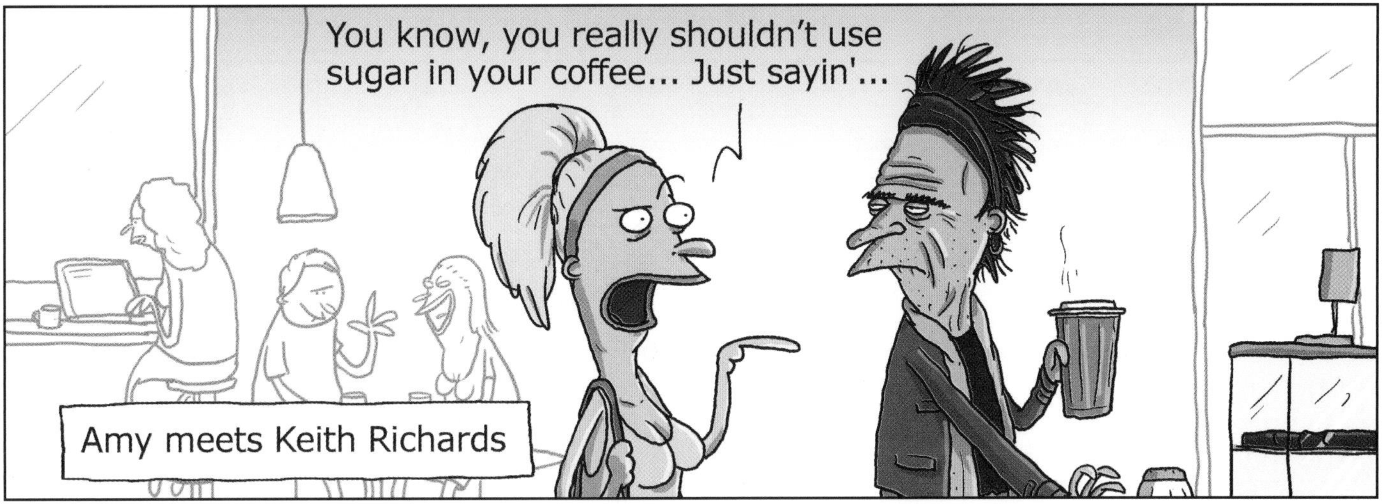
You know, you really shouldn't use
sugar in your coffee... Just sayin'...
Amy meets Keith Richards

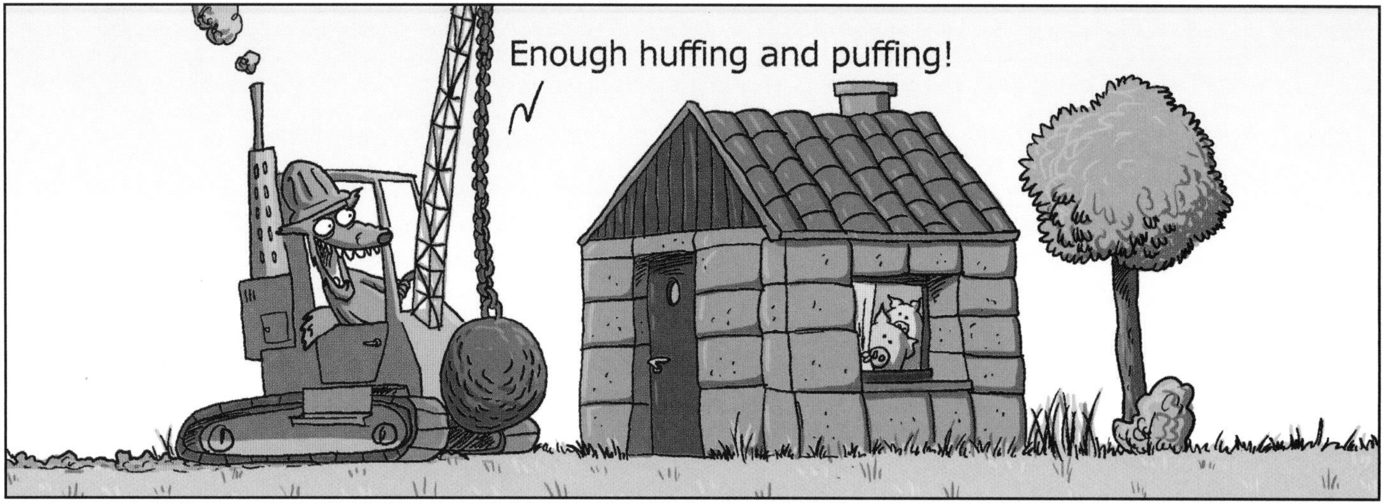
Enough huffing and puffing!

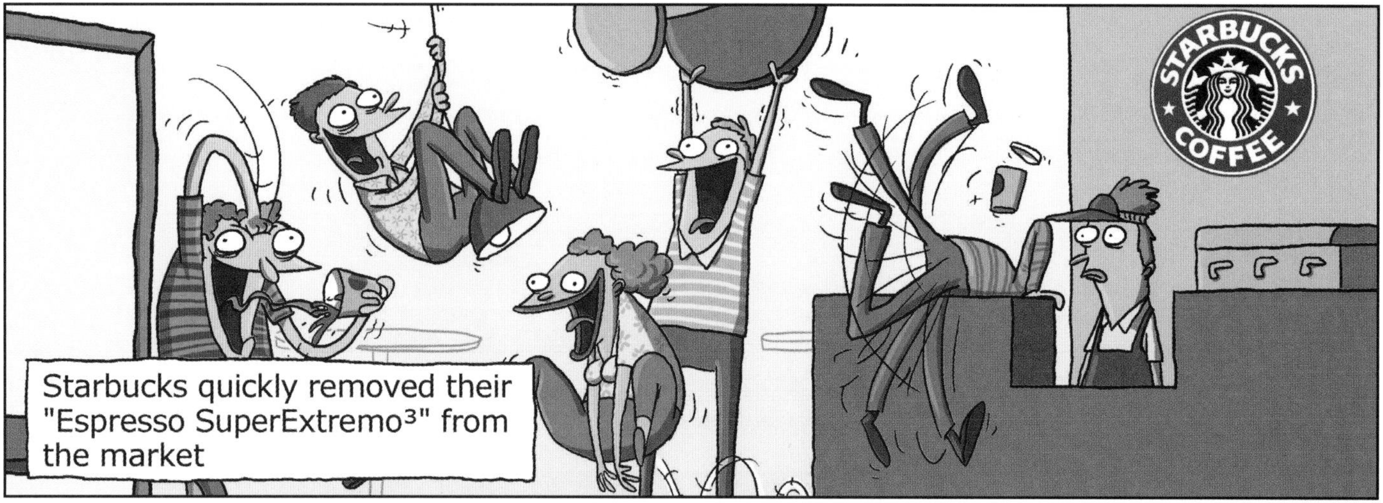
STARBUCKS COFFEE
Starbucks quickly removed their "Espresso SuperExtremo³" from the market

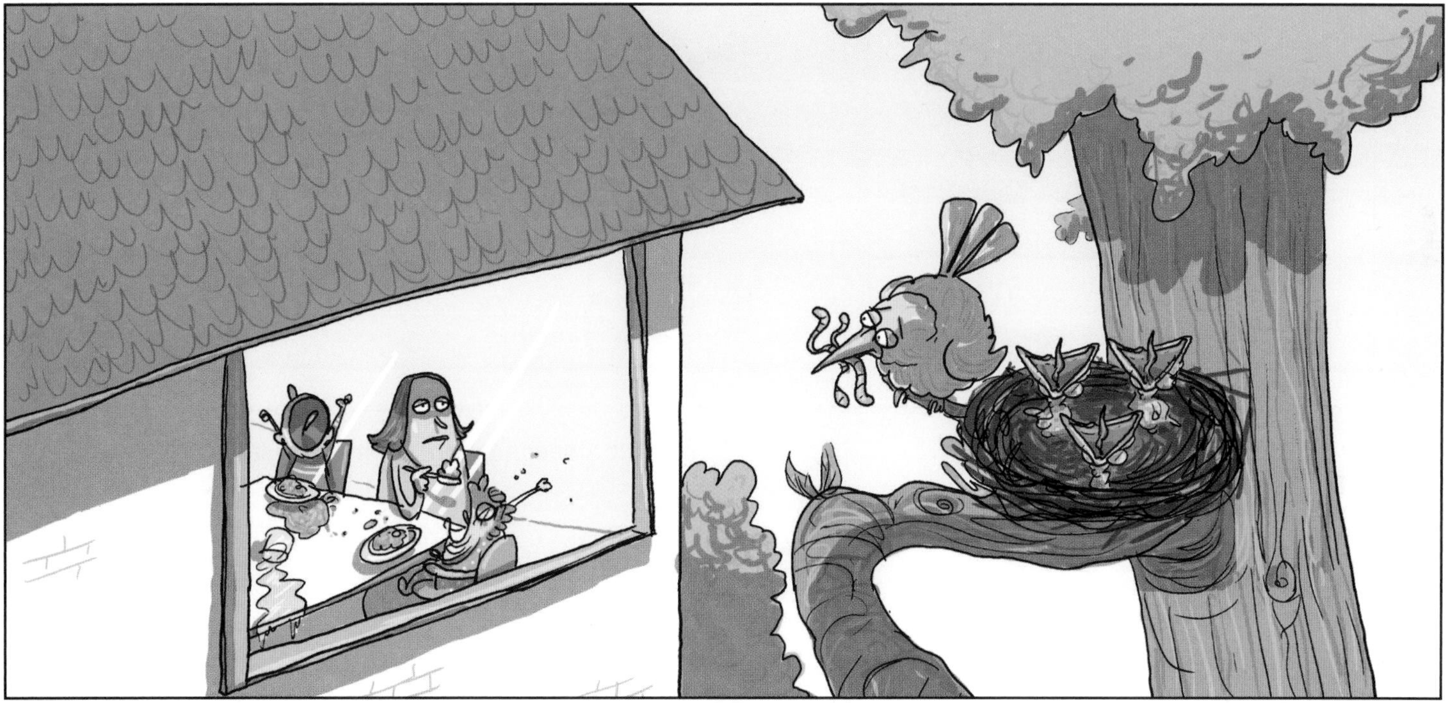

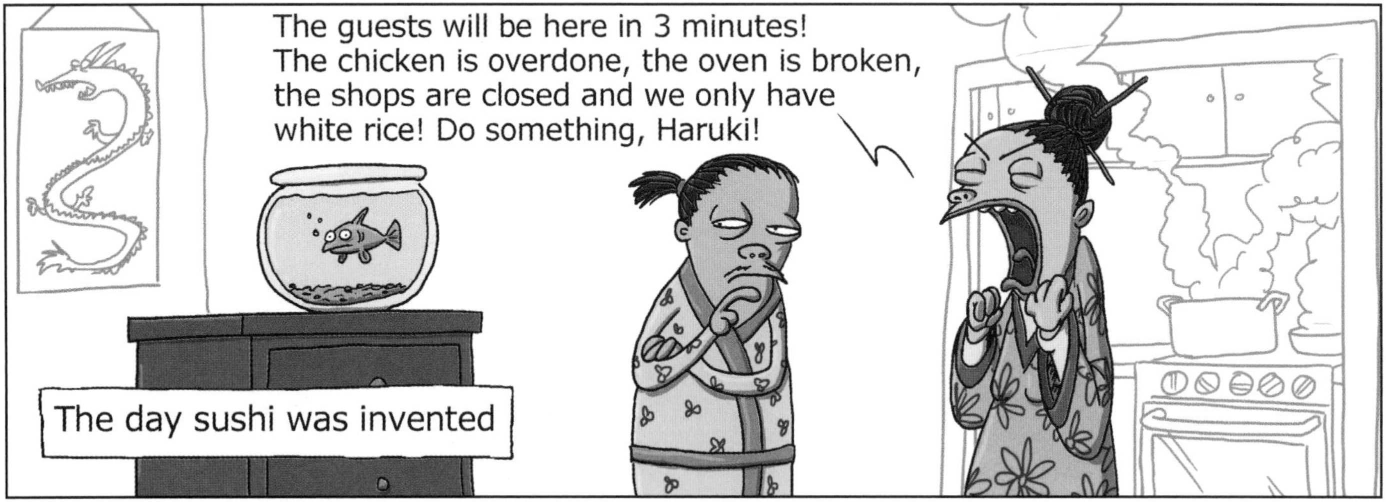
The guests will be here in 3 minutes!
The chicken is overdone, the oven is broken, the shops are closed and we only have white rice! Do something, Haruki!
The day sushi was invented

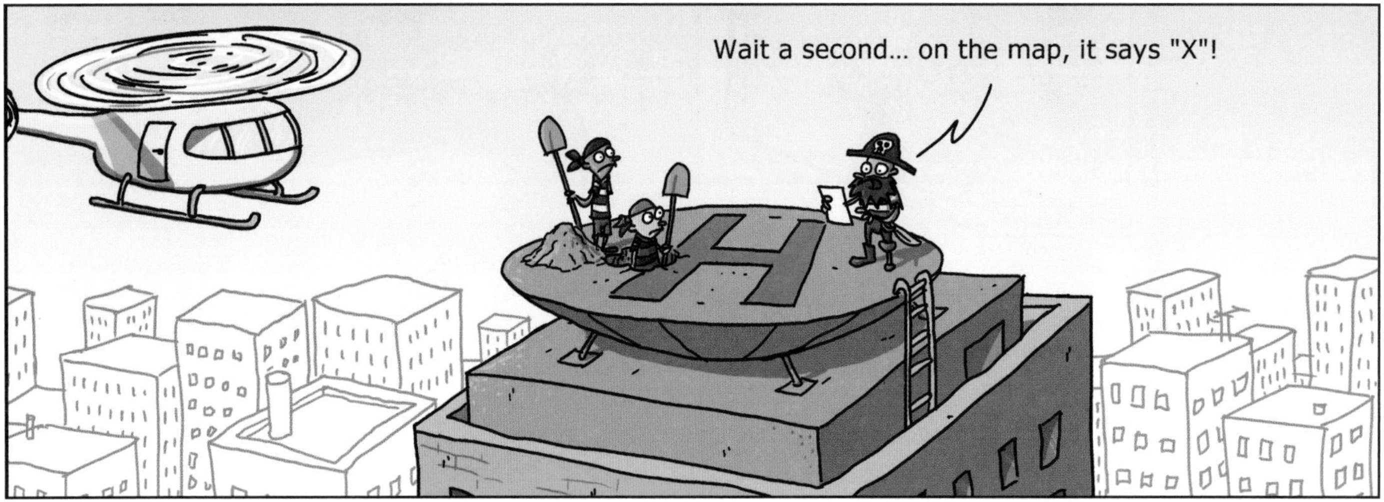
Wait a second... on the map, it says "X"!

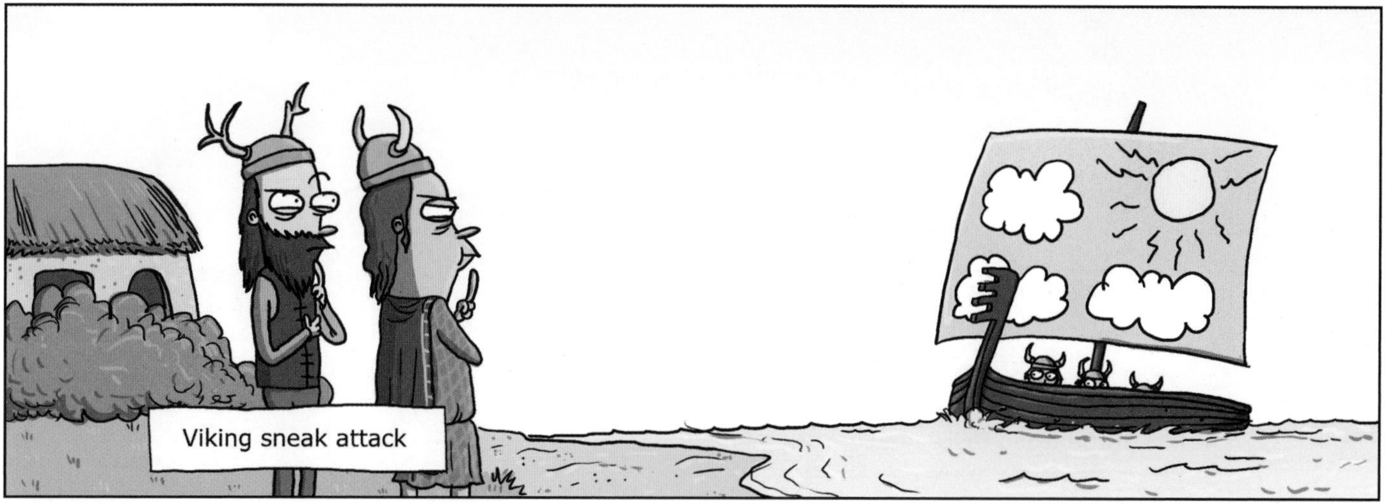
Viking sneak attack

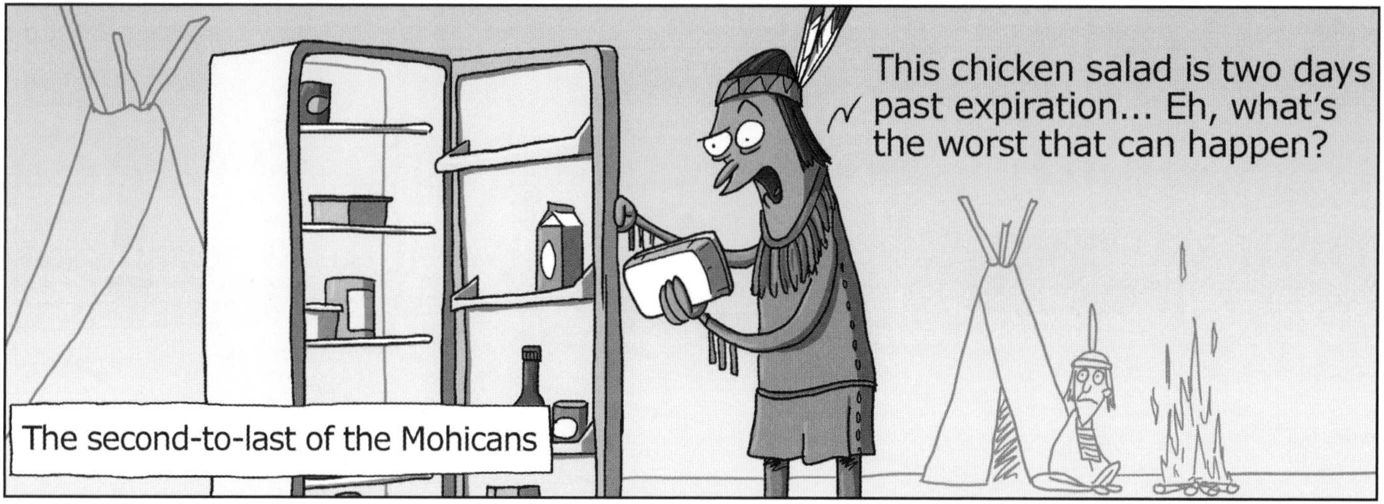
This chicken salad is two days past expiration... Eh, what's the worst that can happen?
The second-to-last of the Mohicans

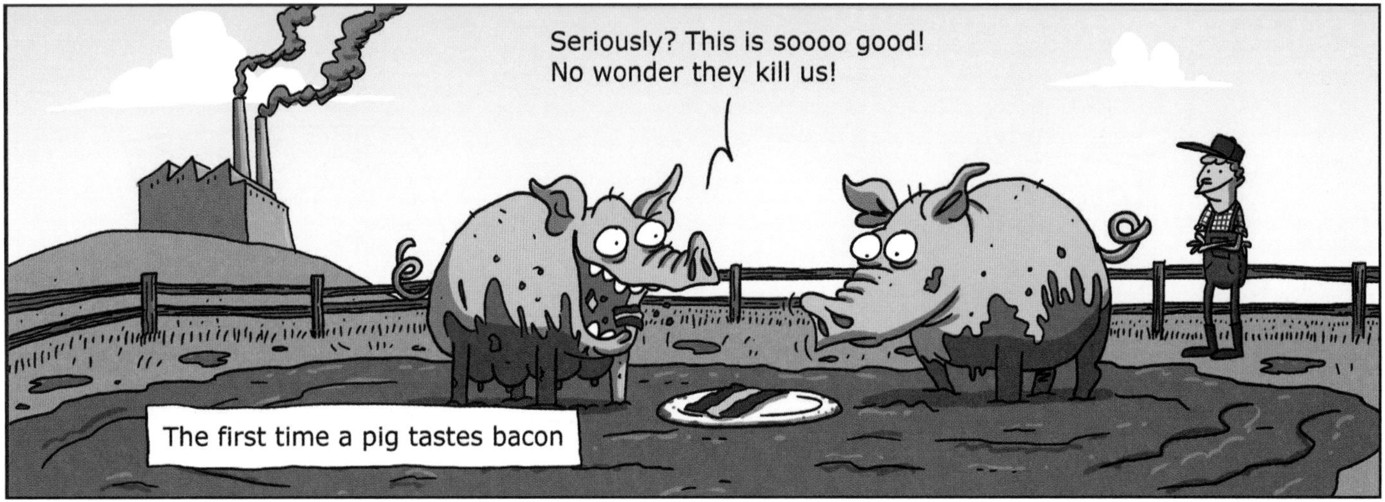
Seriously? This is soooo good!
No wonder they kill us!
The first time a pig tastes bacon

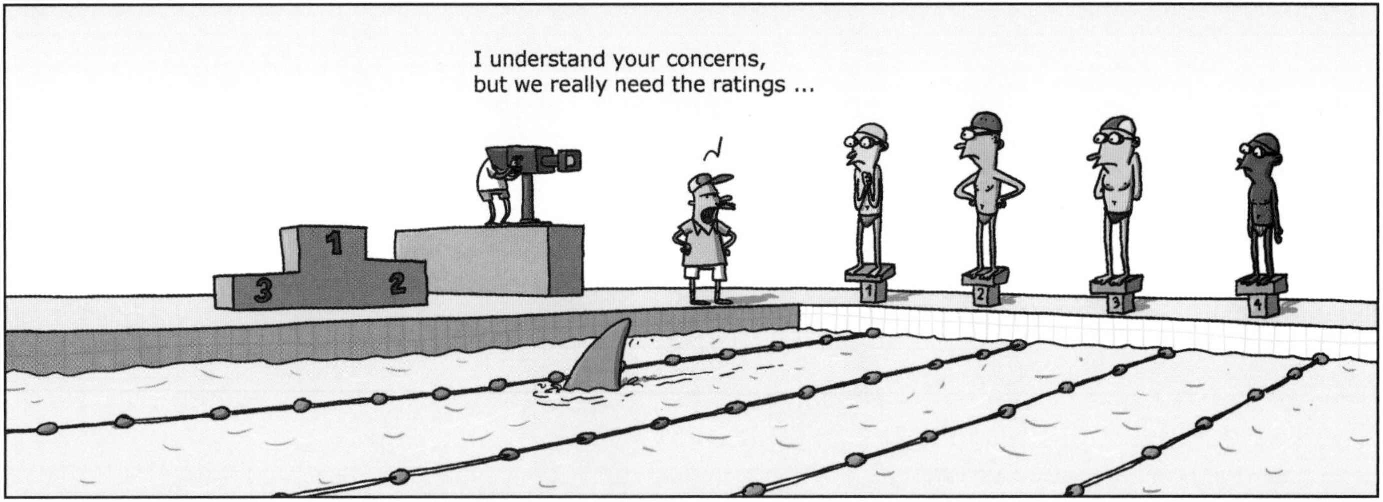
I understand your concerns,
but we really need the ratings ...
1
2
3
1
2
3
4

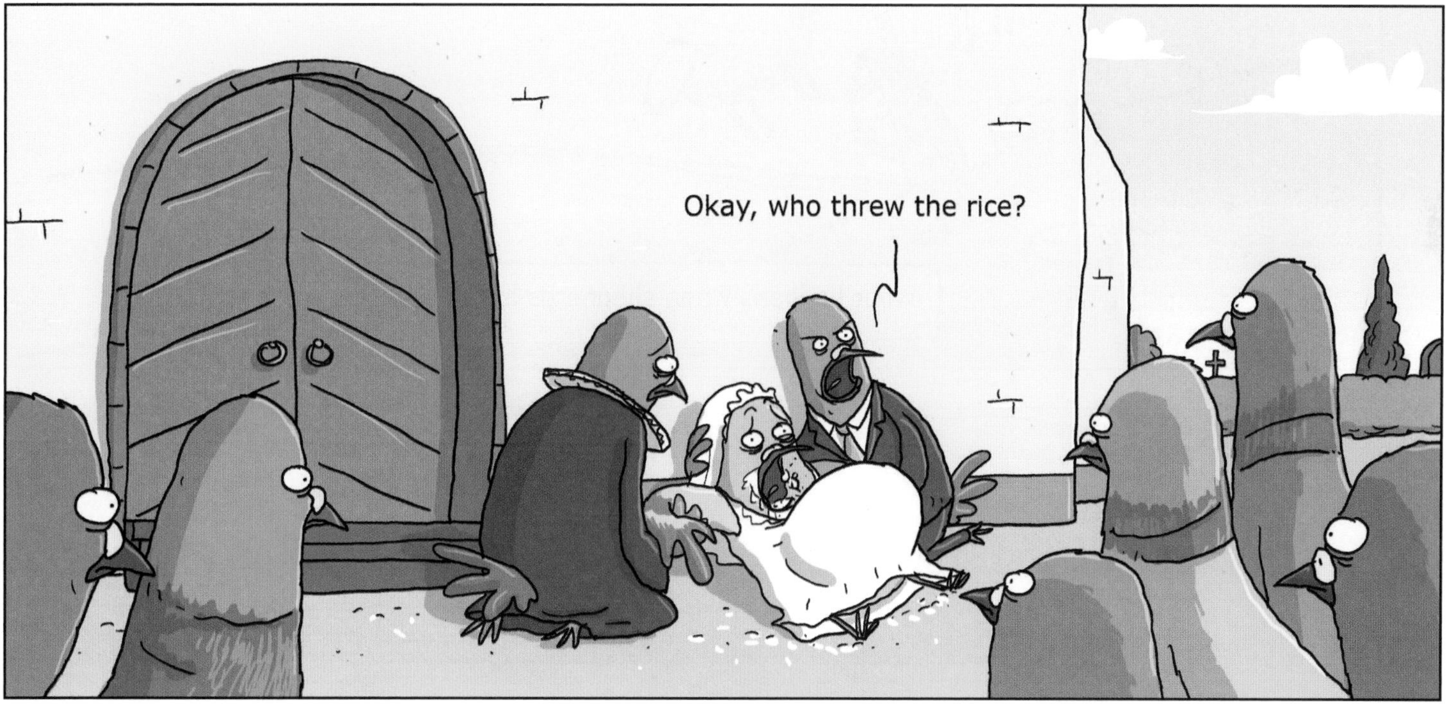
Okay, who threw the rice?

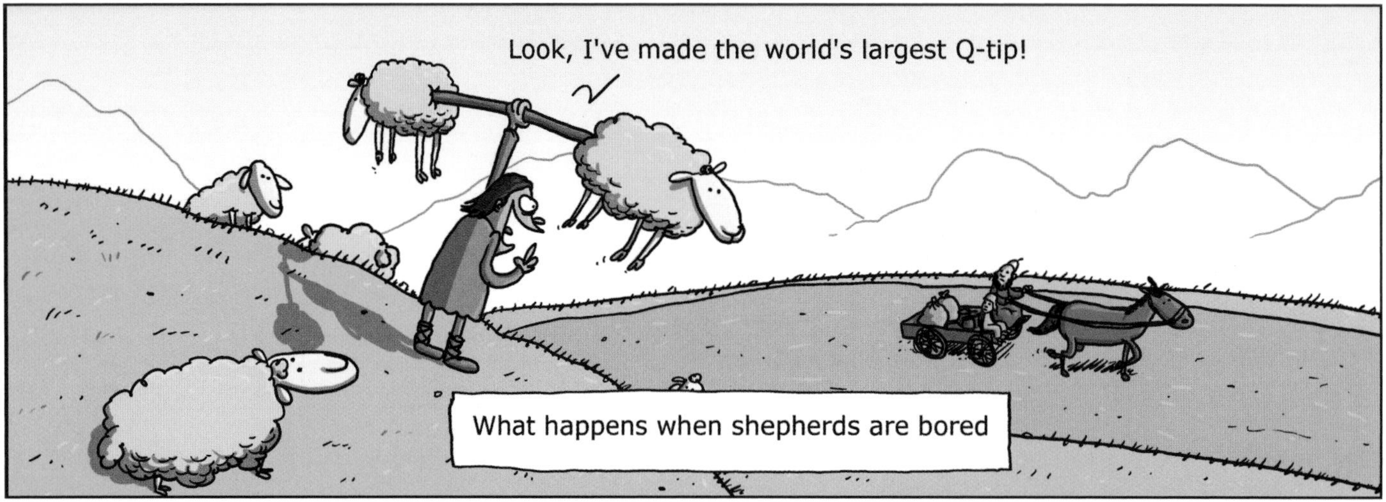
Look, I've made the world's largest Q-tip!
What happens when shepherds are bored

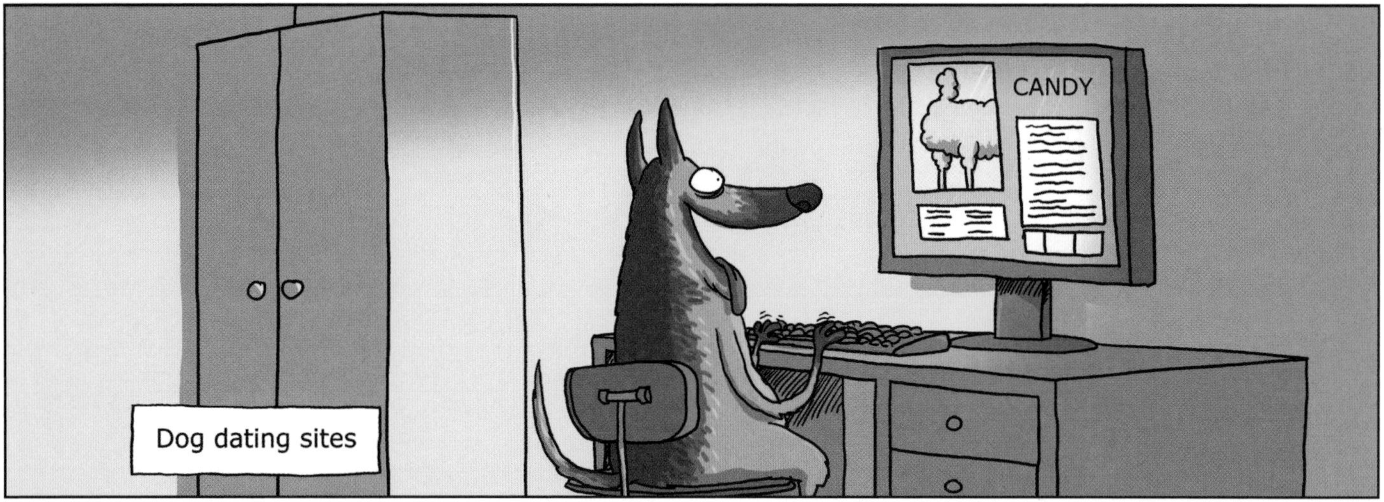
CANDY
Dog dating sites

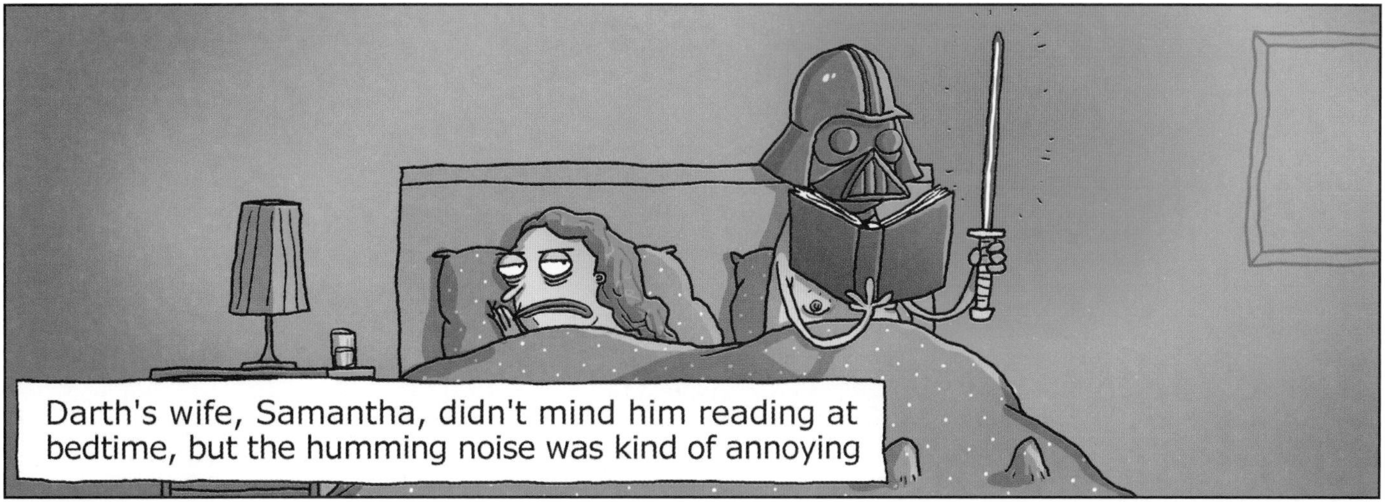
Darth's wife, Samantha, didn't mind him reading at bedtime, but the humming noise was kind of annoying

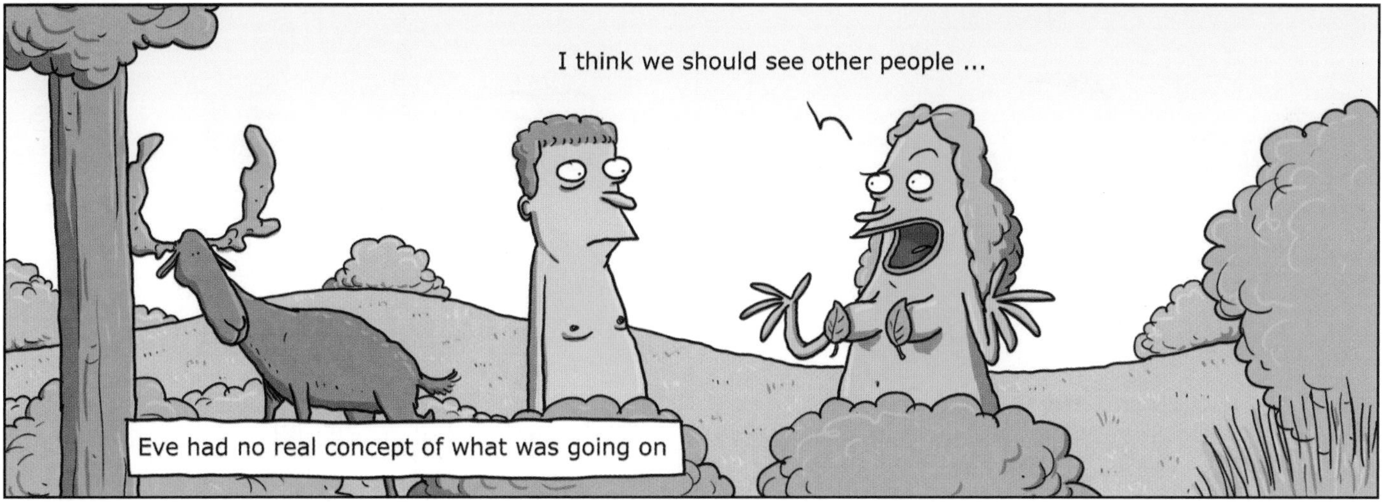
I think we should see other people ...
Eve had no real concept of what was going on

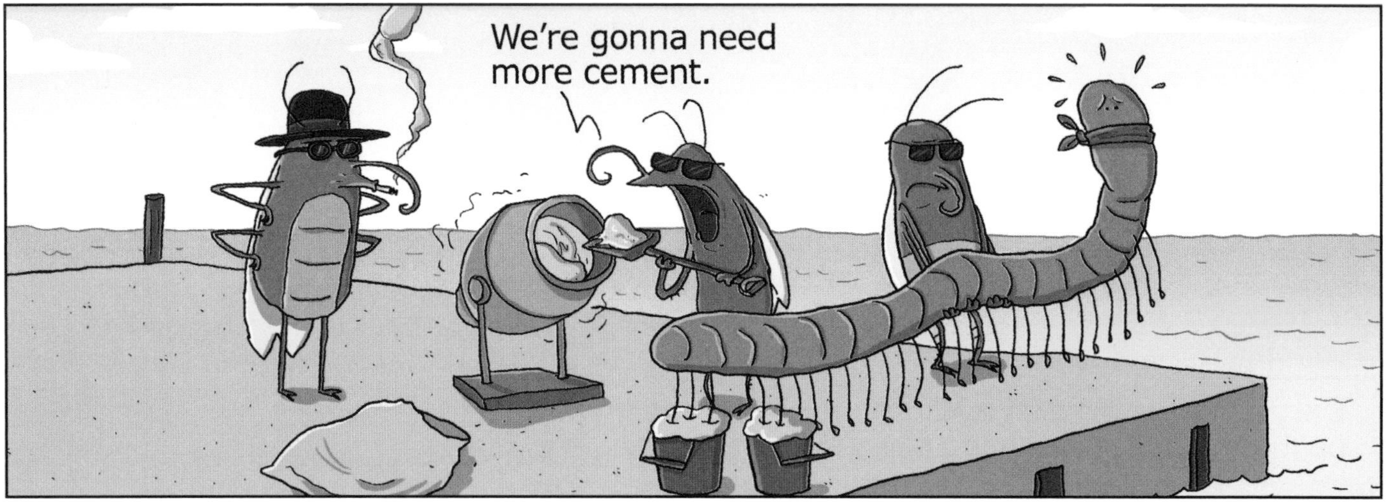
We're gonna need more cement.

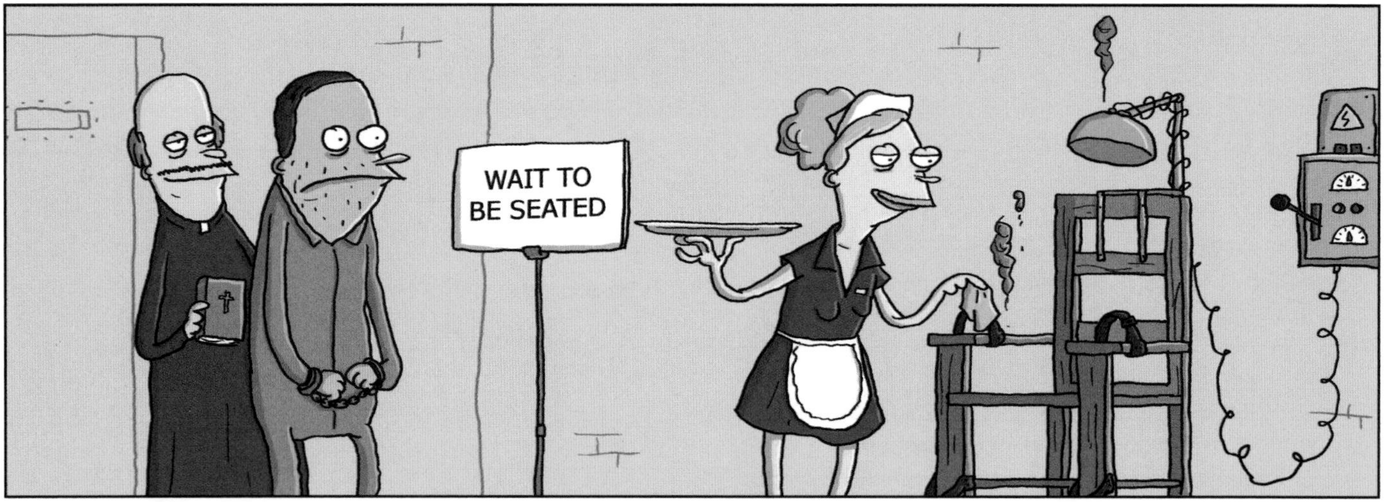
WAIT TO BE SEATED

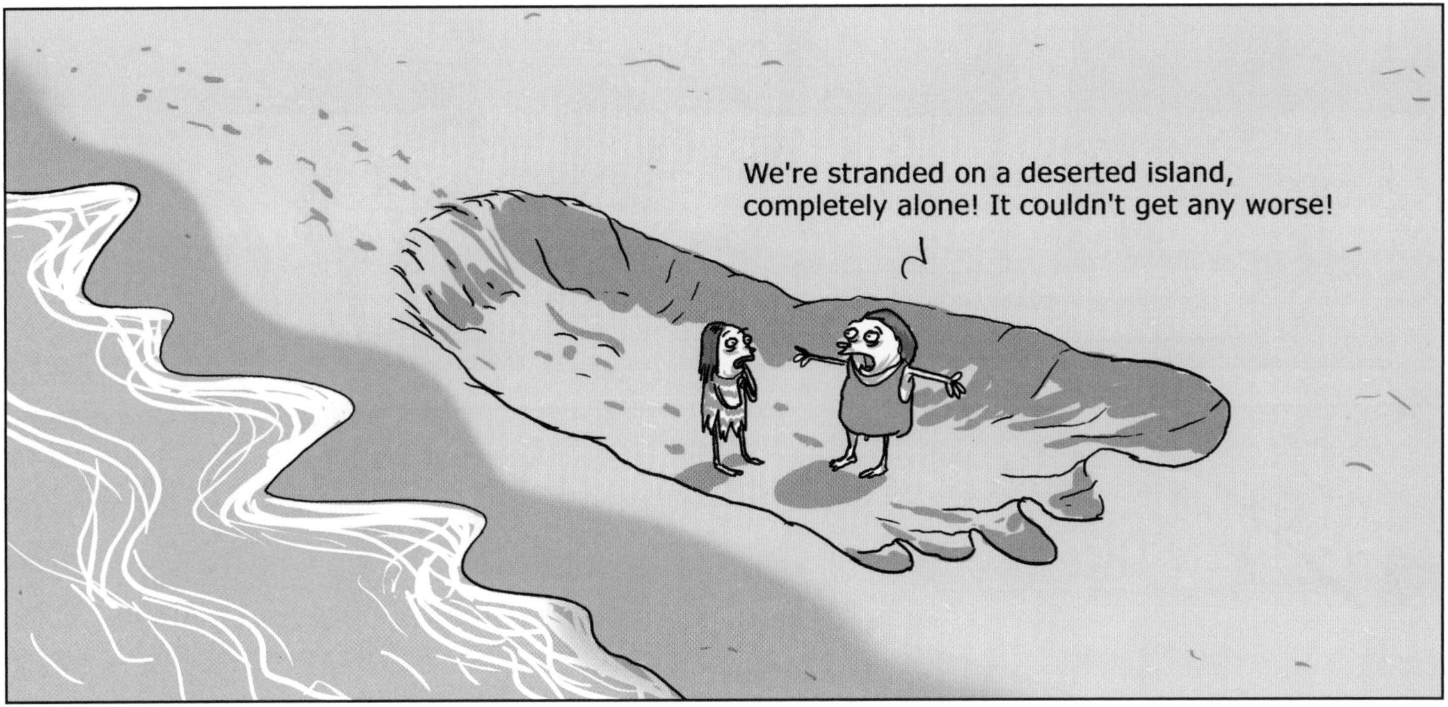
We're stranded on a deserted island, completely alone! It couldn't get any worse!

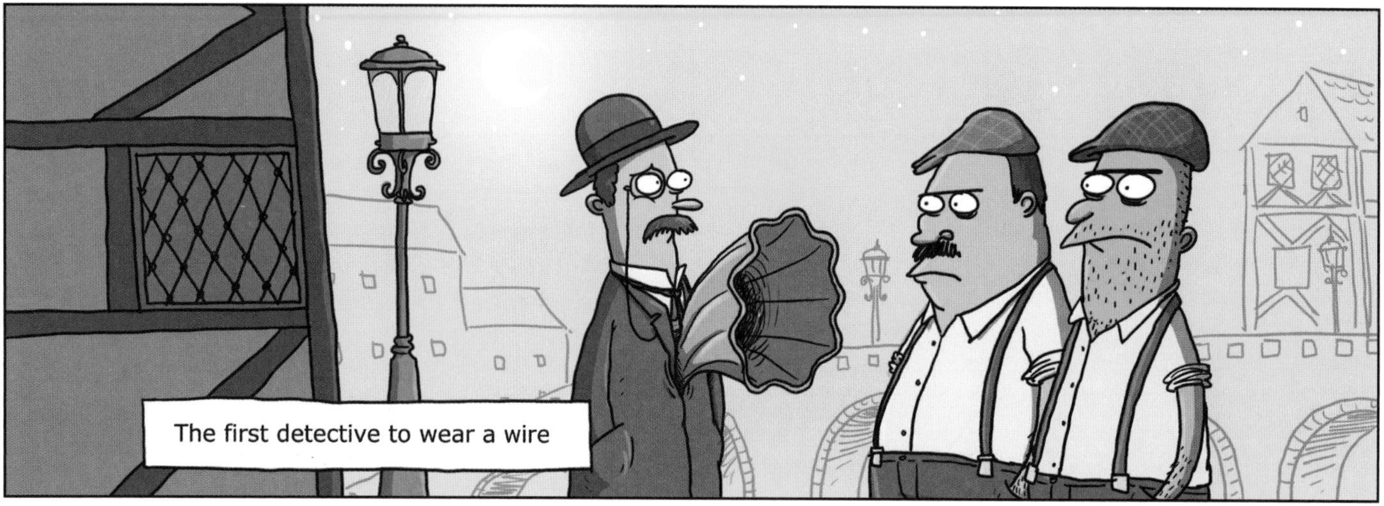
The first detective to wear a wire

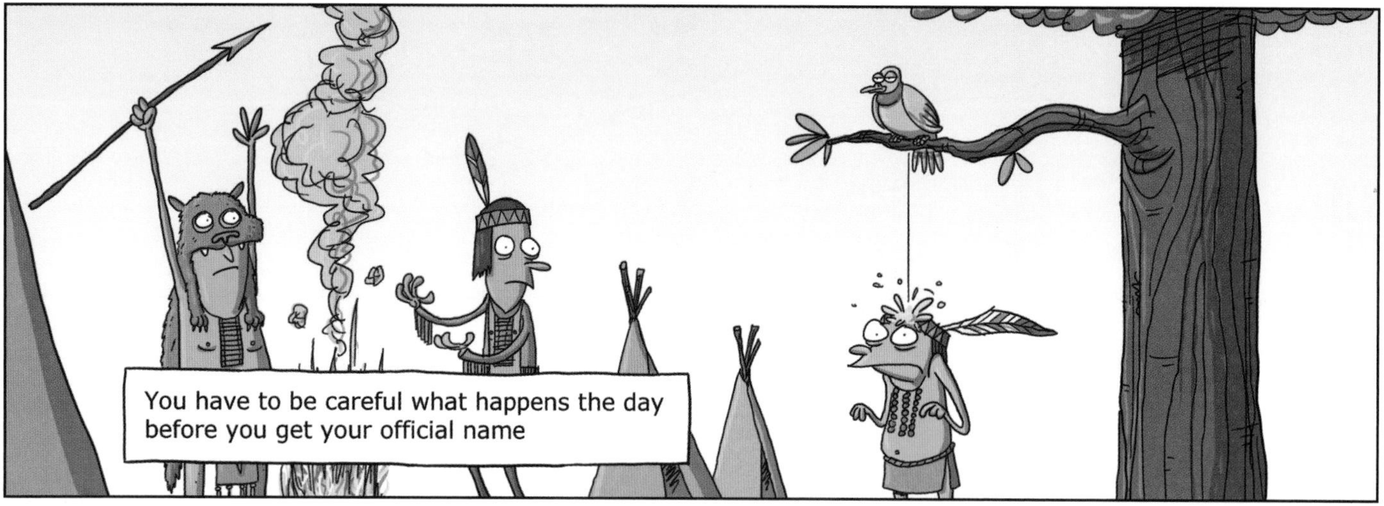
You have to be careful what happens the day before you get your official name

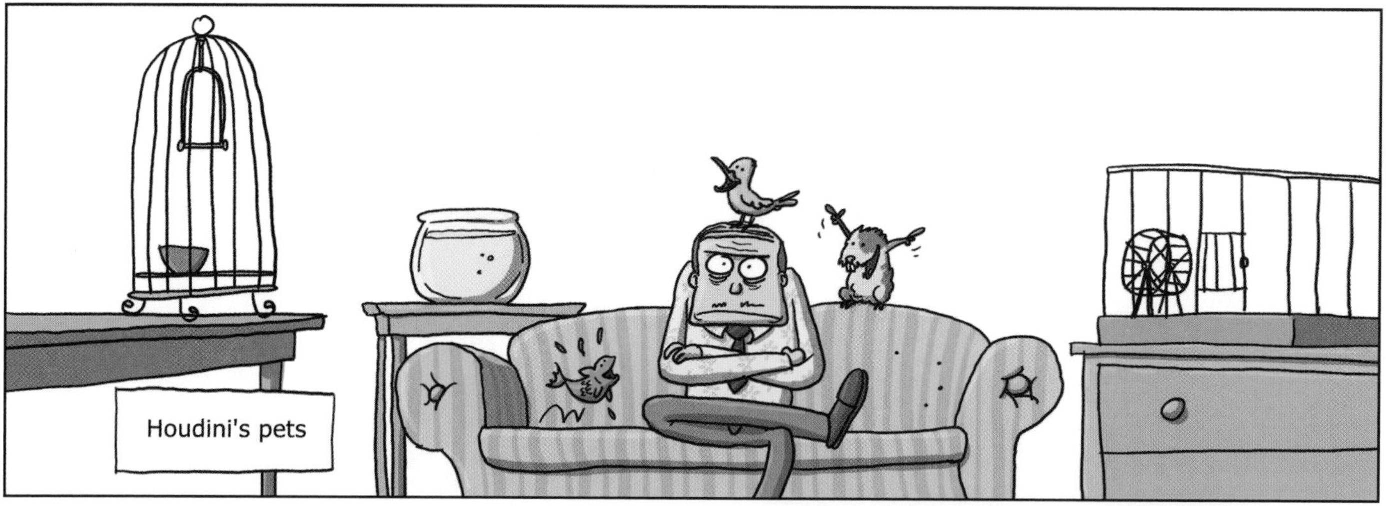
Houdini's pets

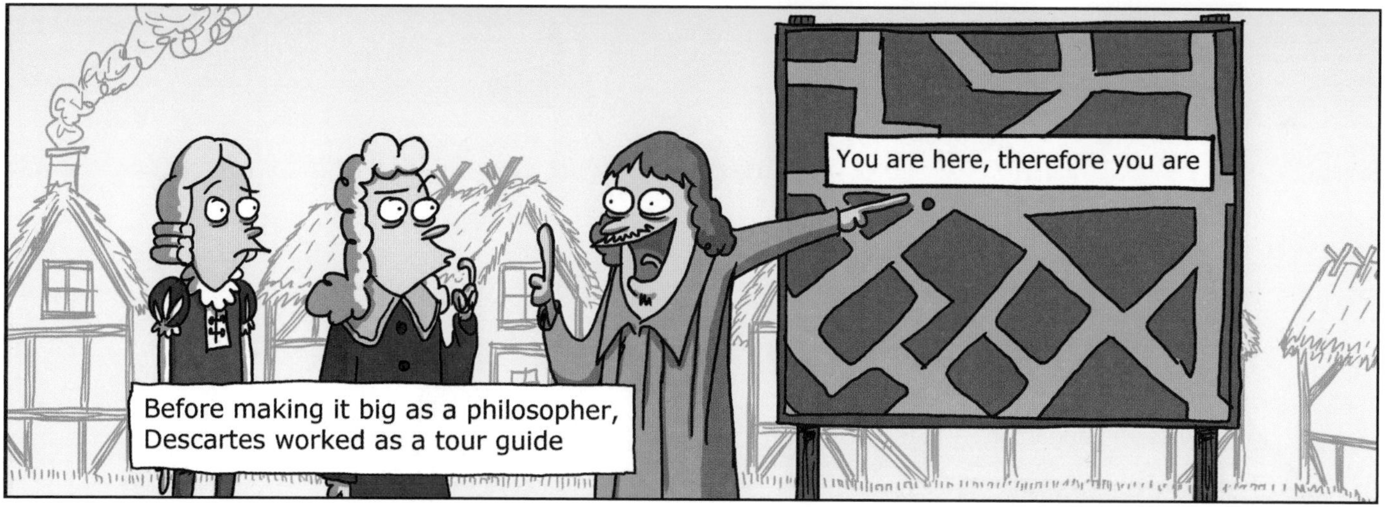
You are here, therefore you are
Before making it big as a philosopher, Descartes worked as a tour guide

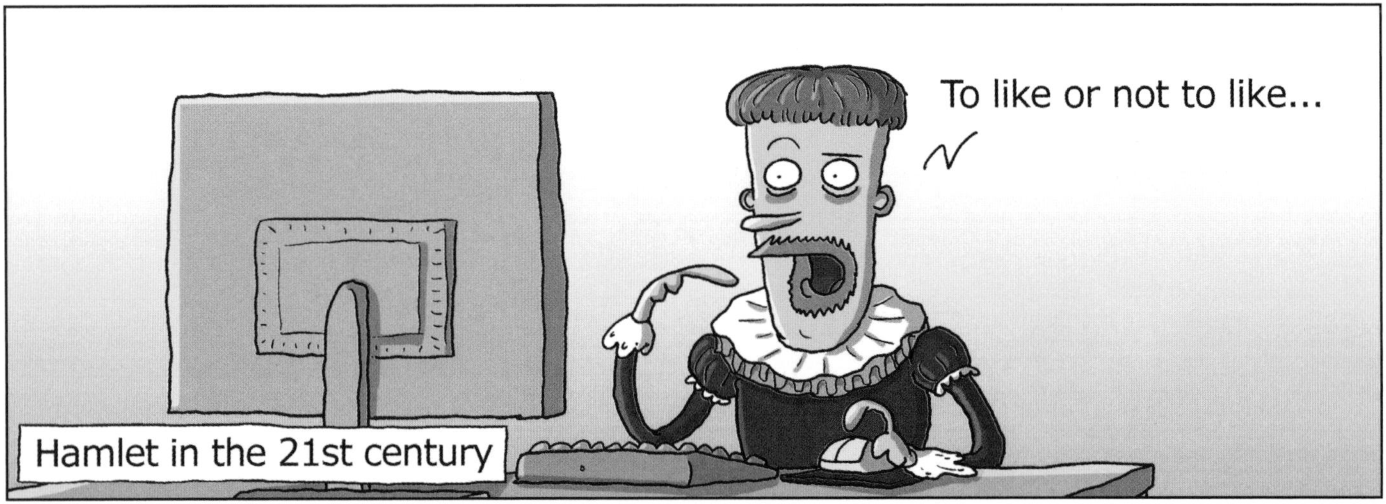
To like or not to like...
Hamlet in the 21st century

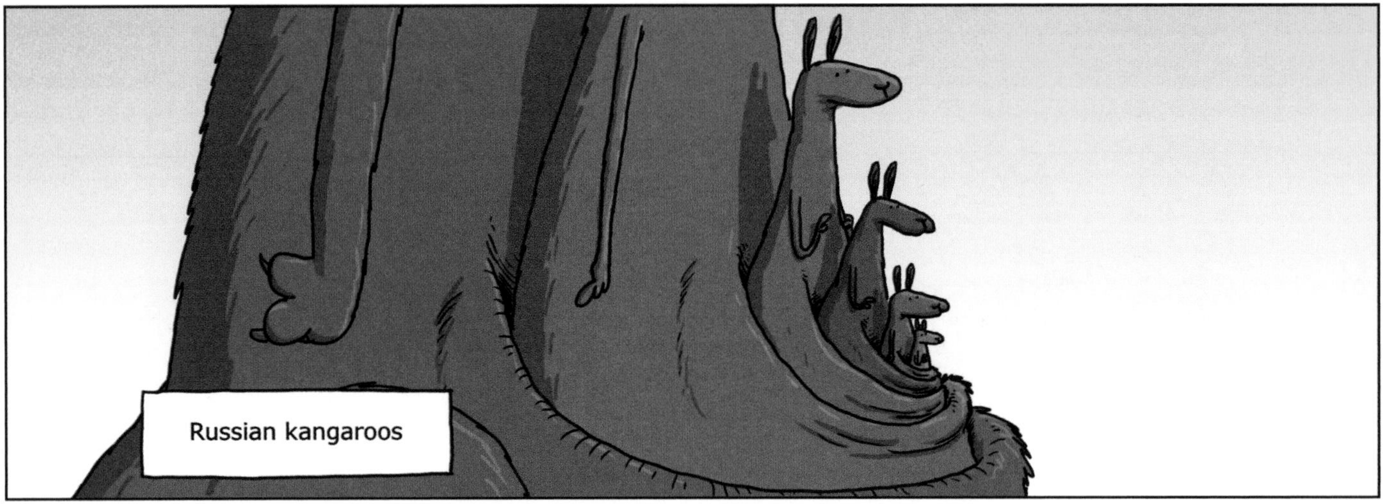
Russian kangaroos

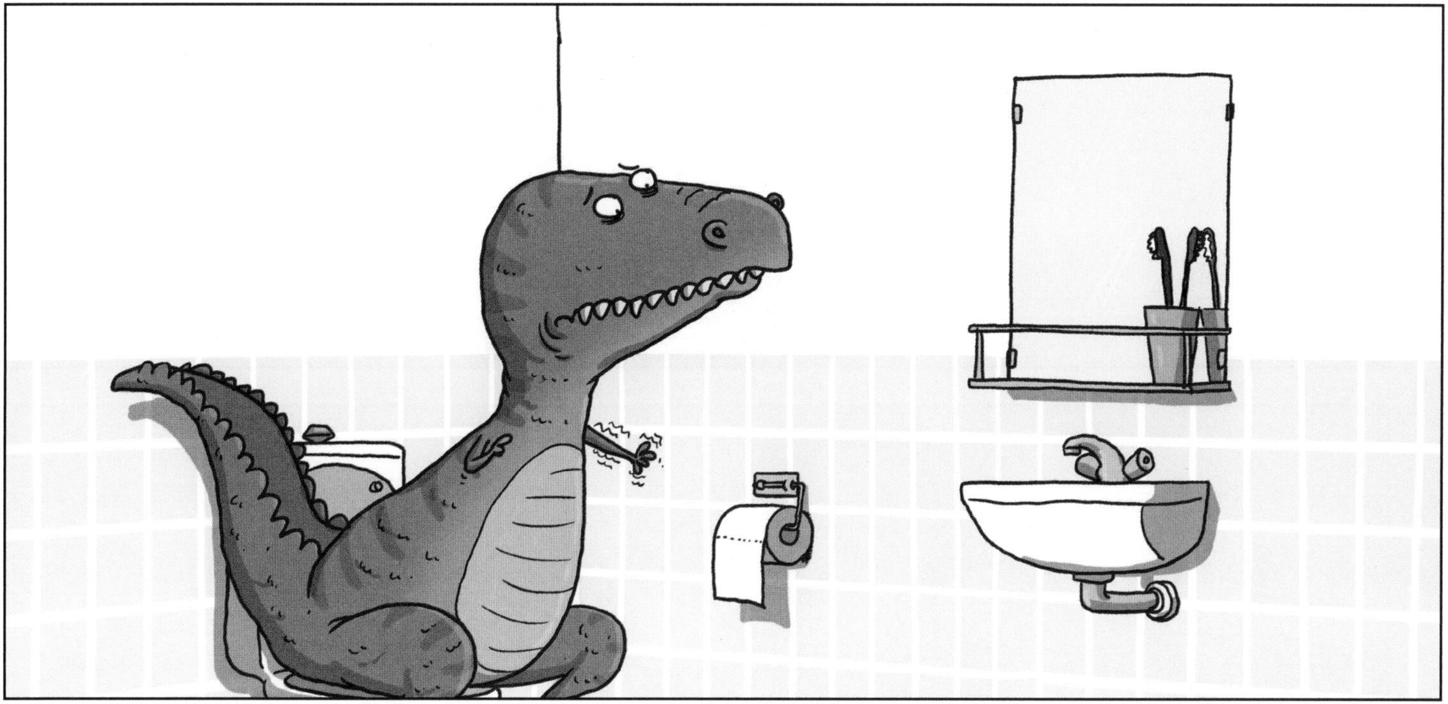

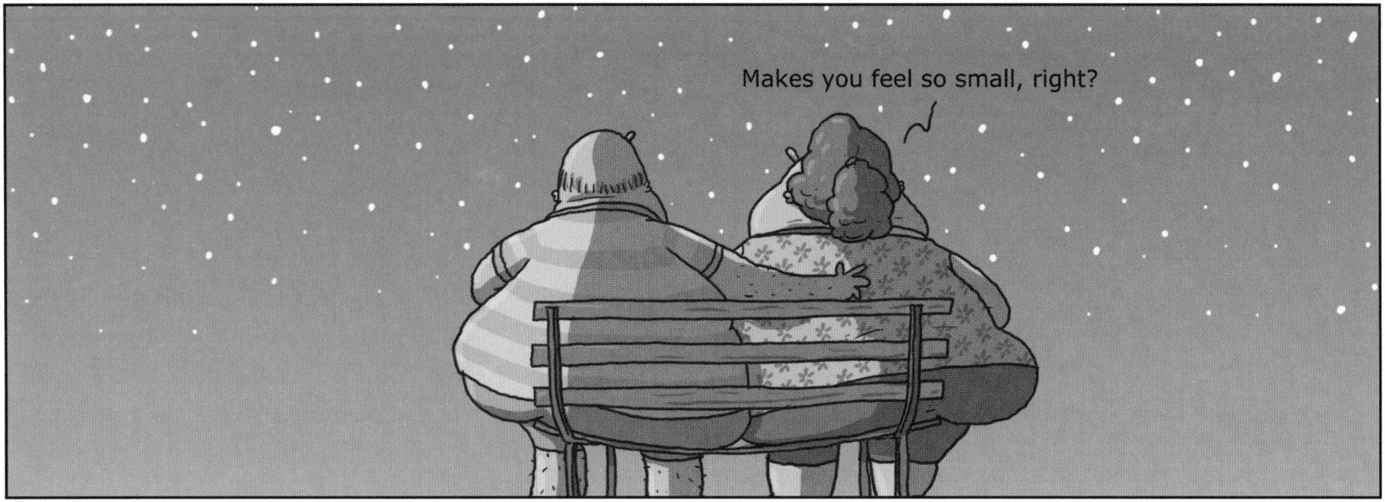
Makes you feel so small, right?

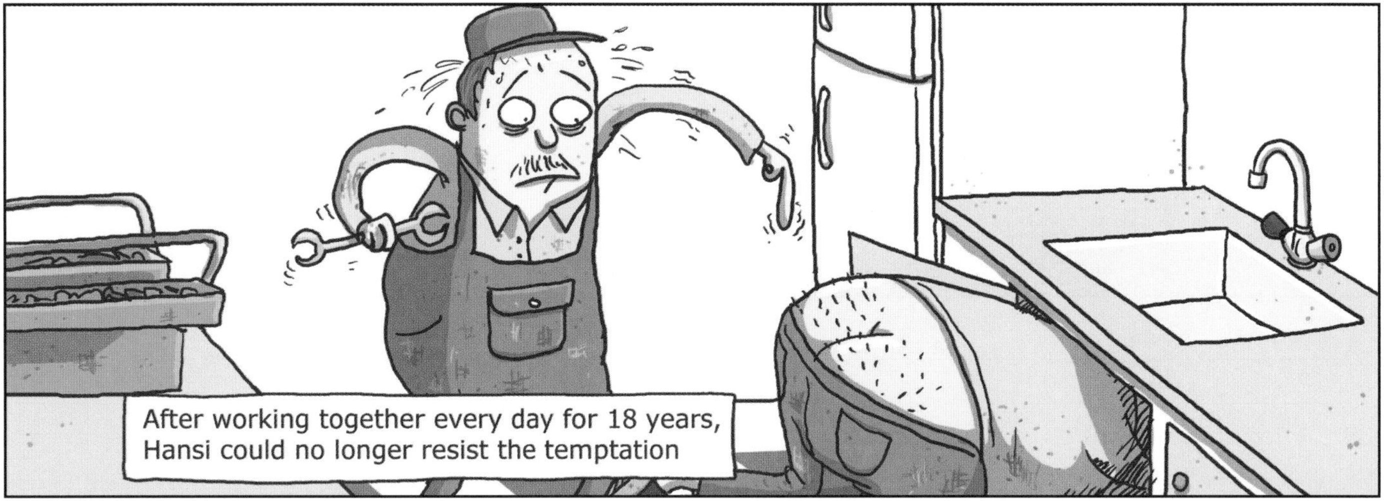
After working together every day for 18 years,
Hansi could no longer resist the temptation

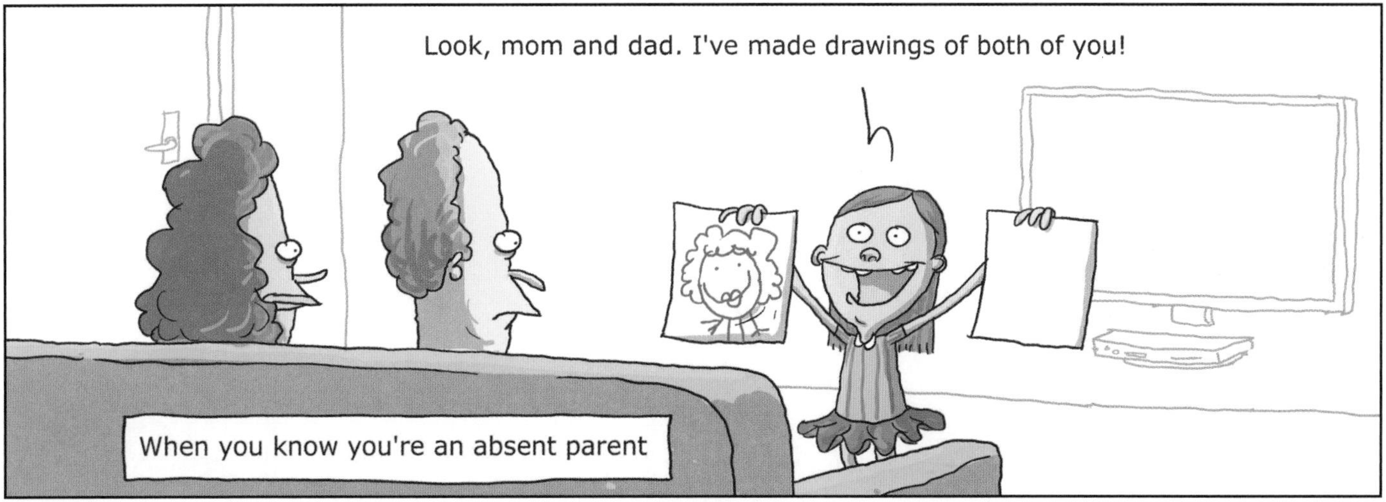
Look, mom and dad. I've made drawings of both of you!
When you know you're an absent parent

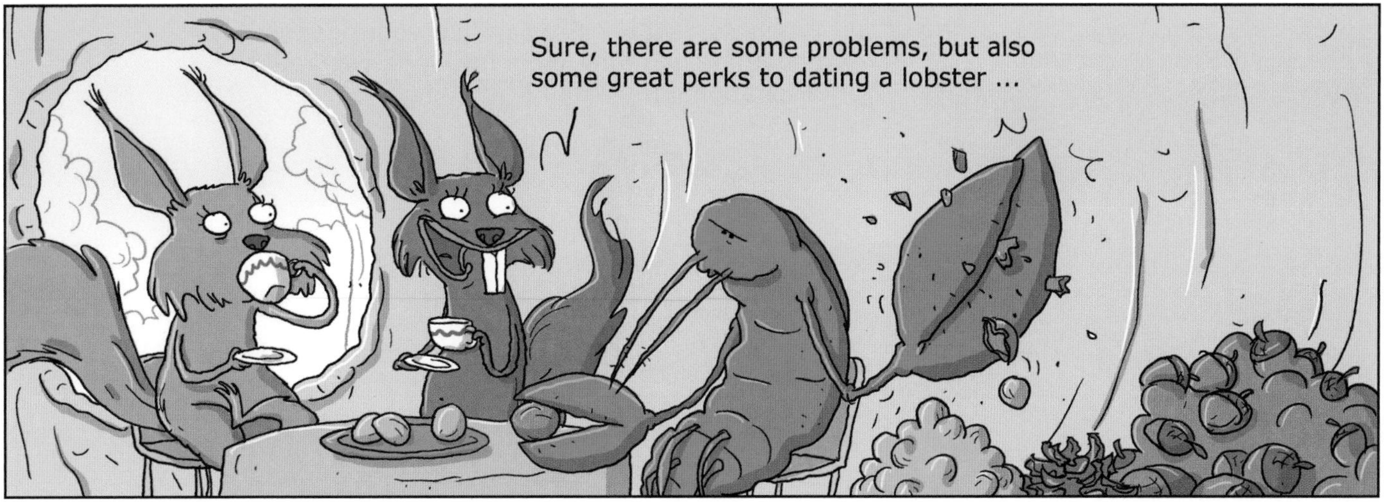
Sure, there are some problems, but also some great perks to dating a lobster ...

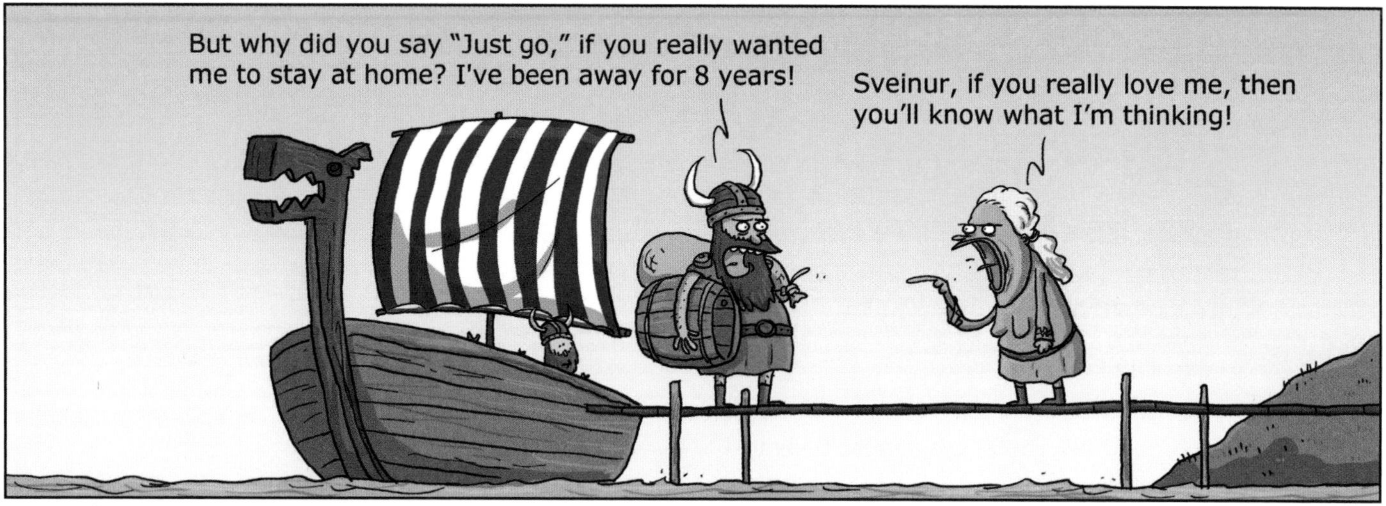
But why did you say "Just go," if you really wanted me to stay at home? I've been away for 8 years!
Sveinur, if you really love me, then you'll know what I'm thinking!

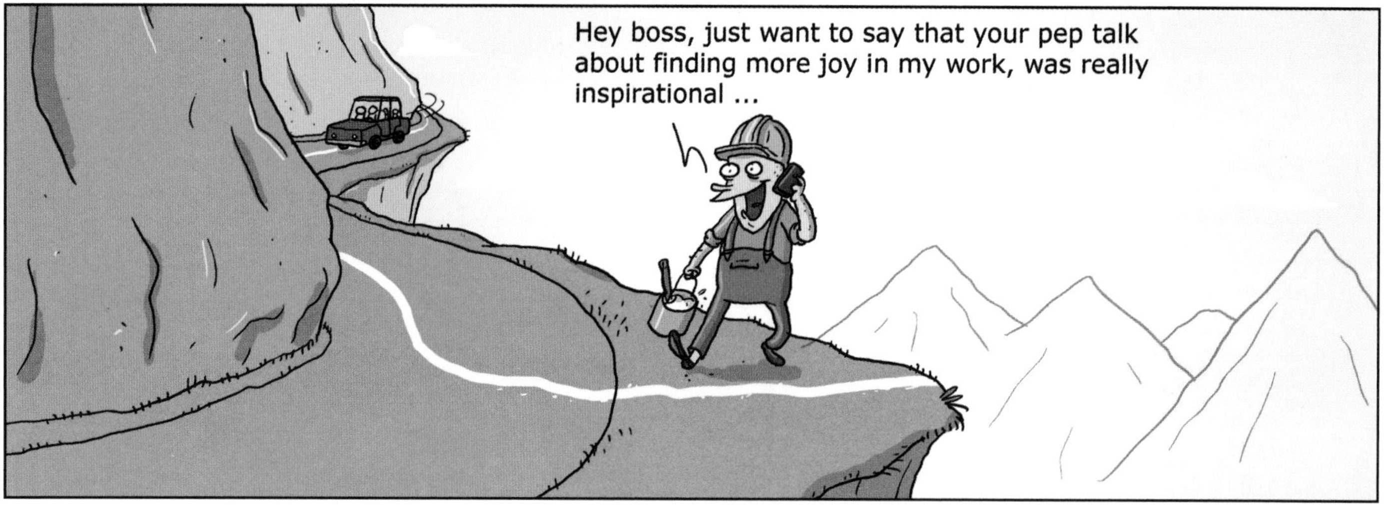
Hey boss, just want to say that your pep talk about finding more joy in my work, was really inspirational ...

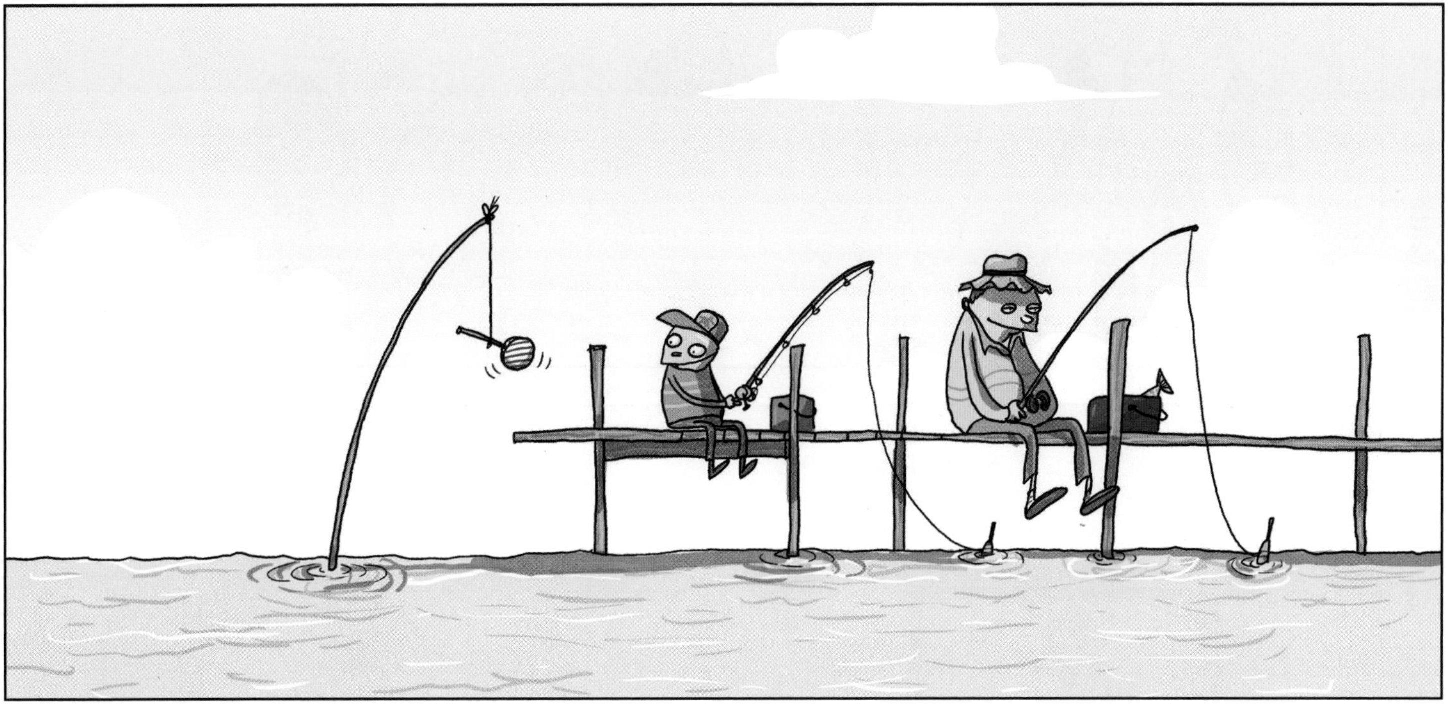

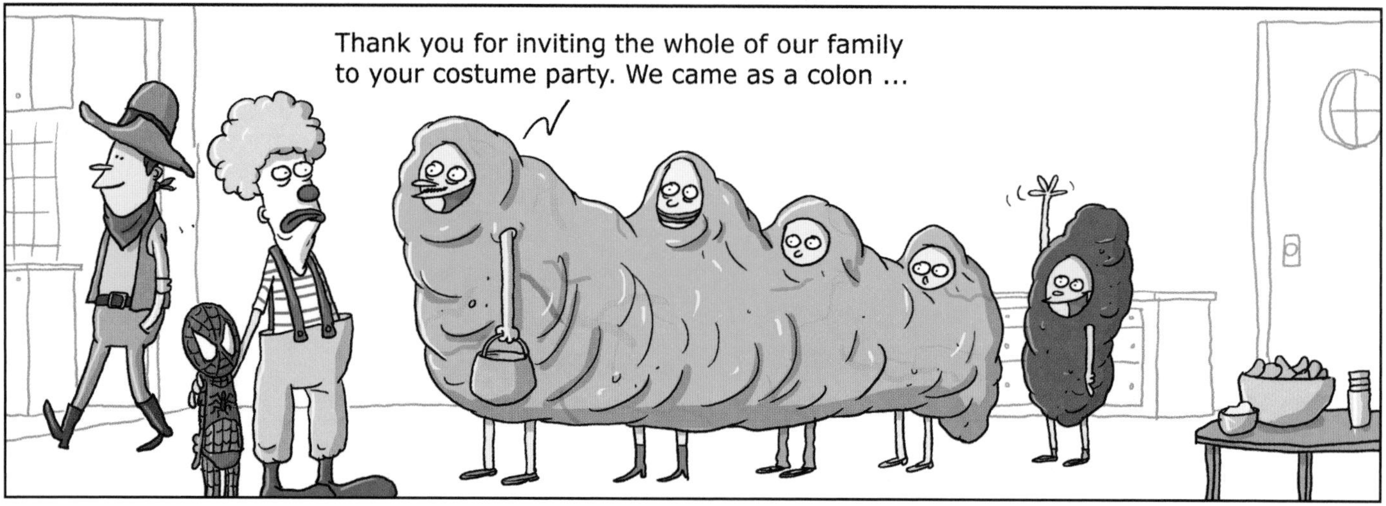
Thank you for inviting the whole of our family
to your costume party. We came as a colon ...

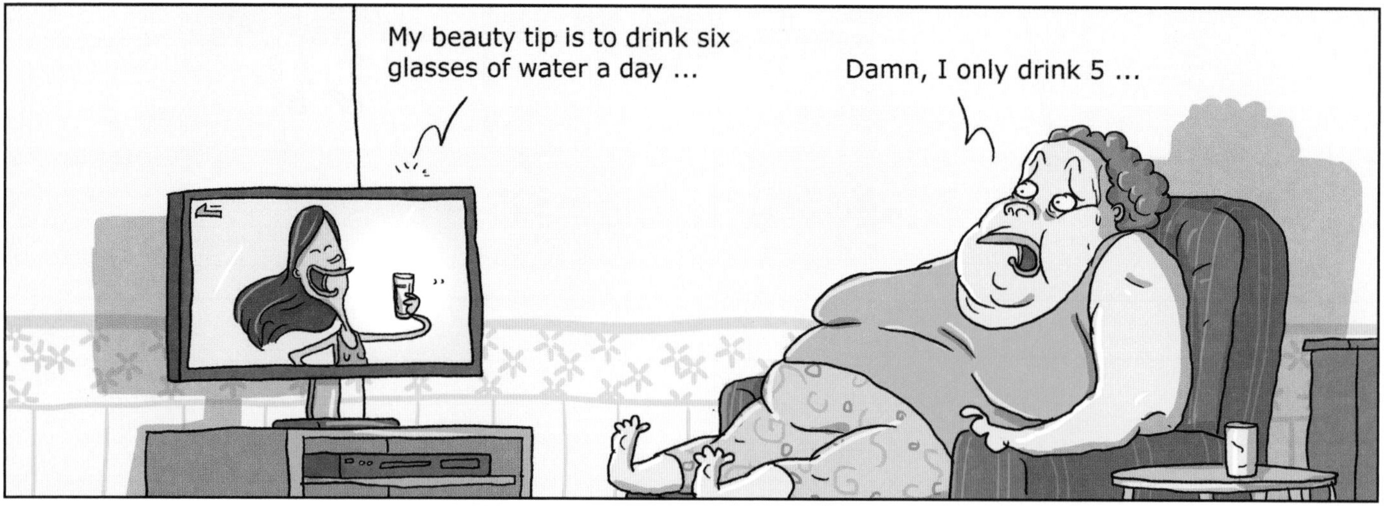
My beauty tip is to drink six
glasses of water a day ...
Damn, I only drink 5 ...

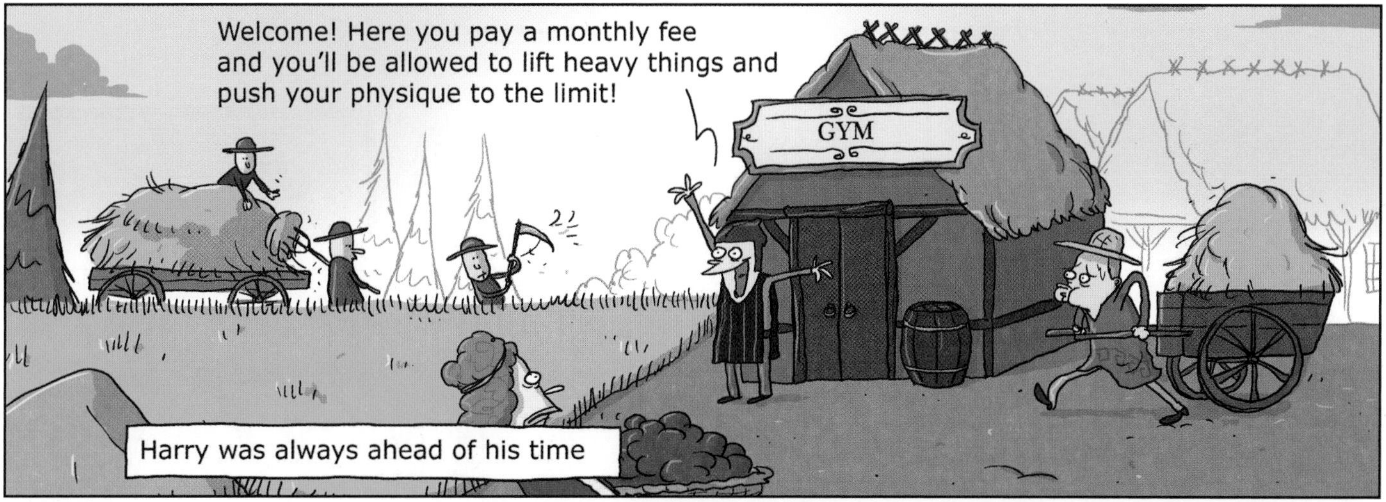
Welcome! Here you pay a monthly fee and you'll be allowed to lift heavy things and push your physique to the limit!
GYM
Harry was always ahead of his time

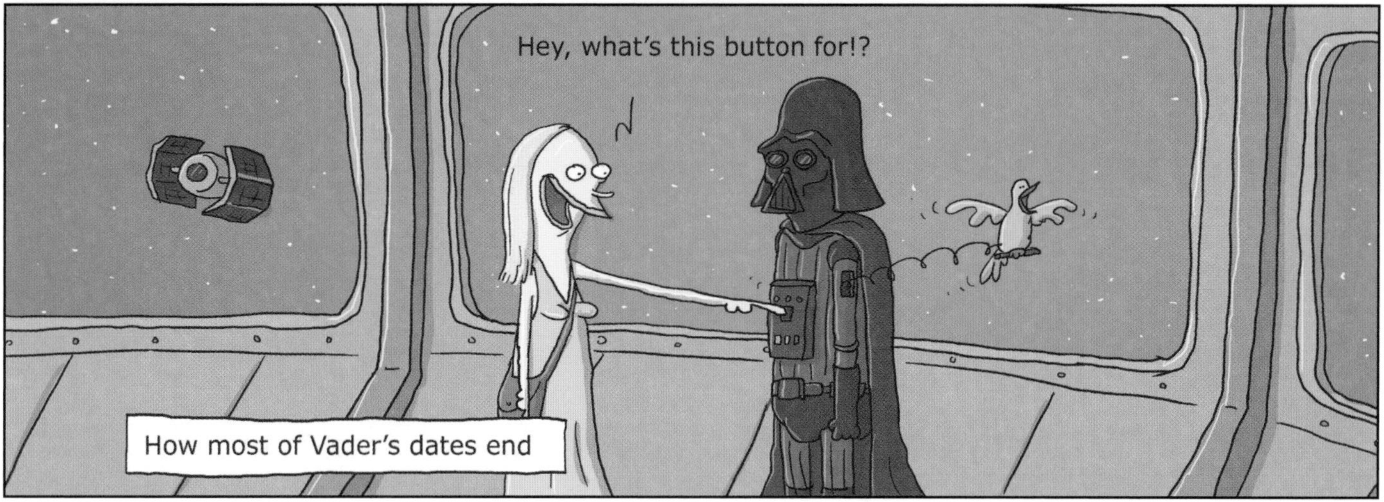
Hey, what's this button for!?
How most of Vader's dates end

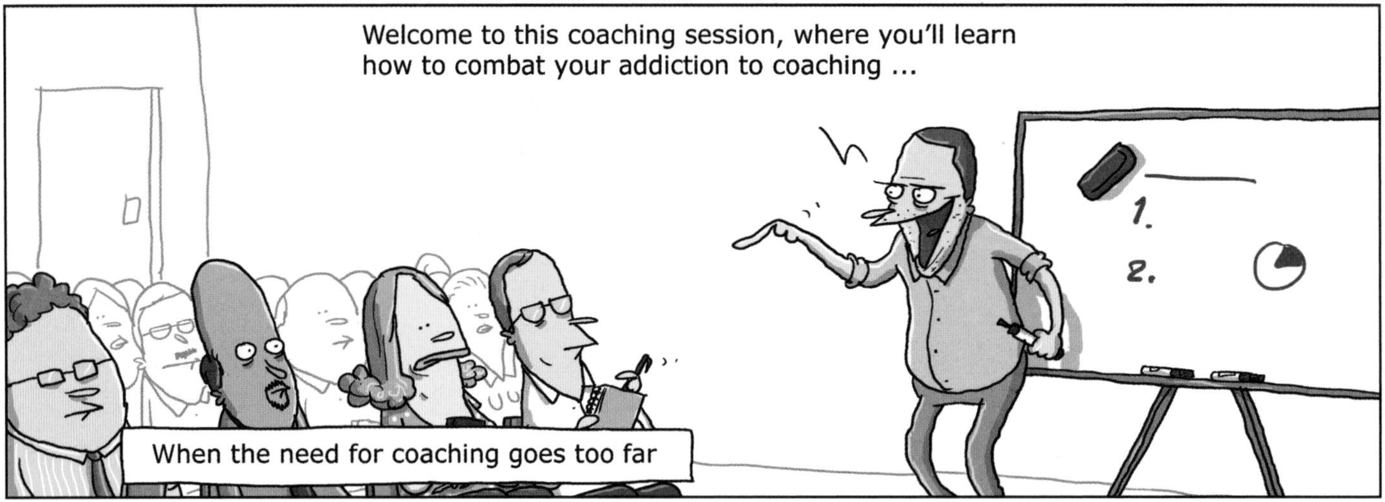
Welcome to this coaching session, where you'll learn how to combat your addiction to coaching ...
1.
2.
When the need for coaching goes too far

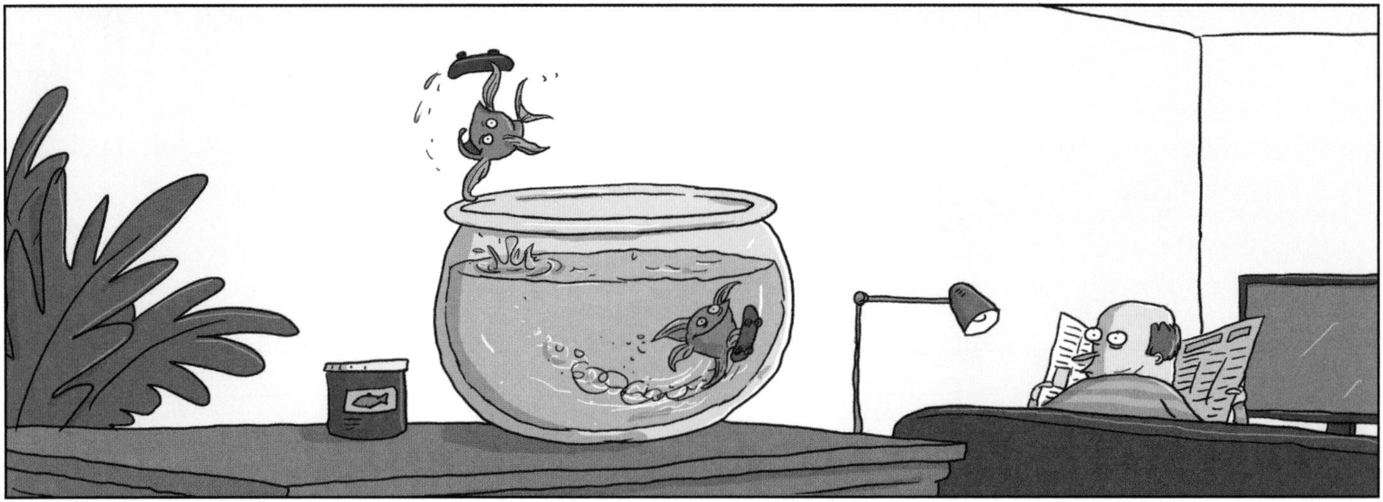

WuMo is distributed by Universal Uclick.

Andrews McMeel Publishing, LLC
an Andrews McMeel Universal company
1130 Walnut Street, Kansas City, Missouri 64106
www.andrewsmcmeel.com

15 16 17 18 19 SDB 10 9 8 7 6 5 4 3 2 1

ISBN: 978-1-4494-6674-9

Library of Congress Control Number: 2014952155

ATTENTION: SCHOOLS AND BUSINESSES
Andrews McMeel books are available at quantity discounts with bulk purchase for educational, business, or sales promotional use. For information, please e-mail the Andrews McMeel Publishing Special Sales Department: specialsales@amuniversal.com.

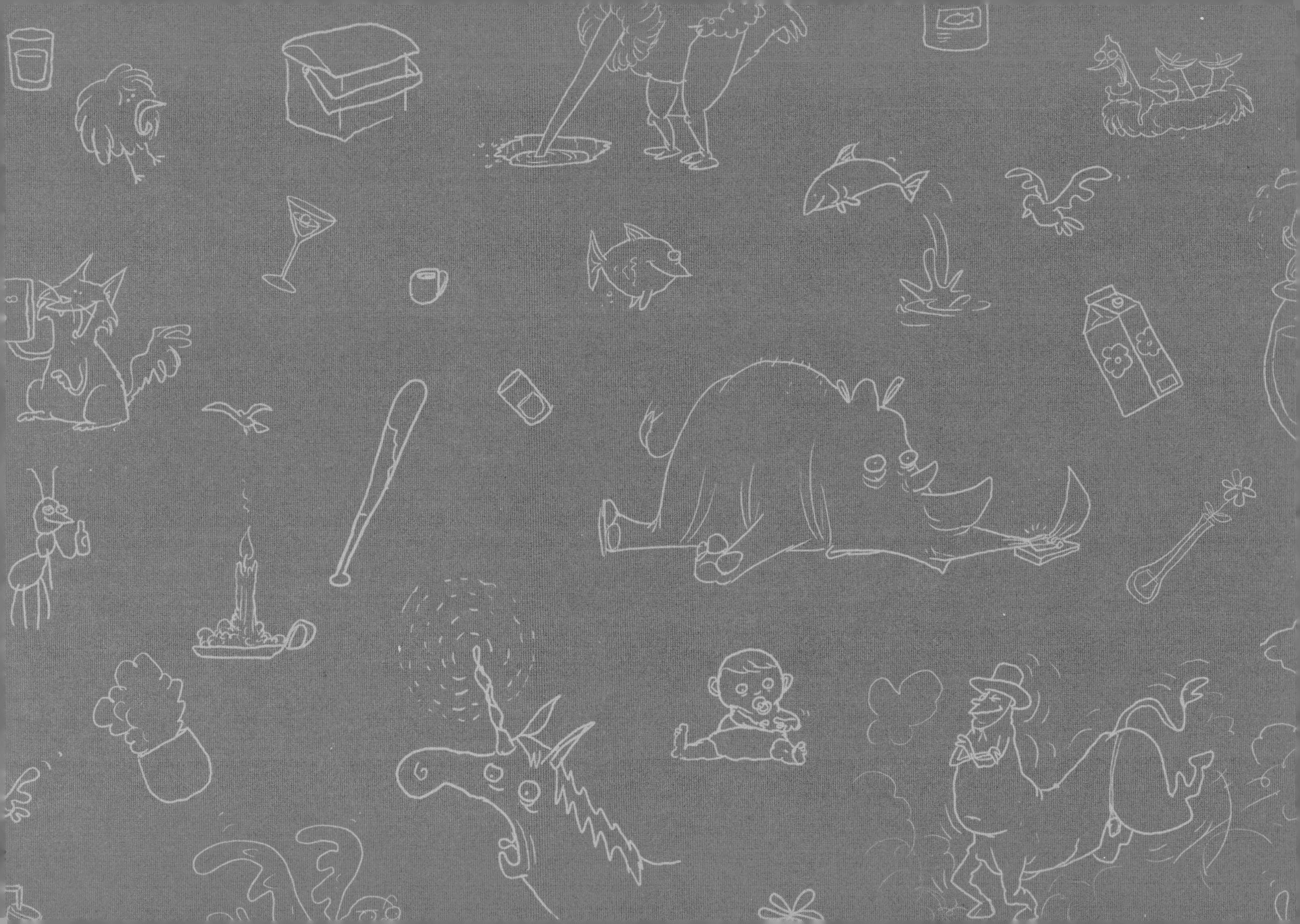